Little White Lies

THE MOVIE QUIZ BOOK

In memory of

Barry Norman (1933–2017)

Jim Bowen (1937–2018)

Jonathan Demme (1944–2017)

Little
White
Lies

THE MOVIE QUIZ BOOK

MIKE McCAHILL
ADAM LEE DAVIES

LAURENCE KING PUBLISHING

CONTENTS

1

The Name of the GAME

Our very own opening title sequence

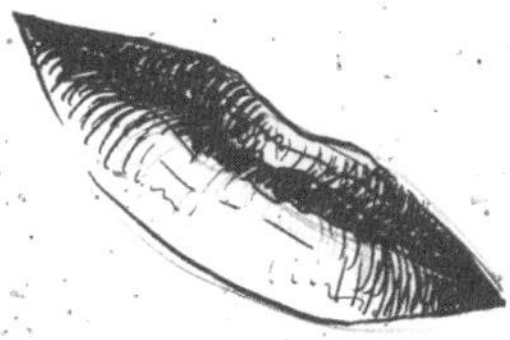

SAY WHAT?

Odd titles

Fill the blanks in these singular movie titles

Julie Newmar, Disney, 8th, Hell, Cheese, Basil, Happiness, Women, Goats, Mom, Mountain, Juice, Zombies, Snogging, Penis

1. *The Incredibly Strange Creatures Who Stopped Living and Became Mixed-Up* _________ (1964)

2. *Can Heironymus Merkin Ever Forget Mercy Humppe and Find True* ______*?* (1969)

3. *The Adventures of Buckaroo Banzai Across the* _______ *Dimension* (1984)

4. *Summer Night with Greek Profile, Almond Eyes and Scent of* ______ (1986)

5. ______ *Comes to Frogtown* (1988)

6. *Cannibal _______ in the Avocado Jungle of Death* (1989)

7. *Stop! Or My _________ Will Shoot* (1992)

8. *The Man with the Smallest __________ in Existence and the Electron Microscope Technician Who Loved Him* (2003 short)

9. *I Killed My Lesbian Wife, Hung Her on a Meat Hook, and Now I Have a Three-Picture Deal at ________* (1993 short, directed by Ben Affleck)

10. *The Englishman Who Went Up a Hill and Came Down a _________* (1995)

11. *To Wong Foo, Thanks for Everything! ___________* (1995)

12. *Don't Be a Menace to South Central While Drinking Your _____ in the Hood* (1996)

13. I *Want Someone to Eat __________ With* (2006)

14. *Angus, Thongs and Perfect __________* (2008)

15. *The Men Who Stare at __________* (2009)

SPELL BOUND

A cinematic spelling test

Spell out the names of the following film folk (no Googling!)

1. The director of *Taxi Driver, Goodfellas* and *The Wolf of Wall Street*.

2. British actress who broke out in *Bend It Like Beckham*, *Pride & Prejudice* and *Atonement*.

3. Played a tattooed gangster in Edgar Wright's *Baby Driver*, but is best known for his lead role in TV's *Mad Men*.

4. Punchy actor (and sporadic performance artist) who served as the hero of Michael Bay's *Transformers* franchise before going on to work with Lars von Trier.

5. Kicked off his career in featherlight romcoms before his transition to an acting heavyweight in films such as *Dallas Buyers Club* and *Interstellar*.

6. Rotund comedian who became a fan favourite as the oddball Alan in the *Hangover* franchise.

7. The Terminator, and the man who killed the original Predator.

8. American actress who can currently be seen playing the role of Black Widow in the Marvel Cinematic Universe.

9. Child star nominated at the tender age of nine for her lead performance in 2012's *Beasts of the Southern Wild*.

10. Reliable stage and screen actor who had a career breakthrough in 2013 as Solomon Northup, the title character of Steve McQueen's *12 Years a Slave*.

11. American funny man whose breakthrough came as the *40-Year-Old Virgin*.

12. Sandy-haired scion of an Irish acting dynasty, first spotted as Bill Weasley in the *Harry Potter* series; more recently A.A. Milne in *Goodbye Christopher Robin*.

13. New York-born, Irish-raised actress, a three-time Oscar nominee for *Atonement*, *Brooklyn* and *Lady Bird*.

14. Fulsomely browed model-turned-actress, a sparky screen presence in 2015's *Paper Towns* and 2017's *Valerian and the City of a Thousand Planets.*

15. Visionary Thai writer-director who took home the Cannes Palme d'Or in 2010 for *Uncle Boonmee Who Can Recall His Past Lives*.

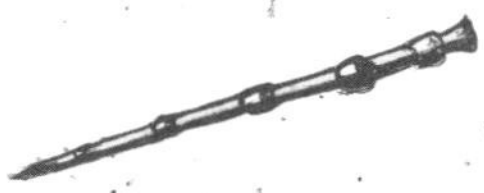

RHAPSODIES IN BLUE

Cerulean cinema

Match these fifteen clues to the fifteen films with 'Blue' in their title listed below.

1. Inspired the long-running British police series *Dixon of Dock Green*

-

2. Found Elvis Presley turning heads on the shores of America's 50th state

-

3. Involved mucky movie mastermind Zalman King investigating a series of murders linked to a strain of LSD

-

4. Featured cameos from dozens of musical legends, plus a young Steven Spielberg as the Cook County clerk

-

5. Provided a showcase for British comedy double-act Cannon and Ball as bumbling cops

-

6. Sent a police helicopter in pursuit of renegade ex-Army colonel Malcolm McDowell

-

7. Saw a youthful Kyle MacLachlan discovering a severed ear and entering into a sadomasochistic relationship

-

8. Was shot under the title *Green Monkey* and later emerged on VHS under the title *Insect*

-

9. Formed a 79-minute meditation on mortality that premiered in British cinemas, on BBC Radio 3 and UK broadcaster Channel 4 on the same night

-

10. Cast Juliette Binoche as the grieving wife of a just-deceased composer

-

11. Comprised an improvised spin-off from 1995's *Smoke*, featuring cameos from the likes of Madonna, Lou Reed and Michael J. Fox

-

12. Found a fresh-faced Ewan McGregor dealing drugs to the denizens of the Cornish surfing scene

-

13. Saw LL Cool J's parrot devoured by a rogue Frankenshark

-

14. Earned Michelle Williams an Oscar nomination for her portrayal of a young wife and mother whose marriage is on the rocks

-

15. Won the Palme d'Or after raising critical eyebrows with its explicit sex scenes

Blue Monkey (1987)
Blue Valentine (2010)
The Boys in Blue (1982)
Blue Sunshine (1977)
Three Colours Blue (1993)
Deep Blue Sea (1999)
The Blue Lamp (1950)
Blue Is the Warmest Colour (2013)
Blue (1993)
Blue Velvet (1986)
Blue Hawaii (1961)
The Blues Brothers (1980)
Blue Juice (1995)
Blue in the Face (1995)
Blue Thunder (1983)

ALTERNATIVE REALITIES

Movies that changed their titles

1. Patriotic 1941 drama *This England* was retitled *Our Heritage* upon its release in which country?

A) Scotland

B) Australia

C) USA

D) Soviet Union

2. The 1994 British historical drama *The Madness of King George III* was released in the US under the shorter title *The Madness of King George*. Why?

A) A pornographic parody bearing the film's original title had already made it to screens

B) Because of a lawsuit filed by owners of the King George III restaurant in Los Angeles

C) Test screenings revealed that audiences read III as 111 and were expecting the film to be a spoof

D) The producers were worried that American audiences would think it was a sequel and decide not to see it because they had missed I and II

3. Which classic rock track shares its name with the US title for 1946 British weepie *A Matter of Life and Death*?

A) 'Don't Bring Me Down' by ELO

B) 'Fly Like An Eagle' by the Steve Miller Band

C) 'In the Air Tonight' by Phil Collins

D) 'Stairway to Heaven' by Led Zeppelin

4. 1986's high school basketball drama *Hoosiers* was rechristened *Best Shot* for its UK release. But what is a Hoosier?

A) A nonsense word invented by the scriptwriter

B) A bald rooster

C) A resident of Indiana

D) A type of jockstrap

5. It was released in the UK as *Shadow Makers*, but who or what does the original title of Roland Joffé's 1989 film *Fat Man and Little Boy* refer to?

A) Warring inventors Thomas Edison and Nikola Tesla

B) Obese ventriloquist Del Parnell and his dummy Captain Quips

C) The two atomic bombs that were detonated over Japan during the First World War

D) Rival American football quarterbacks Johnny Unitas and Joe Namath

6. Under what title was the 1991 Robbie Coltrane comedy *The Pope Must Die* released in the US after exhibitors voiced concerns about attracting protests?

A) *The Pope Mustn't Die*

B) *The Pope Must Diet!*

C) *The Eight Deadly Sins*

D) *Holy Commotions*

7. Film titles translated into other languages can undergo some surprising changes. Which of the following is NOT an actual Chinese translation of the

corresponding American film ...?

A) *Just Send Him to University Unqualified* (*Risky Business*)

B) *He's a Ghost!* (*The Sixth Sense*)

C) *Ugly Man Go in Wood Chipper* (*Fargo*)

D) *Run! Run! Cloudzilla!* (*Twister*)

8. And what about the rest of the world? Which of the following is NOT true?

A) In the Czech Republic *Bad Santa* is known as *Mummy, why is Santa Drunk?*

B) In Japan *Leaving Las Vegas* is known as *I'm Drunk and You're a Prostitute*

C) In Malaysia *Austin Powers: The Spy Who Shagged Me* is known as *The Spy Who Behaved Very Nicely Around Me*

D) In Peru *Knocked Up* is known as *Slightly Pregnant*.

9. How was 1996's *Scream* titled on the front page of Kevin Williamson's original screenplay?

A) *A Case of the Munchies*

B) *Scary Movie*

C) *Not Another Teen Movie*

D) *The Jock, the Cheerleader, the Nerd & the Virgin*

10. The 1998 heartstring-twanger known in the UK and Ireland as *Waking Ned* was suffixed with Ned's surname upon its US release. What was it?

A) Kelly

B) O'Reilly

C) Wakeman

D) Devine

11. What altogether more interesting title was Tom Cruise sci-fi actioner *Edge of Tomorrow* set to be released as until 11th-hour jitters caused a change of mind?

A) *Flow My Tears, the Soldier Said*

B) *Greenwich Means Time*

C) *The Steppenwolf Diaries*

D) *All You Need Is Kill*

12. Although the original script for 2006's *Snakes on a Plane* bore that title, for a lengthy period the film was set to be released as *Pacific Air Flight 121*. What caused it to change back?

A) Pan Am cargo plane Flight 121 crashed in Utah a month before the film's release

B) Hundreds of thousands of Guns N' Roses soundtrack CDs had already been pressed

C) An online petition signed by over 500,000 people

D) Star Samuel L. Jackson demanded it, claiming the title was the only reason he agreed to be in the film

13. American distributors felt obliged to prefix the title of Michael Winterbottom's 2005 comedy *A Cock and Bull Story* with the title of the book it was adapted from. Was it ...?

A) *Elmer Gantry*

B) *Quentin Slaughter*

C) *Fanny Hill*

D) *Tristram Shandy*

14. How is the 2010 J-horror parody *Big Tits Zombie* known in the US?

A) *Big Tits Kabuki*

B) *Big Tits: Kamikaze Sorority*

C) *Big Tits Over Tokyo*

D) *The Big Tits Dragon*

15. It's *Zootopia* in the US, and *Zootropolis* in the UK. But what was Disney's 2016 animation called in Germany?

A) *Zoophilia*

B) *Zoomania*

C) *Zoologischer Garten*

D) *Zooropa*

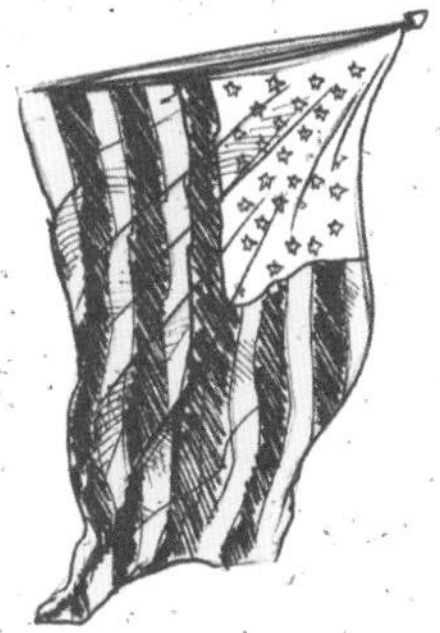

ALL ABOUT US

Films with 'American' in their title

1. What luxury would ultimately prove too expensive for George Lucas to include in 1973's car-crazy comedy *American Graffiti*?

A) The Batmobile

B) A cameo by Paul Newman

C) Elvis Presley songs

D) A flying saucer scene

2. Wim Wenders' 1977 thriller *The American Friend* is an adaptation of which of Patricia Highsmith's Tom Ripley novels?

A) *The Talented Mr. Ripley*

B) *Ripley's Game*

C) *Ripley Down-Under*

D) *Mr. & Mrs. Ripley*

3. Which song became a hit after it was used over the opening sequence of Paul Schrader's 1980 film *American Gigolo*?

A) 'Love is a Battlefield' by Pat Benatar

B) 'Hai Karate' by Chrome Panther

C) 'Call Me' by Blondie

D) 'Just a Gigolo' by David Lee Roth

4. What's the name of the unwelcoming Yorkshire pub our backpacker heroes stray into in 1981's *An American Werewolf in London*?

A) The Goat and Compasses

B) Tapping the Admiral

C) The Bucket of Blood

D) The Slaughtered Lamb

5. To whom or what does the title of 1996's adaptation of David Mamet's play *American Buffalo* refer?

A) John F. Kennedy

B) A racehorse

C) John Q. Public

D) A rare coin

6. Which pseudonym did maverick director Tony Kaye try (and fail) to have his credit changed to after falling out with producers of 1998's *American History X*?

A) Adolf Hitler

B) Anne Frank

C) Humpty Dumpty

D) I.P. Freely

7. Which actress doubled down in 1999 by appearing in both *American Pie* and *American Beauty*?

A) Tara Reid

B) Thora Birch

C) Annette Bening

D) Mena Suvari

8. Speaking of *American Pie*, which of the following is NOT the subtitle of one of the franchise's direct-to-disc spin-offs?

A) *The Book of Love*
B) *Band Camp*
C) *The Naked Mile*
D) *Tijuana Hot Pocket*

9. Which track is playing as *American Psycho*'s Patrick Bateman (Christian Bale) takes a hatchet to Jared Leto's unfortunate Paul Allen?
A) 'I Just Died in Your Arms Tonight' by Cutting Crew
B) 'Careful with that Axe, Eugene' by Pink Floyd
C) 'Hip to Be Square' by Huey Lewis and the News
D) 'Rock Me Amadeus' by Falco

10. On what grounds is a potentially redemptive last-reel softball game in 2001's *Wet Hot American Summer* cancelled?
A) An alligator attack
B) A bad batch of corn dogs
C) A forest fire
D) Triteness

11. 2003's *American Splendor* takes us inside the troubled imagination of which comic-book legend, played by Paul Giamatti?
A) Alan Moore
B) Robert Crumb
C) Harvey Pekar
D) Frank Miller

12. Around which sport does John Badham's 1985 coming-of-age drama *American Flyers* – starring a young Kevin Costner – revolve?
A) Cycling
B) Hang gliding
C) Frisbee golf
D) Bobsledding

13. Which of the following is NOT an entry in the *American Ninja* series?
A) The Confrontation
B) Blood Hunt
C) Dojo of Death
D) The Annihilation

14. Jennifer Lawrence's Rosalyn in 2013's *American Hustle* takes particularly good care of her nails. What does her preferred choice of nail polish smell of?
A) 'Week-old Pop Tarts'
B) 'Champagne and gunfire'
C) 'Flowers with garbage'
D) 'Nancy Reagan's bathroom'

15. The 2014 documentary *American Interior* saw director Gruff Rhys follow in the footsteps of his forebear John Evans, who set off from the UK in 1792 in search of what?
A) A portal to the centre of the Earth rumoured to be located in Oklahoma
B) A fabled tribe of Welsh-speaking Native Americans
C) A herd of woolly mammoth that were still said to roam the plains
D) Recipes for the first cookbook to be published in the New World

THE NAMESAKE

Films that share titles

1. A formative American silent epic, and a riposte of sorts – released a century later – which sought to redress the earlier film's suspect racial politics?

2. Claire Denis's tart 1988 survey of a childhood in colonial Africa, and an altogether gooier Lasse Hallström confection from 2000?

3. A knockout 2013 indie centring on a housewife exploring her sexuality, and a shakier Will Smith drama released two years later?

4. A brakes-off J.G. Ballard adaptation of 1996, and a much written-off Oscar Best Picture winner from the Noughties?

5. A tasty Marx Brothers romp, and a no less absurd Laurel and Hardy short released six years earlier?

6. Two hard-as-nails dramas of football hooliganism, and a slick Nineties vehicle for salaryman Tom Cruise?

7. A chillingly plausible 2010 thriller set on a stalled ski lift, and one of Disney's biggest hits of recent years?

8. An Eddie Murphy buddy comedy of 1999, a less vital James Dean biopic of 2015, and a flatlining *Alien* knock-off from 2017?

9. A featherlight John Travolta comedy, and a clinical 2011 drama about an Austrian paedophile?

10. A canonical Russian silent of 1926, an Albert Brooks comedy of 1996, a dark Korean thriller of 2009, and – to some degree – a 2017 Jennifer Lawrence freakout?

11. An infamous Hitchcock classic, and a bigger-than-life biopic of a prominent gangster rapper?

12. A reliable Hal Hartley comedy, and a David Schwimmer-directed thriller centred on online grooming?

13. A Robert Benton detective drama that saw Paul Newman walking into the sunset, and the opening entry in one of this century's most successful franchises?

14. A train-related British silent of 1927, a Palme d'Or winner of the mid-Nineties, and a gritty British club-scene thriller of 1998?

15. A magical Michael Winterbottom portrait of pre-millennial London, and a grimier 2003 biopic dramatizing the downfall of porn star John Holmes?

Match answers to questions

Life
Notorious
Duck Soup
Concussion
Twilight
Frozen
Chocolat
Mother(!)
Crash
Michael
The Firm
The Birth of a Nation
Wonderland
Underground
Trust

LOST IN TRANSLATION

Transliterated titles

1. Which post-war American classic labours under the somewhat less poetic name *Sludge on the Dock* whenever it's revived in Portuguese cinemas?

2. Which Disney animation opened across Latin America as *The Night of the Cold Noses*?

3. Which specific Woody Allen film was handed the title *Urban Neurotic* in Germany?

4. What's the more commonly known title of the landmark genre movie that opened in Hungary as *The Eighth Passenger Was ... Death*?

5. Which mid-Eighties Michael J. Fox vehicle was sold to Brazilian audiences as *The Boy from the Future*?

6. And which of this era's standout teen movies went by the title *Expert in Fun* across Latin America?

7. Which Sam Raimi film opened in Japan under the title *Captain Supermarket*?

8. Which multiple Oscar winner went under the title *Mr. Cat Poop* in Hong Kong, reportedly as its protagonist's name translates as such for native audiences?

9. Which major British international hit from the same year went by the name *Six Naked Pigs* in China?

10. Which Adam Sandler vehicle was slapped with the title *Dimwit Surges Forth* in Thailand?

11. The Czech title of which blockbusting teen movie translates, somewhat bluntly, to *Boobs, Boobs, Boobies*?

12. Which sensitive turn-of-the-millennium drama, recipient of multiple gongs for its breakthrough star, was known in China as *17-Year-Old Girl's Medical Chart*?

13. Which recent American crowdpleaser is known in the Czech Republic by the not inaccurate *Bez Kalhot* – literally *Without Trousers*?

14. And which critically reviled all-star non-comedy now sits unloved in Czech bargain bins bearing the bizarrely florid title *Unapproachable Youth*?

15. Which beloved 21st-century indie is known as *Meetings and Failures in Meetings* in Brazil, *Between the Words* in Poland, and *Love is a Strange Place* in Portugal?

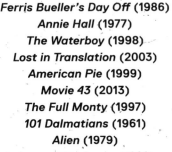

Match answers to questions

Ferris Bueller's Day Off (1986)
Annie Hall (1977)
The Waterboy (1998)
Lost in Translation (2003)
American Pie (1999)
Movie 43 (2013)
The Full Monty (1997)
101 Dalmatians (1961)
Alien (1979)
Army of Darkness (1992)
Girl, Interrupted (1999)
On the Waterfront (1954)
As Good as It Gets (1997)
Magic Mike (2012)
Teen Wolf (1985)

BEAT THE DEVIL

P.S. I Love You: Notable postscripts and subtitles

Complete the title – no half marks here.

1. 2014's *Birdman, or* ....

2. 1919's *Broken Blossoms, or* ....

3. 1927's *The Lodger:* ....

4. 1965's *Those Magnificent Men in their Flying Machines, or* ....

5. 1985's *Police Academy II:* ....

6. 1999's *Freeway II:* ....

7. 2000's *Battlefield Earth:* ....

8. 2006's *Borat!:* ....

9. 2006's *The Santa Clause 3:* ....

10. 2008's *Il Divo:* ....

11. 2008's *Gingerdead Man 2:* ....

12. 2008's *Louise Bourgeois:* ....

13. 2009's *Precious:* ....

14. 2011's *Spy Kids 4:* ....

15. Finally, 2006's *Wristcutters*, 2009's *Dogging* and 2017's *Toilet* all share which subtitle? ....

Say What?: Odd titles

1. *Zombies*, 2. *Happiness*, 3. *8th*, 4. *Basil*, 5. *Hell*, 6. *Women*, 7. *Mom*, 8. *Penis*, 9. *Disney*, 10. *Mountain*, 11. *Julie Newmar*, 12. *Juice*, 13. *Cheese*, 14. *Snogging*, 15. *Goats*

Spellbound: A cinematic spelling test

1. Martin Scorsese, 2. Keira Knightley, 3. Jon Hamm, 4. Shia LaBeouf, 5. Matthew McConaughey, 6. Zack Galifianakis, 7. Arnold Schwarzenegger, 8. Scarlett Johansson, 9. Quvenzhané Wallis, 10. Chiwetel Ejiofor, 11. Steve Carell, 12. Domhnall Gleeson, 13. Saoirse Ronan, 14. Cara Delevingne, 15. Apichatpong Weerasethakul

Rhapsodies in Blue: Cerulean cinema

1. *The Blue Lamp*, 2. *Blue Hawaii*, 3. *Blue Sunshine*, 4. *The Blues Brothers*, 5. *The Boys in Blue*, 6. *Blue Thunder*, 7. *Blue Velvet*, 8. *Blue Monkey*, 9. *Blue*, 10. *Three Colours Blue*, 11. *Blue in the Face*, 12. *Blue Juice*, 13. *Deep Blue Sea*, 14. *Blue Valentine*, 15. *Blue Is the Warmest Colour*

Alternative Realities: Movies that changed their titles

1. a, 2. d, 3. d, 4. c, 5. c, 6. b, 7. c (it's actually known as *Murder Mystery in Snowy Cream*), 8. a (it's actually known as *Santa is a Pervert*), 9. b, 10. d, 11. d, 12. d, 13. d, 14. d, 15. b

All about US: Films with 'American' in their title

1. c, 2. b, 3. c, 4. d, 5. d, 6. c, 7. d, 8. d, 9. c, 10. d, 11. c, 12. a, 13. c, 14. c, 15. b

The Namesake: Films that share titles

1. *The Birth of a Nation*, 2. *Chocolat*, 3. *Concussion*, 4. *Crash*, 5. *Duck Soup*, 6. *The Firm*, 7. *Frozen*, 8. *Life*, 9. *Michael*, 10. *Mother(!)*, 11. *Notorious*, 12. *Trust*, 13. *Twilight*, 14. *Underground*, 15. *Wonderland*

Lost in Translation: Transliterated titles

1. *On the Waterfront*, 2. *101 Dalmatians*, 3. *Annie Hall*, 4. *Alien*, 5. *Teen Wolf*, 6. *Ferris Bueller's Day Off*, 7. *Army of Darkness*, 8. *As Good as It Gets*, 9. *The Full Monty*, 10. *The Waterboy*, 11. *American Pie*, 12. *Girl, Interrupted*, 13. *Magic Mike*, 14. *Movie 43*, 15. *Lost in Translation*

P.S. I Love You: Notable postscripts and subtitles

1. (*The Unexpected Virtue of Ignorance*), 2. *The Yellow Man and the Girl*, 3. *A Story of the London Fog*, 4. *How I Flew from London to Paris in 25 Hours and 11 Minutes*, 5. *Their First Assignment*, 6. *Confessions of a Trickbaby*, 7. *A Saga of the Year 3000*, 8. *Cultural Learnings of America for Make Benefit Glorious Nation of Kazakhstan*, 9. *The Escape Clause*, 10. *The Spectacular Life of Giulio Andreotti*, 11. *Passion of the Crust*, 12. *The Spider, the Mistress and the Tangerine*, 13. *Based on the Novel 'Push' by Sapphire*, 14. *All the Time in the World*, 15. *A Love Story*

ANSWERS

2

The Early YEARS

Cinema's baby steps

BLUFFER'S GUIDE

Pen portraits of movie pioneers

1. This Ohio-born innovator – flush after inventing the lightbulb – spent the late 19th century cornering the market in recording and exhibiting images.

2. Often regarded as American cinema's founding father, this controversial figure directed the silent era's first blockbuster, a thunderous historical epic that remains a site of contention today.

3. Known as 'the Biograph Girl', she was one of the most popular female stars of the early screen, but struggled to adapt to the talkies, committing suicide in 1938 by swallowing a mixture of cough syrup and ant powder.

4. This industry lynchpin oversaw Hollywood's first feature-length venture – 1914's *The Squaw Man* – before going on to craft biblically epic spectacles, notably two separate takes on *The Ten Commandments.*

5. These doe-eyed sisters positioned themselves among the nascent industry's most luminous stars with their performances in 1918's First World War drama *Hearts of the World* – guided, as they would so often be, by the director in Question #2.

6. Born Lazar Meir in Minsk in 1884, this cinema owner turned studio chief provided one of the initials for a studio still in action today.

7. Although born in Canada, she became known as 'America's Sweetheart' after a run of successful films in the 1910s; in the Twenties, she married the legendary screen swashbuckler with whom she had formed the studio United Artists.

8. This Italian-born Casanova became silent cinema's pre-eminent heartthrob in 1921 after appearing in back-to-back sensations *The Four Horsemen of the Apocalypse* and *The Sheik*.

9. Tall, bespectacled and often found wearing a boater hat, this popular silent-comedy star endures in the imagination for his staggering, unfaked stunts – most memorably clinging from a clock face in 1923's *Safety Last*!

10. This very able French director rallied the European film industry in 1927 with his stirring five-hour, three-screen biopic of Napoleon Bonaparte.

11. This Brooklyn-born boy wonder oversaw the production of such enduring works as *Ben-Hur* (1925) and *A Night at the Opera* (1935).

12. This actress escaped childhood poverty to become an overnight sensation after starring in 1927's *It*, thereby becoming the first recipient of the popular press's now-common 'It Girl' tag.

13. The man who married 'America's Sweetheart' (Question #7), he became a huge star off the back of *The Mark of Zorro* (1920) and played the title roles in *Robin Hood* (1922) and *The Thief of Bagdad* (1924).

14. This Kansas-born performer, noted for her distinctive bobbed haircut, redefined screen eroticism with her turn as the doomed Lulu in 1929's *Pandora's Box*.

15. A reliably bankable performer in the 1920s, this German Shepherd was rescued from the battlefields of the First World War, returning the compliment by saving the day in such titles as 1926's *While London Sleeps* and 1927's *A Dog of the Regiment*.

Match answer to question

Florence Lawrence, Louise Brooks, Abel Gance, Thomas Edison, Rin Tin Tin, Mary Pickford, D.W. Griffith, Douglas Fairbanks, Louis B. Mayer, Clara Bow, Irving G. Thalberg, Dorothy and Lillian Gish, Harold Lloyd, Rudolph Valentino, Cecil B. DeMille

IN THE BEGINNING

Cinematic firsts

1. In October 1888, Frenchman Louis Aimé Augustin Le Prince recorded the first motion picture images in Leeds, England. What did the film capture?

A) The Leeds United football team practising penalty kicks
B) His son playing an accordion
C) A cockfight
D) Trams going by the window of his studio

2. Le Prince intended to exhibit his groundbreaking films across Europe and America. What stopped him doing so?

A) Thomas Edison sued him for breach of copyright
B) A maid mistakenly threw his negatives out during a spring clean
C) Crippling doubt
D) He mysteriously disappeared during a train journey from England to Paris

3. Among the Edison Company's early hits was an 1894 short called *Carmencita*, directed by William Dickson. Who or what was the eponymous subject?

A) A fishing boat
B) A bullfight
C) A flamenco dancer
D) A two-headed donkey

4. The first film to be presented for the public on a screen was the Lumière brothers' *La Sortie des Ouvriers de l'Usine Lumière* (*Employees Leaving the Lumière Factory*) in 1895. How many people turned up to see it?

A) 0
B) 1
C) 200
D) 5000

5. The first film to be officially registered for copyright was produced in 1894. What was it called?

A) *Dora's Feigned Surprise*
B) *Ramsey Lauder's Dilemma*
C) *Mona's Lucky Escape*
D) *Fred Ott's Sneeze*

6. Which band of brothers prove themselves the heroes of D.W. Griffiths' groundbreaking 1915 film *Birth of a Nation*?

A) The Sioux
B) The British
C) The Ku Klux Klan
D) The Confederate Army

7. The British pairing of Birt Acres and Robert W. Paul entered the expanding marketplace in 1896 with footage of which two events?

A) The Oxford–Cambridge boat race and the Derby horse race

B) Buffalo Bill's Wild West Show and the funeral of Queen Victoria

C) The opening of Parliament and a kangaroo race across Tower Bridge

D) The Camden Lock Dwarf-Tossing finals and trapeze act The Tumbling Titfields

8. 1897's *The Corbett-Fitzsimmons Fight* – depicting a boxing match between James J. Corbett and Robert Fitzsimmons – is regarded as the first full-length documentary film. But what were the fighters' respective nicknames?

A) Gentleman Jim and the Freckled Wonder

B) The Milwaukee Mastodon and Feudin' Fitzsimmons

C) Clobbering Corbett and Robert the Bruce

D) Ol' Thunderguns and the Pugilistic Paragon

9. Why did the first full-length feature, 1906's *The Story of the Kelly Gang*, end up having to shoot its leading man at some distance?

A) He was serving time in prison

B) He had filed a restraining order against hot-headed director Charles Tait

C) He was an extra drafted in after the original lead ran off

D) After seeing early footage from the film, the producers deemed him 'distractingly ugly'

10. The first full-length literary adaptation was a 1909 film version of which seminal text?

A) *Faust*

B) *Les Misérables*

C) *Wuthering Heights*

D) *The Inferno*

11. What cinematic first was bestowed on Charles Dickens's *Oliver Twist* in 1912?

A) It was the first film in which a zoom lens was used

B) It was the first film to be banned (by Tsar Nicholas II of Russia)

C) It was the basis of the first feature films made in both the UK and the US

D) It was the first film screened at Buckingham Palace

12. Al Jolson ushered cinema into the age of sound in 1927's *The Jazz Singer*. What were the first lines spoken?

A) 'Wait a minute, wait a minute ... you ain't heard nothin' yet!'

B) 'Hey, someone get me a drink of water ... I got something stuck in my throat!'

C) 'Somebody better call the cops ... we got a riot goin' on!'

D) 'Oh baby, oh mammy ... we're cookin' now!'

13. 1929 British sound effort *Blackmail* was directed by which future cinema legend?

A) Sinden Smallbridge

B) Alfred Hitchcock

C) David Lean

D) Milford Haven

14. Opening its doors in 1887, which of the following is considered to have been the world's first cinema?

A) Drexler Auditorium in Chicago

B) Le Cinéma de Fausses Nouvelles in Paris

C) The Wintergarten in Berlin

D) The Griffin Playhouse in London

15. Which nation had to wait until the 1990s to complete production on its first full-length feature?

A) Liechtenstein

B) Samoa

C) Laos

D) Saudi Arabia

FIRST FLOURISHES

Landmark silents

1. The Lumière brothers reportedly caused panicked audiences to flee screaming in fear when they screened a film of what in 1895? [Clue: the French title is *L'arrivée d'un [???] en Gare de La Ciotat*]

2. Which household pet makes a lively appearance in the brothers' *La Sortie des Ouvriers de l'Usine Lumière*?

3. That film was remade (after a fashion) one year later in a short that showed Portuguese workers exiting which type of building?

4. Thomas Edison produced a 1896 short that features cinema's first depiction of which intimate act?

5. The Lumières' 1895 short *L'Arroseur Arrosé* forms a textbook illustration of a time-honoured practical joke, in which a young boy treads on which garden implement?

6. Edwin S. Porter's 1903 short *The Great Train Robbery* draws to a shock ending when one of the robbers points what directly at the audience?

7. India's first full-length feature, 1913's *Raja Harishchandra*, was made by director Dadasaheb Phalke. He was inspired to turn his hand to filmmaking after seeing a film called *The Life of...*

8. The French director Louis Feuillade made a celebrated silent serial *Les Vampires* in 1915 which sees a cat-suited maiden patrolling the rooftops of Paris. Her name is an anagram of the word 'vampire', but what is it?

9. Swedish director Victor Sjöström's 1921 silent *The Phantom Carriage* is believed to have inspired a memorable bathroom sequence in a claustrophobic Eighties horror touchstone. Which one?

10. What was historically notable about Oscar Micheaux, director of 1920's race-relations drama *Within Our Gates*?

11. Sergei Eisenstein's 1925 landmark *Battleship Potemkin* features a tumultuous sequence in which bodies (and a pram) go tumbling down what in the midst of gunfire?

12. That same sequence later inspired a key shootout in which Prohibition-set US action movie of 1987, which netted Sean Connery his only Oscar?

13. When Fritz Lang signed off on his 1927 sci-fi opus *Metropolis*, he probably didn't envision it being given a 'disco remix' six decades later. Which Italian producer and musician provided that version's soundtrack?

14. The 1928 masterpiece *The Passion of Joan of Arc* was directed by which celebrated Danish director?

15. The 1962 French film *Vivre Sa Vie* contains a scene in which the actor Anna Karina gazes up at footage of Dreyer's Joan, Renée Falconetti. Name the director of the film.

THE PALEFACE

Buster Keaton

1. Born Joseph Keaton in 1895, the silent comedy maestro took the name Buster because ...

A) It came to him in a fever dream following a swim in a fetid lake

B) He was a fan of Phil Collins caper film *Buster*

C) It featured in a quip made by Harry Houdini, who saw him fall, unharmed, down a flight of stairs

D) It's a combination of his favourite mode of transport and his favourite river – the Ter in Essex, England

2. Which stage name was young Buster assigned upon starting to perform with his family's touring acrobatic troupe at the age of three?

A) The Human Mop

B) Jeremy K. Dwyer

C) Stakka Bo

D) Michael Keaton

3. As a child, Keaton lost his right index finger in an accident – how?

A) He was grating a frozen banana and got carried away

B) He caught it in a mangle

C) A seagull took off with it, along with his half-eaten Reuben sandwich

D) He cut it off as a blood offering to a local Yakuza chief

4. Keaton's first full-length star vehicle was 1920's *The Saphead*, made after starring in a series of shorts headlined by which plus-sized star?

A) Jelly Ramclasp

B) Blubber Hardstirrup

C) Lardy Hamsaddle

D) Fatty Arbuckle

5. In the 1921 short *The Playhouse*, Keaton plays every credited role, including a conductor, members of a minstrel troupe, and ...

A) A talking hot dog

B) A primate

C) The inventor of the Biro

D) Amanullah Khan, Emir of Afghanistan

6. 1923's classic *Our Hospitality* charts a feud between Southern clans the Canfields and the McKays. But what is the source of the ongoing discord?

A) Keaton's Willie McKay defiled Grandma Canfield's grave with turtle entrails

B) The McKay kids kept throwing their Frisbee on to the Canfields' kitchen extension

C) Willie laughed at Joseph Canfield's mispronunciation of the word 'gala'

D) No-one can actually remember

7. Keaton's 1925 *Seven Chances* (100% on Rotten Tomatoes) provided the inspiration

for 1999's Chris O'Donnell romcom *The Bachelor*. How many percentage points fewer did the latter earn?

A) 99%

B) 91%

C) 45%

D) It too has a 100% score

8. How did the British artist and filmmaker Steve McQueen pay homage to Keaton in his 1997 work *Deadpan*?

A) It opens with McQueen intoning: 'I bloody love you, Buster Keaton.'

B) He recreated a key stunt from 1928's *Steamboat Bill, Jr.*

C) He films himself making a life-sized statue of Keaton out of flour and water

D) He reads out Keaton's autobiography in Greek

9. Which of the following was a stipulation in the punitive contract Keaton unwisely signed with MGM in the late 1920s?

A) The actor must forswear sex during production

B) The actor must submit to regular blood alcohol tests

C) The actor must never smile on screen

D) The actor must never do his own stunts

10. Which card game can Keaton be observed playing during his comeback cameo in 1950's *Sunset Boulevard*?

A) Whist

B) Bridge

C) Uno

D) Top Trumps

11. The actor James Mason played an unexpected part in preserving Keaton's early work, after coming into several rare film reels in the 1950s. How so?

A) He rescued them from a skip

B) His daffy aunt was using the film cans to prop up her hamster cage

C) He won them in a strip poker game

D) He moved into Keaton's one-time LA abode

12. In which film about a washed-up comedian does Keaton share the stage with Charlie Chaplin?

A) *Monsieur Verdoux*

B) *Limelight*

C) *A Countess from Hong Kong*

D) *A King in New York*

13. *Singin' in the Rain* star Donald O'Connor played Keaton in 1957 biopic *The Buster Keaton Story*. How much was Buster paid for the story rights?

A) $50,000

B) $1

C) The title deeds to Lelu Island in Micronesia

D) A lifetime's eat-all-you-like free pass at the Paramount canteen

14. Keaton starred in a 1965 short named *Film*, made with legendary playwright Samuel Beckett. What did the *Times* critic Dilys Powell have to say about it?

A) 'A remarkable fusion of classic-era Hollywood and visionary theatrical experimentation.'

B) 'Samuel Beckett is making Irish experimental film great again.'

C) 'A load of old bosh.'

D) 'The best Marvel movie so far this year.'

15. At the age of 70 and terminally ill with cancer, Keaton played his final screen role in 1966's *A Funny Thing Happened on the Way to the Forum*. How did he shock fellow cast members?

A) He poured beer over his feet between takes

B) He wouldn't stop swearing

C) He insisted on doing his own stunts

D) He claimed he was able to levitate between the hours of 9pm and 11pm

SEND IN THE CLOWN

Charlie Chaplin

True or false?

1. Chaplin was born in 1889 in the London borough of Southwark.

2. In 1897, Charlie appeared with a troupe of child dancers who were known as Seven Kent Kiddies.

3. One of Chaplin's first major stage credits was the 1904 premiere of that beloved and oft-performed pantomime *Peter Pan*.

4. The young Chaplin was fired from his job as a butler at one swanky London residence after being caught playing an electric cello while on duty.

5. While touring with the Fred Karno company, Chaplin was understudied by the legendary screen clown Stan Laurel.

6. Nabel Mormand was the name of the popular comedienne with whom Chaplin came to appear many times over the first years of his career.

7. *Making a Living* was the title of the first film Chaplin appeared in for Mack Sennett's Keystone Studios, released in 1914.

8. Chaplin made his directorial debut in 1914, with the comic short *Caught in the Rain*. At a screening of the film, his colleagues demurred and told him he'd never be a great director.

9. During the iconic cabin dinner scene in 1925's *The Gold Rush*, Charlie had his now established Tramp perform a tabletop dance number with a tin of creamed corn and a mouldy kumquat.

10. Chaplin fondly referred to his Beverly Hills home as 'Tramp Towers'.

11. In the 1940 film *The Great Dictator*, Chaplin plays a ranting, mustachioed fascist named Adenoid Hynkel.

12. Chaplin was married four times. His shortest marriage was to his second wife, Lita Gray, which lasted from 1924 to 1927.

13. In 1972, Chaplin took to the stage of the Dorothy Chandler Pavilion in Los Angeles to receive an honorary Oscar, cueing the longest standing ovation in Academy Award history – a full 12 minutes.

14. Oona Chaplin, born in 1986 and star of saucy TV fantasy saga *Game of Thrones*, is Charlie's granddaughter.

15. British comedian Rik Mayall played Chaplin in 2001's *The Cat's Meow*, Peter Bogdanovich's film about the enduring mystery surrounding the death of movie mogul Thomas Ince.

BLOCK HEADS

Laurel and Hardy

1. Before he teamed up with Stan, Oliver Norvell Hardy found minor fame working under his nickname. What was it?

A) Stinko
B) Lardy
C) Rollo
D) Babe

2. What was the name of the 1927 silent short in which Stan and Ollie 'officially' appeared together as comedy duo 'Laurel And Hardy'?

A) *A Philadelphia Gorilla in Brooklyn*
B) *Trick Golf*
C) *Love Me, Love My Biscuits*
D) *Putting Pants on Philip*

3. What did Stan do to develop his character's distinctive onscreen gait?

A) Hold a drinking straw between the cheeks of his bottom
B) Sleep at a 45-degree angle
C) Cut off the heels of his shoes
D) Wear underwear two sizes too small for him

4. Ollie played a major role in a 1925 film that would be remade some years later to far greater acclaim. Was it ...?

A) *The Maltese Falcon*
B) *The Wizard of Oz*
C) *Around the World in 80 Days*
D) *The Treasure of the Sierra Madre*

5. What was the name of the pop-eyed Scots actor who became the boys' regular foil (and was also reputedly the inspiration for Homer Simpson's 'D'oh!')?

A) James Finlayson
B) Hymie Henderson
C) Wylie Watson
D) Jock Masterson

6. 1927's insurance-scam comedy *The Battle of the Century* climaxes with what culinary calamity?

A) Stan accidentally swallows a budgerigar
B) The boys get sucked into a toffee-making machine
C) A colossal custard pie fight
D) Ollie burns down his house while cooking Cherries Jubilee

7. 1929's *Big Business* finds Stan and Ollie selling which item door-to-door?

A) Christmas trees
B) Encyclopedias
C) Asbestos insulation
D) Ladies underwear

8. How did emergent blonde bombshell Jean Harlow raise a few early eyebrows at the climax of the boys' 1929 romp *Double Whoopee*?

A) She sucked a hot dog out of its bun
B) Her nipples were clearly visible through her

wet blouse during portions of the film's famous firehouse finale

C) Her skirt was whipped off by a departing taxi cab

D) She used an American flag as a picnic blanket

9. What task proves difficult for the boys in the 1932 short *The Music Box*?

A) Disguising the audible fact that they've eaten too many beans

B) Evading the advances of two amorous opera singers

C) Teaching a chimpanzee to play the drums

D) Carrying a piano up a long flight of stairs

10. What pressing problem do the boys have to deal with while crossing a rickety rope bridge in 1938's *Swiss Miss*?

A) A territorial gorilla

B) A drunken yodeller

C) An aggrieved yak

D) Both are desperate to relieve themselves

11. Stan Laurel roomed with Charlie Chaplin during a 1912 US tour. How did he later describe the beloved comic genius?

A) Smelly, lazy and possessing a debilitating fear of cats

B) Mean, cheap and showing signs of insanity

C) Gullible, obscene and a degenerate gambler

D) Easily offended and alcoholic but surprisingly good with kids

12. 'The Trail of the Lonesome Pine' was the breakout song from the boys' 1937 film *Way Out West*. Where would you pick up the trail?

A) 'In the hills and hollers of Kentucky'

B) 'From the Redwood Forest to the Gulf Stream waters'

C) 'In the Blue Ridge Mountains of Virginia'

D) 'On top of Old Smokey, all covered with snow'

13. One of the boys' most cherished films is the 1930 short *Laughing Gravy*. But who or what is 'Laughing Gravy'?

A) Ollie's gold-digging girlfriend

B) An oil well

C) Their new restaurant

D) Their pet dog

14. In 1942 Stan and Ollie appeared in a short film for the US Department of Agriculture that reminded Americans about the importance of wood and forestry management in the war effort. What was it called?

A) *Wood, What Is it Good For?*

B) *Careful with that Match!*

C) *The Tree in a Test Tube*

D) *Plastic Schmastic!*

15. The Laurel and Hardy Appreciation Society is informally known as ...?

A) The Sugar Daddies

B) The Blockheads

C) The Bacon Grabbers

D) Sons of the Desert

BEAT THE DEVIL

Shock of the New: early Surrealists and Expressionists

1. What was the name of the hulking creative who wrote, directed and starred in two screen versions of the Golem legend, before being appointed the Nazis' 'Actor of the State'?

2. The titular health professional in 1920's *The Cabinet of Dr. Caligari* was reputedly modelled on which gloomy German philosopher?

3. Who was the leading man of F.W. Murnau's landmark 1922 horror *Nosferatu*, to whom Tim Burton later paid homage when naming Christopher Walken's character in *Batman Returns*?

4. A Fritz Lang thriller of 1922 established the character of a gambler-turned-criminal mastermind who was to loom large over German cinema in subsequent decades. What was his name?

5. 1929's *Un Chien Andalou*, directed by Luis Buñuel and Salvador Dalí, made audiences wince by cutting from clouds crossing the moon to which grisly image?

6. Buñuel, anticipating audience unrest that didn't follow, reportedly carried what in his pocket to the film's premiere?

7. Which song, later covered by the Beatles, Kevin Ayers and Christina Aguilera, was first made famous by Marlene Dietrich in Josef von Sternberg's 1930 melodrama *The Blue Angel*?

8. On which exotic island did Murnau shoot his lush 1931 melodrama *Tabu*?

9. Which indie curio of 2000 offered an alternative history of the making of 1922's *Nosferatu*?

10. Buñuel receives unlikely thanks in the credits of which gonzo Noughties comedy?

Bluffer's Guide: Pen portraits of movie pioneers

1. Thomas Edison, 2. D.W. Griffith, 3. Florence Lawrence, 4. Cecil B. DeMille, 5. Dorothy and Lillian Gish, 6. Louis B. Mayer, 7. Mary Pickford, 8. Rudolph Valentino, 9. Harold Lloyd, 10. Abel Gance, 11. Irving G. Thalberg, 12. Clara Bow, 13. Douglas Fairbanks, 14. Louise Brooks, 15. Rin Tin Tin

In the Beginning: Cinematic firsts

1. b, 2. d, 3. c, 4. c, 5. d, 6. c, 7. a, 8. a, 9. c, 10. b, 11. c, 12. a, 13. b, 14. c, 15. d (*Sinbad, the Little Sailor* in 1990)

First Flourishes: Landmark silents

1. A train, 2. A dog, 3. A factory, 4. A kiss, 5. A hose, 6. A gun, 7. Christ, 8. Irma Vep, 9. *The Shining*, 10. He was the first African-American filmmaker, 11. Steps (the Odessa Steps, to be specific), 12. *The Untouchables*, 13. Giorgio Moroder, 14. Carl Dreyer, 15. Jean-Luc Godard

The Paleface: Buster Keaton

1. c, 2. a, 3. b, 4. d, 5. b, 6. d, 7. b (at a measly 9%), 8. b, 9. c, 10. b, 11. d, 12. b, 13. a, 14. c, 15. c

Send in the Clown: Charlie Chaplin

1. True, 2. False – they were called Eight Lancashire Lads, 3. True, 4. False – he was playing a trumpet, 5. True, 6. False – it's Mabel Normand, 7. True, 8. False – they loved it and laughed heartily, 9. False – it was two bread rolls, 10. False – he nicknamed it Breakaway House, 11. True, 12. False – he was married to first wife, Mildred Harris, for two years (1918–20), 13. True, 14. True, 15. False – it was Eddie Izzard

Blockheads: Laurel and Hardy

1. d, 2. d, 3. c, 4. b, 5. a, 6. c, 7. a, 8. c, 9. d, 10. a, 11. b, 12. c, 13. d, 14. c, 15. d

Shock of the New: Early Surrealists and Expressionists

1. Paul Wegener, 2. Arthur Schopenhauer, 3. Max Schreck, 4. Dr Mabuse, 5. A razorblade slicing an eyeball, 6. Stones, 7. 'Falling in Love Again (Can't Help It)', 8. Bora Bora, 9. *Shadow of the Vampire*, 10. *Jackass: Number Two*

ANSWERS

3

The Shot

CALLERS

They made the movies.

PEEPING TOM

Alfred Hitchcock

1. What was the young Hitch's first position in the London offices of the Famous Players-Lasky film company?

A) Focus puller
B) Tea boy
C) Graphic artist
D) Runner

2. What provides the backdrop for the grand finale of 1929's *Blackmail*, Hitchcock's first sound feature?

A) The Tower of London
B) A Suffragette rally
C) The British Museum
D) Crowds ice skating on the River Thames

3. Which of the following is NOT the title of one of Hitch's early directorial efforts?

A) *An Elastic Affair*
B) *The Manxman*
C) *Elstree Calling*
D) *A Frightful Blunder*

4. What was notable about the filming of 1948's *Rope*?

A) It was shot in just one day
B) It was shot to look like one uninterrupted take
C) Hitchcock wasn't actually there for the shoot
D) It was shot using only a fish-eye lens

5. And what was unusual about Hitchcock's 1956 film *The Man Who Knew Too Much*?

A) Filmed on location in Marrakesh, it was the first American film shot entirely outside the US
B) It was shown in cinemas with an added laugh track
C) It was a remake of Hitchcock's own 1934 film of the same name
D) None of the lead actors were ever seen together in the same frame

6. What explanation is given for the homicidal behaviour of our feathered friends in 1963's *The Birds*?

A) Boredom
B) The polarity of the world's magnetic field has reversed
C) None
D) They have been driven mad by airborne pollutants

7. What object was repeatedly knifed to simulate the sound of Janet Leigh being stabbed in *Psycho*?

A) A dead goose
B) A hot water bottle filled with sausagemeat
C) A cushion wrapped in a leather jacket
D) A watermelon

8. Which of the following is an actual quote from the Master of Suspense?

A) 'I always sleep with the lights on.'

B) 'I still have my childhood teddy bear. Doesn't everyone?'

C) 'I'm frightened of eggs.'

D) 'I telephone my mother twice a day without exception.'

9. Which piece of music has passed into legend as the theme tune of TV's *Alfred Hitchcock Presents*?

A) Saint-Saëns' 'Danse Macabre'

B) Gounod's 'Funeral March of a Marionette'

C) Rachmaninov's 'The Isle of the Dead'

D) Mussorgsky's 'Night on Bald Mountain'

10. Who did Hitchcock bring in to design the dream sequences for his 1943 mental asylum thriller *Spellbound*?

A) Salvador Dalí

B) Walt Disney

C) Aleister Crowley

D) Chuck Jones

11. According to Hitchcock's daughter Patricia, what film was one of her father's cinematic guilty pleasures?

A) *Herbie Rides Again*

B) *Debbie Does Dallas*

C) *Animal House*

D) *Smokey and the Bandit*

12. Which future Oscar winner played the thug who tramples Cary Grant's fingers as he dangles from Mount Rushmore in the gripping climax of 1959's *North by Northwest*?

A) Martin Landau

B) George Kennedy

C) Gene Hackman

D) Jack Nicholson

13. Tippi Hedren famously played one of Hitch's iciest blondes in 1964's *Marnie*. But why did his first choice, Grace Kelly, decline the role?

A) She hated her prospective co-star Sean Connery with a passion

B) Kelly was by then Princess Grace of Monaco and her well-to-do subjects objected to her taking the part

C) She thought the name of the film's eponymous heroine sounded 'too common'

D) She was too traumatized by the recent death of President Kennedy

14. Anthony Hopkins played the Master in 2012's biopic *Hitchcock*. But which prominent actress met her end in that film's shower sequence while playing *Psycho*'s Janet Leigh?

A) Sienna Miller

B) Kristen Stewart

C) Jennifer Lawrence

D) Scarlett Johansson

15. What item does the serial killer in Hitch's 1972 film *Frenzy* use to murder his female victims?

A) A trouser press

B) A coat hanger

C) His tie

D) His shoe

FEMALE GAZE

Women directors, established and emerging

1. The world's first female director, Alice Guy-Blaché, made her debut in 1896 with which film?

A) *A Baguette for Claudette*

B) *The Dumpling Queen*

C) *The Cabbage Fairy*

D) *The Cheese Eaters*

2. What was Patty Jenkins' only previous feature (way back in 2003) before she took the comic-book movie world by storm with 2017's *Wonder Woman*?

A) *The Shipping News*

B) *Monster*

C) *In the Cut*

D) *Mona Lisa Smile*

3. In 1997 Mimi Leder directed the first feature film to be released by newly formed studio DreamWorks. What was it called?

A) *Dante's Peak*

B) *The Relic*

C) *The Peacemaker*

D) *The Devil's Own*

4. German director Leni Riefenstahl is unquestionably most famous for her Nazi propaganda film *Triumph of the Will*, but she directed other films as well. Which of the following is NOT one of them?

A) *The Blue Lamp*

B) *Lowlands*

C) *The White Ecstasy*

D) *Olympia*

5. Ida Lupino was one of the first American actresses to make the move behind the camera, and in doing so became the only person to both appear in and direct episodes of which TV series?

A) *Bewitched*

B) *Star Trek*

C) *I Love Lucy*

D) *The Twilight Zone*

6. Angelina Jolie's 2011 directorial debut *In the Land of Blood and Honey* is a love story set against the backdrop of ...?

A) The Russian Revolution

B) The Crusades

C) The Bosnian War

D) The 1986 World Cup

7. How does Colin Farrell's character meet his end in Sofia Coppola's steamy 2017 Civil War-set drama *The Beguiled*?

A) He is pushed down a well

B) He is buried up to his neck and left to die

C) He is fed poisoned mushrooms

D) He has an allergic reaction to a bee sting

8. What track provided the cue for a memorable in-car singalong in Penelope Spheeris' 1992 comedy *Wayne's World*?

A) Alice Cooper's 'School's Out'
B) Nirvana's 'Smells Like Teen Spirit'
C) Right Said Fred's 'I'm Too Sexy'
D) Queen's 'Bohemian Rhapsody'

9. Which of the following actresses was NOT a member of the all-star baseball team in Penny Marshall's historical drama *A League of Their Own*?

A) Madonna
B) Geena Davis
C) Rosie O'Donnell
D) Roseanne Barr

10. In Nora Ephron's textbook 1993 romcom *Sleepless in Seattle*, which films are claimed to be the weepies of choice for women and men respectively?

A) *Love Story* and *Mean Streets*
B) *An Affair to Remember* and *The Dirty Dozen*
C) *Now, Voyager* and *The Godfather*
D) *Rosemary's Baby* and *Planet of the Apes*

11. To what does the title of Kathryn Bigelow's 2002 film *K-19: The Widowmaker*, starring Harrison Ford, refer?

A) A dog
B) A tornado
C) A submarine
D) A food additive

12. To what does the title of Ava DuVernay's celebrated Netflix documentary *13th* refer?

A) The Thirteenth Amendment to the United States Constitution
B) The thirteenth inning of the 1989 World Series
C) The thirteenth man to walk on the moon
D) The thirteenth floor of the Empire State Building

13. Which British colloquialism did Andrea Arnold blurt out when picking up her Best Short Film Oscar for *Wasp* in 2005?

A) 'Christ on a bike!'
B) 'Ecky thump!'
C) 'Well, I'll go to the foot of our stairs!'
D) 'This is the dog's bollocks!'

14. *Green Street*, Lexi Alexander's 2005 film about East End football hooligans, boasted which surprising American lead?

A) Johnny Galecki
B) Neil Patrick Harris
C) Elijah Wood
D) Wil Wheaton

15. How did director Haifaa al-Mansour get around strict Saudi Arabian customs that effectively banned her from filming exterior shots for her 2012 film *Wadjda*?

A) She disguised herself as a man
B) She used a drone to keep up with the action
C) She gave directions from a van parked nearby
D) She gave HD cameras to tourists and asked them to shoot scenes for her

WEIRD WORLD

David Lynch

1. Why did David Lynch's family move around the US when he was a child?

A) Because of his father's roving job with the Department of Agriculture

B) Because he won a 'See All 50 Spooky States' competition on the back of a cereal box

C) Because of the publicity commitments that came with his famous, shock-haired appearance in a nationwide shampoo ad campaign

D) Because he was thrown out of a series of schools for repeatedly 'rejecting the premise' of Math class

2. Which future rock 'n' roll frontman did Lynch get thrown out of the college dorm room they shared at the Boston School of Fine Arts for being 'too weird'?

A) Jello Biafra of Dead Kennedys

B) Peter Wolf of The J. Geils Band

C) Brad Delp of Boston

D) Clem Fandango of Slippery Thistle

3. What is the name of the LA diner Lynch visited after lunch every day for seven years in the *Blue Velvet* years?

A) The Mulholland Drive-In

B) Bob's Big Boy

C) Pee-Wee's Gobblebag

D) Twin Perks

4. His regular order was a chocolate milkshake chased down by several cups of coffee. What did he insist his shake arrive in?

A) A silver goblet

B) A coyote's skull

C) A replica of one of Judy Garland's ruby slippers from *The Wizard of Oz*

D) A 'What Made Milwaukee Famous ...' mug, custom made for him by his pen pal, imprisoned serial killer Jeffrey Dahmer

5. David Lynch's daughter Jennifer is also a film director. What was the name of her 1993 debut movie in which *Twin Peaks* star Sherilyn Fenn had her limbs lovingly removed by a smitten Julian Sands?

A) *Lopping Laural*

B) *Boxing Helena*

C) *Portable Patty*

D) *Simone's Stumps*

6. Lynch's long-running comic strip in the *LA Reader* was called *The Angriest ________ in the World*?

A) George Lucas

B) Dog

C) Samaritan

D) Feminist

7. After the success of 1980's *The Elephant Man*, Lynch was invited to helm which hit 1983 movie?

A) *Octopussy*

B) *Mr. Mom*

C) *WarGames*

D) *Return of the Jedi*

8. What band was the unlikely choice to provide the soundtrack for Lynch's troubled 1984 adaptation of Frank Herbert's classic sci-fi novel *Dune*?

A) Duran Duran

B) Abba

C) Oingo Boingo

D) Toto

9. Lynch's 1997 film *Lost Highway* features the last screen appearance of which comedian?

A) Bill Hicks

B) Richard Pryor

C) Jerry Lewis

D) Meryl 'Screwface' Myers

10. Laura Harring, who starred opposite Naomi Watts in 2001's *Mulholland Drive*, boasts which two other claims to fame?

A) She was a former Miss America who went on to marry the great-great-grandson of German chancellor Otto von Bismarck

B) Her father was the inventor of the car alarm, and in 2009 she was the first woman to skateboard across Australia

C) Her competition-winning high school poem 'Why We Dream' was to be read on the moon by Neil Armstrong, only for the astronaut to forget to bring it. She later had a star named after her.

D) She played the baby in Roman Polanski's 1968 film *Rosemary's Baby*. She would later publicly walk off the 2003 Cannes Film Festival jury upon learning it was chaired by Polanski

11. In a 2002 web series, Lynch fashioned an otherwise conventional studio-shot sitcom that starred only ...?

A) Actors wearing Bill Clinton masks

B) Garden gnomes

C) Rabbits

D) His family

12. How did Lynch promote his 2006 film *Inland Empire* to the Oscar committee?

A) By sending each member a goody bag that included a map of Nebraska and a tiny chunk of the Berlin Wall

B) By dressing in an Oscar costume and asking *Inland Empire* star Laura Dern to marry him live on the Conan O'Brien talk show

C) By taking out a full page ad in *Variety* offering free psychiatric help to any voter that did not nominate *Inland Empire* for Best Picture

D) By standing on a street corner in Hollywood with a live cow and a sign that read 'Without cheese there wouldn't be an *Inland Empire*'

13. What's the name of Lynch's own brand of coffee, launched in 2006?

A) Damn Fine

B) Black Lodge

C) Signature Cup

D) Rinky Dink

14. Lynch lent his voice to Gus, the bartender in which animated TV show?

A) *Rick and Morty*

B) *Maude's Moods*

C) *The Kookytown Casebook*

D) *The Cleveland Show*

15. In 2005 Lynch set up the David Lynch Foundation to promote ...?

A) Experimental techniques for filming the spirit world

B) Compulsory banjo lessons in American high schools

C) Transcendental meditation and world peace

D) Research into the rejuvenating properties of the cherry

THE MAGNIFICENT ANDERSONS

Wes, Paul Thomas and Paul W.S. Anderson

1. Paul Thomas Anderson's father Ernie creeped out Cleveland during the 1960s as 'Ghoulardi', host of a late-night TV horror show. Where does that name pop up in PTA's later life?

A) It's what he named his first son
B) He has the name tattooed on his arm
C) It's the name of his production company
D) It's the name of the drug ring in *Inherent Vice*

2. Which lauded writer served as the young PTA's English teacher at Emerson College during the early 1990s?

A) Anne Rice
B) Chuck Palahniuk
C) J.D. Salinger
D) David Foster Wallace

3. Which inadvisable activity provides the narrative thrust for Paul W.S. Anderson's 1994 thriller *Shopping*?

A) Drunk dialling
B) Glue sniffing
C) Credit card fraud
D) Joyriding

4. PWS's follow-up film was an adaptation of which hit video game?

A) Super Mario Bros.
B) Earthworm Jim
C) Streetfighter
D) Mortal Kombat

5. According to scriptwriter David Peoples, *Soldier*, PWS's 1998 sci-fi shoot-em-up starring Kurt Russell, takes place in the same fictional universe as which of the writer's other films?

A) *Battlefield Earth*
B) *Alien*
C) *12 Monkeys*
D) *Blade Runner*

6. In which font do the credits of Wes Anderson's films generally appear?

A) Van Nostrand
B) Geneva
C) Futura Bold
D) Caldecot Chubb

7. Wes Anderson came to most people's attention with 1998's *Rushmore*, but what was the name of his 1996 debut that starred Owen and Luke Wilson?

A) *Bottle Rocket*
B) *Dime Bag*
C) *Cotton Candy*
D) *Soda Jerks*

8. Wes Anderson loves a friendly face, and has worked with many of the same actors throughout his career. But who is his most frequent collaborator?

A) Owen Wilson
B) Bill Murray

C) Jason Schwartzman

D) Anjelica Huston

9. Daniel Day Lewis won the second of his three Best Actor Oscars for his part in P.T. Anderson's 2007 drama *There Will Be Blood*. What was his character's name?

A) Jeremiah Greengrass

B) Daniel Plainview

C) Eli Masterson

D) Justice Clearwater

10. What was the name of Steve Zissou's boat in Wes Anderson's 2004 comedy *The Life Aquatic with Steve Zissou*?

A) The *Robeson*

B) The *Belmondo*

C) The *Aznavour*

D) The *Belafonte*

11. For insurance purposes, PTA was appointed as backup director on which 'mature' filmmaker's project?

A) Martin Scorsese's *Silence*

B) Woody Allen's *Midnight in Paris*

C) Robert Altman's *A Prairie Home Companion*

D) Ridley Scott's *Alien: Covenant*

12. The bespoke luggage featured in Wes's continent-hopping 2007 curio *The Darjeeling Limited* was created by which designer?

A) Tom Ford

B) John Galliano

C) Marc Jacobs

D) Stella McCartney

13. What was the title and subject of P.W.S. Anderson's eruptive 2014 disaster movie?

A) *Pompeii*

B) *Vesuvius*

C) *Eyjafjallajökull*

D) *Krakatoa*

14. PTA won praise for coaxing a raw dramatic performance from which comedian in 2002's *Punch-Drunk Love*?

A) Will Ferrell

B) Tina Fey

C) Cedric the Entertainer

D) Adam Sandler

15. Wes Anderson's *The Life Aquatic* features Portuguese actor Seu Jorge performing idiosyncratic acoustic versions of songs by which legendary rock act?

A) The Beach Boys

B) Bob Dylan

C) The Rolling Stones

D) David Bowie

CROSSING OVER

Actors-turned-directors

True or false?

1. *The Out-Of-Towners* is the name of Gene Kelly's first full-length directorial credit – a film in which he also starred.

2. A major element in Charles Laughton's sole directorial credit, *The Night of the Hunter* from 1955, involved Robert Mitchum creepily chanting the hymn 'Leaning on the Everlasting Arms'.

3. Emerging British helmer Amma Asante (*Belle, A United Kingdom*) appeared in the popular British TV series *Eastenders* during her teenage years.

4. In recent years, Peter Berg has become Hollywood's go-to director for tough true-life survival tales (*Lone Survivor*, *Deepwater Horizon*, *Patriots Day*). But in the late Eighties, he had a small role in the beloved erotic thriller *9½ Weeks*.

5. Spanish writer-director Icíar Bollaín (*Take My Eyes*, *Even the Rain*, *The Olive Tree*) appeared as a flame-haired socialist in the Ken Loach film *Land and Freedom*.

6. 1996's *Big Night*, directed by Campbell Scott and Stanley Tucci, is about two brothers who work in an abattoir.

7. In 1997 Johnny Depp directed an awful movie called *The Brave* about a guy who is tricked into being involved in a snuff movie.

8. British performer Kathy Burke has won the Best Actress prize at the Cannes Film Festival.

9. Danny DeVito scored a major critical and commercial hit with his 2002 directorial effort *Death to Smoochy*.

10. Sarah Polley, the Canadian writer-director responsible for 2006's *Away from Her* and 2012's *Stories We Tell*, has acted in more films for David Cronenberg than she has for Atom Egoyan.

11. In 2009, Samantha Morton directed a hard-hitting drama called *The Unloved*, in which a young girl goes through the British foster care system.

12. Drew Barrymore's effervescent 2009 debut as director is called *Whip It*, and it centres on the character Bliss Cavendar (played by Ellen Page) who is a small-town dominatrix.

13. Philip Seymour Hoffman also starred in his sole directorial credit, released in 2010, and called *Jack Goes Boating*.

14. Carol is the heroine of writer-director-star Lake Bell's 2013 film *In a World ...*. Her job is a voiceover artist for movie trailers.

15. Arthouse muse Julie Delpy turned to writing and directing her own material in response to the poorly characterized dross major studios were sending her way. She did, however, make a brief cameo training Scarlett Johansson's Black Widow to kick butt in 2015's *Avengers: Age of Ultron*.

THE OUTSIDERS

Directors from other disciplines

1. Which American pop artist is responsible for the 1967 opus *Four Stars* (also known as ****), which runs at 18 hours and 20 minutes?

2. *Maidstone* is the title of a 1970 curio that saw a famed American novelist directing himself as a filmmaker making a doomed Presidential bid. Who was that novelist?

3. The 1973 film *Westworld* provided the inspiration for a recent HBO series. Yet its author had already made a mark on TV by creating the enduring medical drama *ER*. Name that author.

4. Who made a new name for himself as a writer-director-star both in and out of the blaxploitation genre, but also as a defensive back for American football's Kansas City Chiefs (nicknamed the Hammer)?

5. 1995's *Blue in the Face*, 1998's *Lulu on the Bridge* and 2007's *The Inner Life of Martin Frost* were all directed by which leading American novelist?

6. Painter Julian Schnabel made his directorial debut in 1996 with a biopic of which fellow artist?

7. Cindy Sherman graduated from photographer to movie director with 1997's *Office Killer*, a cult black comedy starring a graduate of *The Breakfast Club*. Which one?

8. Promo director and skateboard entrepreneur Spike Jonze became a fully fledged film director with 1999's *Being ...*?

9. Which British artist and photographer smoothed *Fifty Shades of Grey*'s passage from book to screen?

10. Which other Young British Artist withdrew her 2004 coming-of-age drama *Top Spot* from UK distribution after it was slapped with an 18 certificate by the British Board of Film Censors?

11. Matthew Barney's multimedia project *Drawing Restraint 9* yielded a 2005 film, set aboard a Japanese whaling ship, that starred which leftfield songstress?

12. 2006's *A 21st Century Portrait* found Scottish video artist Douglas Gordon training multiple cameras on the feet and form of which illustrious French footballer?

13. Dutch photographer Anton Corbijn made his directorial debut with 2007's acclaimed Ian Curtis portrait *Control*. Thirteen years earlier, he'd overseen the promo video for 'Love and Tears', the sole UK chart hit for which supermodel?

14. Which American hard rocker counts a remake of *Halloween* as among his increasingly numerous directorial credits?

15. Between his work alongside Robert Rodriguez on the two *Sin City* movies, what comic-book supremo made an ill-fated attempt to reconfigure his superhero yarn *The Spirit* for the big screen?

Match answer to question

Paul Auster, Fred Williamson, Rob Zombie, Björk, Jean-Michel Basquiat, Frank Miller, Molly Ringwald, Michael Crichton, Andy Warhol, Tracey Emin, Norman Mailer, Zinedine Zidane, John Malkovich, Sam Taylor-Johnson (formerly Taylor-Wood), Naomi Campbell

MASTER KEYS

Hitchcock's McGuffins

Can you identify which of Alfred Hitchcock's masterworks these reference:

The 39 Steps, Strangers on a Train, Psycho, The Birds, Vertigo, Rear Window, North by Northwest, Suspicion, Frenzy, Dial M for Murder

1

2

3

4

5

6

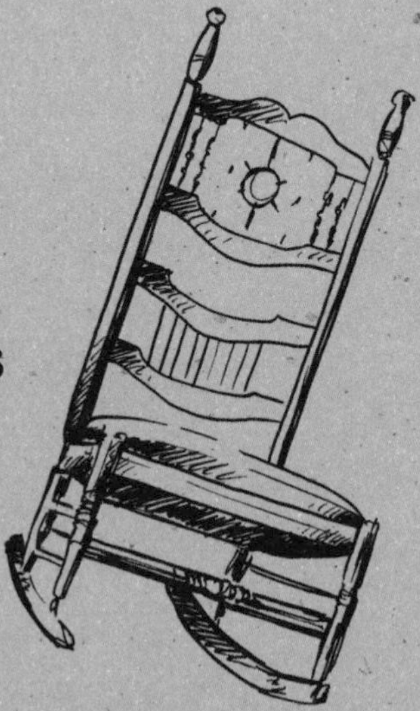

7

8

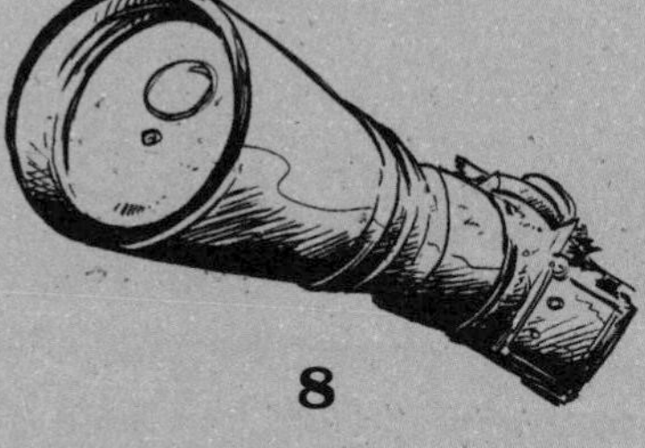

9

10

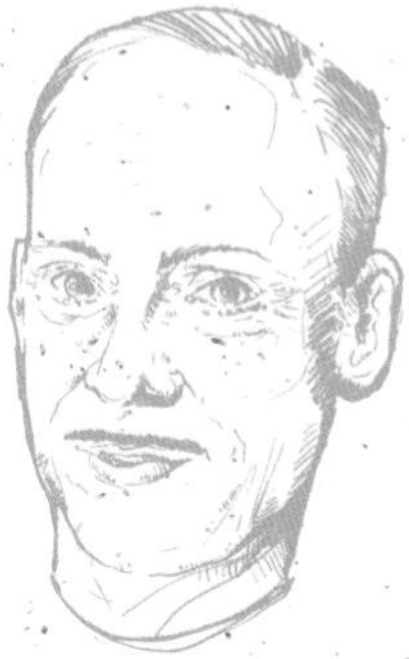

JUST ADD WATERS

The wit and wisdom of John Waters

Ten of the following are bona fide quotes by cult shockmeister Waters; five are fake news. Which are true, and which are false?

1. 'Catholics have more extreme sex lives because they're taught that pleasure is bad for you. Who thinks it's normal to kneel down before a naked man who's nailed to a cross? It's like a bad leather bar.'

2. 'Did you see *Gigli*? Turns out there may be such a thing as too much camp.'

3. 'Everyone wants to see everyone in every movie naked. That's why we have movies.'

4. 'I always say that people have been exposed to my movies – you know, just as you're exposed to pornography, or a virus.'

5. 'I don't trust anyone that hasn't been to jail at least once in their life. You should have been, or something's the matter with you.'

6. 'If you go home with someone and they don't have books, don't fuck 'em!'

7. 'I mean, seriously, is there any real difference between eating dogshit and eating a Hershey bar?'

8. ‘I’m not saying that standards in Hollywood have dropped, but they gave Jessica Simpson a shot at a movie career.’

9. ‘I pride myself on the fact my work has no redeeming social value.’

10. ‘Touching yourself when you see art can be poetry.’

11. ‘I was in an *Alvin and the Chipmunks* movie, which was a real bucket list item.’

12. ‘My dad saw *A Dirty Shame*. I felt bad about my dad knowing what felching was.’

13. ‘Oh God, I think about killing movie people all the time. I spent most of *Meet Joe Black* imagining which of the “creatives” involved would be first up against the wall.’

14. ‘The only insult I’ve ever received in my adult life was when someone asked me, “Do you have a hobby?” A HOBBY?! DO I LOOK LIKE A FUCKING DABBLER?!’

15. ‘I want to meet Eminem, because he has no desire to meet me.’

BEAT THE DEVIL

French Connection: Jean-Luc Godard

1. Godard used the pseudonym Hans Lucas in his early review for which still-running French film journal?

2. He stars in *Le Quadrille*, a 1950 experimental short, directed by which fellow New Wave auteur? (Hint: he went on to direct the surreal classic *Celine and Julie Go Boating*.)

3. In 1960's breakthrough *Breathless*, fast-talking crim Michel Poiccard (Jean-Paul Belmondo) strikes up an affair with a newspaper seller played by which tragic American-born leading lady?

4. In 1964's *Bande à Part*, the three central protagonists claim to have set a record for running through which gigantic Parisian art gallery?

5. Alpha-60 was the name of the Big Brother-like computer overseeing events in which 1965 sci-fi film directed by JLG?

6. 1967's *La Chinoise* punctuated its proto-revolutionary action with naggingly catchy bursts of a song devoted to which little red book-loving world leader?

7. Formed in 1968, Godard's revolutionary filmmaking collective was named after which Soviet film figure who directed *Man with a Movie Camera* – often considered the greatest documentary ever made?

8. What did Godard sign in order to secure funding for his eccentric 1987 version of *King Lear* with Cannon Films?

9. At Cannes in 2004, Godard declared that 'Post-war filmmakers gave us the documentary, Rob Reiner gave us the mockumentary, and Michael Moore [being feted for his *Fahrenheit 9/11*] gave us the "crockumentary".' True or false?

10. The subtitles for 2010's *Film Socialisme* were composed by Godard in a very specific variant of English. What was it?

Peeping Tom: Alfred Hitchcock
1. c, 2. c, 3. d, 4. b, 5. c, 6. c, 7. d, 8. c, 9. b, 10. a, 11. d, 12. a, 13. c, 14. d, 15. c

Female Gaze: Women directors, established and emerging
1. c, 2. b, 3. c, 4. c (she merely acted in this charming 1931 effort), 5. d, 6. c, 7. c, 8. d, 9. d, 10. b, 11. c, 12. a, 13. d, 14. c, 15. c

Weird World: David Lynch
1. a, 2. b, 3. b, 4. a, 5. b, 6. b, 7. d, 8. d, 9. b, 10. a, 11. c, 12. d, 13. c, 14. d, 15. c

The Magnificent Andersons: Wes, Paul Thomas and Paul W.S. Anderson
1. c, 2. d (Wallace's unfinished novel *The Pale King* was posthumously nominated as one of the three finalists for the 2002 Pulitzer Prize for Fiction, but no award was given that year), 3. d, 4. d, 5. d, 6. c, 7. a, 8. b, 9. b, 10. d, 11. c, 12. c, 13. a, 14. d, 15. d

Crossing Over: Actors-turned-directors
1. False – it's *On the Town*, 2. True, 3. False – she was in *Grange Hill*, 4. False – he was in *The Last Seduction*, 5. True, 6. False – they work in a restaurant, 7. True, 8. True – for her role in the Gary Oldman-directed *Nil By Mouth*, 9. False – it crashed and burned, 10. False, 11. True, 12. False – it's about roller derby, 13. True, 14. True, 15. True

The Outsiders: Directors from other disciplines
1. Andy Warhol, 2. Norman Mailer, 3. Michael Crichton, 4. Fred Williamson, 5. Paul Auster, 6. Jean-Michel Basquiat, 7. Molly Ringwald, 8. John Malkovich, 9. Sam Taylor-Johnson (formerly Taylor-Wood), 10. Tracey Emin, 11. Björk, 12. Zinedine Zidane, 13. Naomi Campbell, 14. Rob Zombie, 15. Frank Miller

Master Keys – Hitchcock's McGuffins
1. *Frenzy*, 2. *Dial M for Murder*, 3. *Vertigo*, 4. *Suspicion*, 5. *Strangers on a Train*, 6. *Psycho*, 7. *The 39 Steps*, 8. *Rear Window*, 9. *North by Northwest*, 10. *The Birds*

Just Add Waters: The wit and wisdom of John Waters
1. True, 2. False, 3. True, 4. False, 5. True, 6. True, 7. False, 8. False, 9. True, 10. True, 11. True, 12. True, 13. False, 14. True, 15. True

French Connection: Jean-Luc Godard
1. *Cahiers du Cinéma*, 2. Jacques Rivette, 3. Jean Seberg, 4. The Louvre, 5. *Alphaville*, 6. Chairman Mao, 7. Dziga Vertov, 8. A napkin, 9. True, 10. 'Navajo English'

ANSWERS

4

The Golden AGE

The growth of an industry

THE HOLLYWOOD STUDIOS

The movie industry's powerhouses

1. Which of these major studios was the first to be formed?

A) 20th Century Fox

B) Disney

C) Warner Bros.

D) Universal

2. Who or what was Rin Tin Tin, Warner Bros.' first major star, who debuted in 1922's *The Man From Hell's River*?

A) A mute Abyssinian juggler Harry Warner met on a train

B) French can-can dancer Renata Tebaldi

C) A cartoon beaver

D) A German Shepherd rescued from a First World War battlefield

3. Who led the 1970 campaign to restore the HOLLYWOOD sign, which had fallen into disrepair by that time?

A) Warner Bros. Studios

B) Shock-rocker Alice Cooper

C) Playboy founder Hugh Hefner

D) Crooner Andy Williams

4. What is the name of the lion that roars out from MGM's logo, first seen on screens in 1916?

A) Sheeba

B) Leo

C) Tony

D) Clarence

5. The lady that graces the Columbia Pictures logo began her long screen career in 1924 – albeit without her now-familiar torch in her hand. What was she holding in those early days?

A) A flaming sword

B) A baseball

C) A cinema ticket

D) A stalk of wheat

6. Harry Cohn, head of Columbia Pictures, was known in Tinseltown circles as 'Harry the Horror' until screenwriter Ben Hecht gave him an altogether more literary nickname. What was it?

A) Cohnan the Barbarian

B) The Moriarty of Melrose Avenue

C) The Scrooge of Sunset Boulevard

D) White Fang

7. The life of Irving Thalberg, production chief at Universal and then MGM, is said to have inspired which novel that was eventually filmed in the 1970s?

A) *The Great Gatsby*

B) *The Day of the Locust*

C) *The Last Tycoon*

D) *The Godfather*

8. Before there was Mickey, Walt Disney enjoyed his first success with a series of shorts featuring what character?

A) Lorenzo the Llama

B) Swanky the Crow

C) Oswald the Rabbit

D) Minnie the Moose

9. Which of the following was NOT a film in MGM's successful *Mr. Moto* series of the 1930s?

A) *Thank You, Mr. Moto.*

B) *Mr Moto in Danger Island.*

C) *Think Fast, Mr. Moto.*

D) *Mr. Moto Is So Sorry.*

10. And which of the following creations did NOT number among the classic Universal horror cycle of the 1930s and 40s?

A) *Son of Frankenstein*

B) *Dracula's Daughter*

C) *Son of Dracula*

D) *Mother of Kong*

11. It may be somewhat forgotten now, but RKO was a proud member of the Golden Age's 'Big Five' studios. What did its initials stand for?

A) Radio Keith Orpheum

B) Rimsky Kenco Olazabal

C) Ransom Kinetoscope Oldham

D) Republican Knight Oscillation

12. What does MGM's Latin motto *Ars Gratia Artis* – as seen on their famous logo – mean?

A) Through Adversity to the Stars

B) Art for Art's Sake

C) To Dare Is to Do

D) Carthage Must Be Destroyed

13. The Bob Hope and Bing Crosby *Road to ...* series was a major money-spinner for Paramount for more than two decades. Where did the boys head off to on their first jaunt in 1940?

A) Paris

B) Des Moines

C) Zanzibar

D) Singapore

14. The studios lost some of their muscle from the 1940s onwards after a US Supreme Court ruling ended the practice of studios doing what?

A) Owning cinema chains

B) Holding exclusivity contracts on actors, preventing them working for other studios

C) Taking more than 50% of theatre ticket prices from cinema owners

D) Paying off electrical store owners not to stock televisions

15. The above ruling weakened Universal's position to such a degree that they were bought out in 1952 by which corporation?

A) The Bell Telephone Company

B) Vandalay Industries

C) The New York Yankees

D) Decca Records

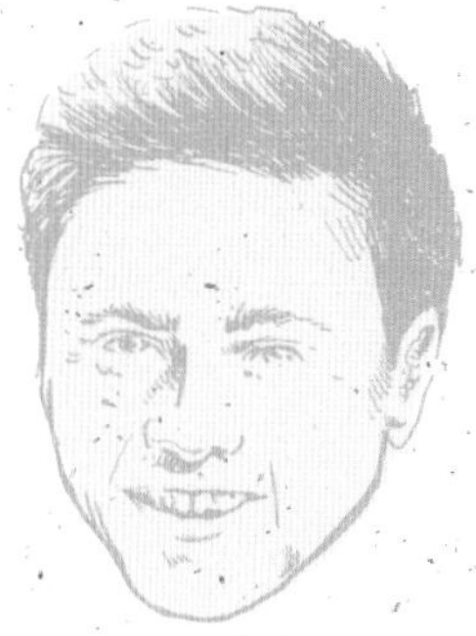

HAPPY FEET

The MGM musical

1. 1944's *Meet Me in St. Louis* climaxes with which event that took place in the city in the spring of 1904?

A) Missouri governor Alphonse J. Tweedy boxing a kangaroo

B) The inaugural baseball World Series

C) The World's Fair

D) The invention of the whoopee cushion (formerly known as the 'Mississippi Fartbag')

2. In *Meet Me in St. Louis*, Judy Garland sang 'Have yourself a merry little Christmas, make the yuletide gay' after she rejected the song's original opening line, which went 'Have yourself a merry little Christmas ...

A) ... being Christian is best'?

B) ... Hitler's boys are on their way'?

C) ... though death is all around'?

D) ... it may be your last'?

3. Where does the bulk of the action in Cecil B. DeMille's demented 1930 musical comedy *Madam Satan* take place?

A) In a church

B) In a submarine

C) On death row

D) On a Zeppelin

4. 1945's *Anchors Aweigh* saw Gene Kelly dance with which beloved animated character?

A) Popeye

B) Jerry (of 'Tom &' fame)

C) Betty Boop

D) Tom (of '& Jerry' fame)

5. What did Mickey Rooney do in 1939's *Babes in Arms* that led to a scene being cut upon the film's re-release in the 1940s?

A) Sing a Nazi drinking song

B) Kiss a six-year-old child on the lips

C) Kick a piglet so hard that it that flew out of frame

D) Mimic President Franklin D. Roosevelt

6. Which of the following is NOT the title of a MGM musical?

A) *Excuse My Dust*

B) *The Bronx Cheer*

C) *Million Dollar Mermaid*

D) *Pagan Love Song*

7. Peter Lawford can be seen duetting with Judy Garland in 1948's *Easter Parade*, but for what would he go on to become more famous?

A) Becoming the first official member of the Church of Scientology

B) Being the voice of animated TV caveman Fred Flintstone

C) Being a founder member of the Las Vegas 'Rat Pack' that included Frank Sinatra, Dean Martin and Sammy Davis Jr.
D) Dying onstage during his opening speech at the 1971 White House Correspondents' Dinner

8. In 1949's furiously fruity sailors-on-shore-leave classic *On the Town*, Frank Sinatra was self-conscious enough about one of his body parts to ...

A) Demand a wiglet to cover his bald patch
B) Have his ears glued back
C) Have the erotic tattoo of Olive Oyl on his forearm surgically removed
D) Request a prosthetic bottom to fill out his Navy uniform

9. Which word or phrase in that film's big hit 'New York, New York' was replaced with 'wonderful' to placate frowning US censors?

A) Sexy
B) Helluva
C) Butt-kicking
D) Ass-grabbing

10. What's the name of the showboat in 1951's *Show Boat*?

A) The *Tub o' Fun*
B) The *Immer Essen*
C) The *Cotton Blossom*
D) The *Salty Bottom*

11. The song 'Singin' in the Rain' is sung to memorably chilling effect in which controversial early-Seventies British film?

A) *A Clockwork Orange*
B) *Straw Dogs*
C) *Confessions of a Window Cleaner*
D) *Adolf Hitler: My Part in His Downfall*

12. To which fictional studio is Gene Kelly's song-and-dance man Don Lockwood contracted in 1952's *Singin' in the Rain*?

A) Monumental Pictures
B) MGM (Margaret 'Gertie' Mandelbaum) Studios
C) Titanic & Co.
D) Lockwood & Lockwood

13. Which 1958 film had the shortest title ever to win a Best Picture Oscar – until matched by 2003's *Argo*?

A) *Iago*
B) *Gigi*
C) *Togo*
D) *Hugo*

14. Complete the title of the film that repackaged classic MGM musical sequences for Seventies audiences: *That's* _____________

A) *Nostalgia*
B) *Regrettable ...*
C) *Entertainment!*
D) *Entertainment?*

15. MGM released its last musical in 1981. What was it?

A) *Concorde!*, starring Goldie Hawn
B) *An American Gondolier*, starring Chevy Chase
C) *Those Hungry, Hungry Hippos ...*, starring John Belushi
D) *Pennies From Heaven*, starring Steve Martin

ATTACK!

Hollywood at war

1. In 1930's *All Quiet on the Western Front*, the lead character is shot by a sniper while doing what?

A) Reaching for a butterfly
B) Playing football
C) Sitting on the lavatory
D) Shooting at a sniper

2. Released in 1939, what was the grabby title of the first Hollywood film to explicitly warn of the threat posed by Hitler's Germany?

A) *A Führer in the Family*
B) *Achtung Baby!*
C) *Confessions of a Nazi Spy*
D) *Jackboots on Union Square*

3. The book *I Was an Alien Spouse of Female Military Personnel Enroute to the United States Under Public Law 271 of the Congress* was turned into which Cary Grant war vehicle?

A) *She Wears the Trousers!*
B) *I Was a Male War Bride*
C) *The Sergeant Wore Stockings*
D) *My Husband the Housewife*

4. What was the nickname of the Boeing B-17 Flying Fortress that would lend itself to a slick screen adaptation some four decades later?

A) The Top Gun
B) The Air Wolf
C) The Memphis Belle
D) The Blue Thunder

5. In *Der Fuehrer's Face*, a Disney cartoon from 1943, Donald Duck slips into a nightmarish state where he's obliged to do what every morning?

A) Eat a never-ending supply of sausages
B) Read *Mein Kampf*
C) Shave off the Hitler moustache that has regrown on his bill
D) Drink an enormous stein of beer

6. What was the barely disguised name of Charlie Chaplin's character in his satire of fascism, *The Great Dictator*, released in 1940?

A) Alfalfa Quickstep
B) Aldous Wiffler
C) Adenoid Hynkel
D) Randolph Tickler

7. Hitler reportedly offered a substantial reward to any German pilot who shot down which star-turned-soldier, a pre-war favourite of der Führer?

A) Betty Grable
B) Clark Gable
C) Robert Mitchum
D) James Stewart

8. Which 1944 production, dramatizing the American response to Pearl Harbor, later provided the title for a song by Cleveland art-rock godheads Pere Ubu?

A) *California Über Alles*

B) *Blue Hawaii*

C) *Thirty Seconds Over Tokyo*

D) *The Battle of Midway*

9. What was the US Marine Corps' response to the 1943 Bugs Bunny war-booster *Super-Rabbit*?

A) They ordered Warner Bros. to withdraw it from cinemas

B) They issued extra carrot rations to all soldiers

C) For a time, all new recruits had a Bugs decal on their helmet above the words 'What's up, Adolf?'

D) They 'enrolled' Bugs into their ranks

10. What did David Niven – who traded the A-list for the British Army for the duration of the Second World War – reply when he was asked to describe his combat experience?

A) 'Nasty business all round.'

B) 'Bit of a brown trouser job, to be honest.'

C) 'Oh, you know, hopped over the Channel, gave the Bosch a bloody nose and home for tea and crumpets.'

D) 'Well, on the whole, I'd've rather been tickling Ginger Rogers' tits.'

11. Niven's BFF Errol Flynn was born in Australia, but became a naturalized American just in time to volunteer for service. For which of these ailments did the hard-living lothario fail his Army medical?

A) A heart murmur

B) Recurrent malaria

C) Latent pulmonary tuberculosis

D) Various venereal diseases

12. US Second World War movies boosted public morale with many stirring and inspirational titles. Some, however, missed the mark. Three of these are actual movie titles. Which one isn't?

A) *We've Never Been Licked*

B) *Mr. Winkle Goes To War*

C) *Charlie Chan: Nazi Buster*

D) *Hillbilly Blitzkrieg*

13. Paramount's dull but lavish 1956 adaptation of *War and Peace* cast which emerging star as Tolstoy's society belle Natasha?

A) Kim Novak

B) Ann-Margret

C) Shirley MacLaine

D) Audrey Hepburn

14. What caused nascent film idol Elvis Presley's draft into the US Army to be delayed by two months?

A) His manager Uncle Tom Parker booked him on a tour of obscure northern American and Canadian towns where he couldn't be reached

B) His mother Gladys was so heartbroken by Elvis's draft letter that she hid it under a rock in the Gracelands reptile tank

C) Elvis personally wrote to the Memphis Draft Board explaining that money and jobs would be lost if he couldn't finish filming his latest film, *Kid Creole*

D) He refused to have his hair shaved off

15. What was the controversial subject of *Let There Be Light*, the John Huston documentary that was suppressed by the US authorities for more than thirty years?

A) Atrocities carried out by US troops in the Arctic Circle

B) Faults in aiming systems that meant many tank commanders had to fire 'blind' throughout the war

C) Extraterrestrial forces in the European conflict

D) Troops returning from the frontline with PTSD

TRADING POST

The memorabilia of the John Wayne Museum

Here are ten items Team LWL purchased during a recent stop-off at the John Wayne Birthplace and Museum gift shop in Winterset, Iowa. Can you match items to price, from cheapest to most expensive?

John Wayne Grill Sauce Set ('recipes reminiscent of the good old days')

A Man's Gotta Do Shot Glass ('with rifle handle')

Old Guys Rule 'Life is Tough' Gray Hat

John Wayne Collapsible Storage Ottoman ('Faux leather covering is durable and easy to clean')

CD copy of Wayne's 1973 spoken-word LP *America, Why I Love Her*

John Wayne Pillow ('lightweight, 100% polyester')

John Wayne Museum Pewter Belt Buckle

John Wayne Birthplace & Museum Golf Shirt, XXX-Large

John Wayne Camp Chair

Signature John Wayne Western-Style Stockade Men's Jacket

$8	**$30**
$10	**$30**
$18	**$50**
$20	**$75**
$24	**$145**

THE WOMEN

The great movie heroines

1. Who remains the only actress to have won the Academy Award for Best Actress four times – for *Morning Glory*, *Guess Who's Coming to Dinner*, *The Lion in Winter* and *On Golden Pond*?

2. Name the leading lady who retired at the height of her stardom at the age of 36? Hint: the year was 1941, and her final film was named *Two-Faced Woman*.

3. Which adventurous, Berlin-born 'Blue Angel' was the first leading lady to kiss another woman on screen?

4. Which of the following actresses did not feature among the multitudinous all-female cast of 1939's *The Women* – Joan Crawford, Rosalind Russell, Joan Fontaine or Ginger Rogers?

5. According to the IRS, which actress was the highest-paid woman in America in 1944, hauling in the princely sum of $400,000? That same year, she played one of the great femme fatales in Billy Wilder's classic noir thriller *Double Indemnity*.

6. The annual Quigley Poll measures American cinemagoers' favourite stars, both male and female. Which semi-forgotten figure – star of *The Beautiful Blonde from Bashful Bend* – topped the favourite actress list seven times between 1942 and 1951?

7. 'She can't talk. She can't act. She's terrific!' was a breathless Louis B. Mayer's lust-filled response to which voluptuous performer's first MGM screen test? Hint: Frank Sinatra developed quite an obsession with her.

8. Which iconic leading lady became an enthusiastic ambassador for the soft drink Pepsi after marrying its CEO in 1956, the same year she starred in Robert Aldrich's *Autumn Leaves*?

9. *Something's Gotta Give* was the name of the (uncompleted) film from which this bombshell superstar was fired just a month before her untimely demise in 1962. Name her.

10. Which Golden Age siren appears on the first poster Andy Dufresne (Tim Robbins) tacks to his cell wall in 1994's *The Shawshank Redemption*?

11. Shockingly, Lauren Bacall had to wait until the 1990s for her first Academy Award nomination – a Best Supporting Actress contender for 1996's *The Mirror Has Two Faces*, in which she played which musical megastar's mother?

12. 1997's James Ellroy period adaptation *L.A. Confidential* featured a high-class escort ring that offered its clients lookalikes of Hollywood sex symbols. Which Golden Age actress had Kim Basinger's Lynn Bracken been styled to resemble?

13. The tragic life of *Carmen Jones* star Dorothy Dandridge, the first black actress to win a Best Actress nomination, spawned a 1999 TV movie toplined by which latter-day A-lister?

14. The 2017 documentary *Bombshell* revealed that an Austria-born interwar screen sensation patented the technology that eventually gifted the modern digital era with WiFi. Name that screen sensation.

15. The inscription on one especially tough movie broad's sarcophagus in LA's Forest Lawn Memorial Park reads: 'She did it the hard way.' Whose tomb?

THE BIG MAN

Orson Welles

1. Orson was, in fact, Welles's middle name. What was his first name?

A) Rupert
B) Tonbridge
C) George
D) Hartley

2. Thanks to a generous inheritance Welles was able to travel through Europe as a young man. In which city did he bluff his way into his first stage role by claiming he was already a Broadway star?

A) London
B) Prague
C) Rome
D) Dublin

3. What was the name of Welles's theatre company, established only three years later?

A) The Mercury Theatre
B) The Fireside Players
C) The Sons of Cain
D) The Kings of Convenience

4. Welles's stage troupe was soon also producing radio shows like *War of the Worlds* – the transmission that made America lose its collective marbles. Which author wrote the book it was based on?

A) H.G. Wells
B) Jules Verne
C) G.B. Harmé
D) Mary Shelley

5. In 1941's *Citizen Kane*, Charles Foster Kane's mansion Xanadu takes its name from which famous poem?

A) 'If' by Rudyard Kipling
B) 'Kubla Khan' by Samuel Taylor Coleridge
C) 'The Road Not Taken' by Robert Frost
D) 'The Mirrored Ball' by O. Newton John

6. What existential zinger does Marlene Dietrich sign off with as Welles's corrupt cop Hank Quinlan lies dying at the end of 1958's *Touch of Evil*?

A) 'One lives one's life, one dies one's death. God is absent.'
B) 'He died like he lived – in a stinking pool of other people's filth.'
C) 'He was some kind of a man. What does it matter what you say about people?'
D) 'Feet sandaled with dreams tread paths of vision leading to wisdom's sharp peaks.'

7. 1947's *The Lady from Shanghai* climaxes with Welles pursuing femme fatale Rita Hayworth through ...?

A) An opium den
B) A wax museum
C) A hall of mirrors
D) A monsoon

8. Welles as cynical Harry Lime in 1949's *The Third Man*: 'In Italy, for thirty years under the Borgias, they had warfare, terror, murder and bloodshed, but they produced Michelangelo, Leonardo da Vinci and the Renaissance. In Switzerland they had brotherly love, they had five hundred years of democracy and peace – and what did that produce?'

A) 'A silly little pocket knife'

B) 'A whole lot of yodelling'

C) 'Fondue'

D) 'The cuckoo clock'

9. It's fair to say that Welles's reach sometimes exceeded even his mighty grasp, and there were many projects that, for one reason or another, were never realized. Which of the following is NOT (known to be) one of them?

A) *Too Much Johnson* – a silent movie comedy pastiche that was never released due to legal wrangles

B) *Dune* – in which Welles was cast as the corpulent Baron Harkonnen in Chilean madman Alejandro Jodorowsky's aborted Seventies tilt at Frank Herbert's sci-fi novel

C) *Satan's Surprise* – a comedy of manners set around the devil's dinner table

D) *The Life of Christ* – Jesus: The Western

10. Welles considered his 1965 Shakespearean mash-up *Chimes at Midnight* – in which he played the boastful, boozy, big-bearded knight Falstaff – to be his best work. But to what did the *New York Times* compare his performance?

A) 'A dissolute, bumbling street-corner Santa Claus.'

B) 'A blind man in a dark room looking for a black cat.'

C) 'An exploded sofa that has suddenly come to life and immediately taken to the bottle.'

D) 'A hippopotamus gargling cacti.'

11. What 1986 film features Welles's final performance?

A) *The Name of the Rose*

B) *Dr. Otto and the Riddle of the Gloom Beam*

C) *Transformers: The Movie*

D) *Night on the Galactic Railroad*

12. What was Welles's verdict on 1970s pop idol Donny Osmond?

A) 'He has Van Gogh's ear for music.'

B) 'They should lock him up in Mormon jail. Or any jail.'

C) 'By far the worst of all Osmonds.'

D) 'The toppermost of the poppermost.'

13. An infamous outtake from an early Seventies recording session finds Welles remorselessly berating studio technicians during a voiceover for what product?

A) Domecq Sherry

B) Reese's Peanut Butter Cups

C) Tidyman's Carpets

D) Findus Frozen Peas

14. Welles died on the same day (10 October 1985) as which other Hollywood icon?

A) Rock Hudson

B) Louise Brooks

C) Yul Brynner

D) Groucho Marx

15. Which masterwork finally toppled *Citizen Kane* from its fifty-year reign at the top of influential British film magazine *Sight & Sound*'s 'Greatest Films' poll in 2012?

A) *The Searchers*

B) *Vertigo*

C) *The Shawshank Redemption*

D) *Goodfellas*

MAKE 'EM LAUGH

Comic capers

1. What was the name of the fourth Marx brother, who signed up to serve in the Army rather than join his siblings in showbiz – and also inspired a 1997 indie movie directed by Harmony Korine?

2. Harold Lloyd is the great-great-uncle of action hunk Casper Van Dien, who made waves as the lantern-jawed star of which subversive 1997 sci-fi extravaganza?

3. He was known as one of the great directors of screwball comedies and counts the Coen brothers as among his biggest fans. Before his movie career he invented kiss-proof lipstick. Name that director.

4. Freedonia was the name of the fictional republic central to which Marx brothers' 1933 comedy classic?

5. 'The Walls of Jericho' is the biblical nickname given to the bedsheet Clark Gable hangs between himself and Claudette Colbert so as to preserve their modesty in which 1934 romantic comedy?

6. One of the most prolific comedy performers of the Thirties and early Forties was Asta, the dog who appeared in 1934's *The Thin Man*, 1937's *The Awful Truth* and 1938's *Bringing Up Baby*. To which breed did he belong? (Be as specific as you care.)

7. More animal crackers: which species of wild cat was Baby, who provided the element of feline chaos in 1938's *Bringing Up Baby*?

8. Which volunteer position does Jefferson Smith (James Stewart), civic-minded hero of 1939's *Mr. Smith Goes to Washington*, occupy before he goes to Washington?

9. *Sylvia Scarlett, The Philadelphia Story, Holiday, Bringing Up Baby* – which iconic male/female combo starred in all of these films.

10. The normal rate of spoken dialogue in American feature films is 90 words per minute. How many wpm does 1940s quickfire screwball *His Girl Friday* clock in at (to the nearest 50)?

11. In 1941's classic *The Lady Eve*, Henry Fonda plays an uptight ophiologist – which is to say, an expert in which species?

12. The lofty passion project that agonized filmmaker John L. Sullivan (Joel McCrea) hopes to bring into existence in 1941's *Sullivan's Travels* gave its name to a later, musically driven Coen brothers production. Which one?

13. The queen of comic timing, Carole Lombard, died in a plane crash at the age of 33. Name the 1942 Shakespeare-referencing screwball – in which a troupe of ham actors take on the Nazis – which was to include her final performance.

14. This 1949 Hepburn/Tracy classic features the pair playing married rival lawyers, with a screwball twist involving a gun made of liquorice. Name this Bible-referencing film?

15. On the American Film Institute's millennial list of its 100 greatest comedies, which of the following titles ranked the highest – *Bringing Up Baby, The Philadelphia Story, His Girl Friday* or *My Man Godfrey*?

BEAT THE DEVIL

After the Golden Age: Notable B-pictures

1. The marine engineer hero of 1942's *Cat People* hails by a name shared by a larger-than-life British screen actor (and chat-show regular) of the Sixties, Seventies and Eighties. What is it?

2. That film's 1944 sequel, *The Curse of the Cat People*, recycled key sets from Orson Welles's troubled follow-up to *Citizen Kane*. Name the film.

3. Richard Fleischer's tremendous train-set thriller *The Narrow Margin* was shot in 1950 but went unreleased until 1952, because the head of the studio responsible had simply forgotten about its existence. Who was this scatterbrained, aviation-loving mogul?

4. Which common kitchen accessory served as the monster in 1955's zero-budget *The Beast with a Million Eyes*?

5. Which car-loving icon of cinematic cool landed his first screen role care of 1958's *The Blob*?

6. How did gimmick-friendly schlockmeister William Castle ensure his 1959 shocker *The Tingler* lived up to its title?

7. When Bela Lugosi died during production of 1959's notorious dud *Plan 9 from Outer Space*, director Ed Wood recruited a man who'd been treating his wife to stand in as a replacement. From which branch of medicine did this stand-in hail?

8. Which up-and-coming young star (who went on to win three Oscars) has a blink-and-you'll-miss-it role as masochistic dental patient Wilbur Force in 1960's original *Little Shop of Horrors*?

9. Which atmospheric 1962 curio shot for a pittance around Salt Lake City, Utah, was the only feature made by director Herk Hervey, and has been cited as a major influence on the work of David Lynch and George A. Romero?

10. 1974's babes-behind-bars saga *Caged Heat* was the first directorial credit for which much-respected Oscar-winner-to-be? Hint: he was also behind a great Talking Heads concert film.

The Hollywood Studios: The movie industry's powerhouses
1. d (in 1912. Warners and Disney were founded in 1923. 20th Century Fox is the baby of the bunch, founded in 1935.), 2. d, 3. c (the other three were among the nine people who paid for the renovation of a letter each), 4. b, 5. d, 6. d, 7. c, 8. c, 9. d (a Moto novel by John P. Marquand not adapted from the series), 10. d, 11. a, 12. b, 13. d, 14. a, 15. d

Happy Feet: The MGM musical
1. c, 2. d, 3. d, 4. b, 5. d, 6. b ('the Bronx Cheer' is a well-known brand of whoopee cushion), 7. c, 8. d, 9. b, 10. c, 11. a, 12. a, 13. b, 14. c, 15. d

Attack!: Hollywood at war
1. a, 2. c, 3. b, 4. c, 5. b, 6. c, 7. b, 8. c, 9. d (he rose to Master Sergeant by the war's end), 10. d, 11. This is our one and only trick question – he had them all, the poor cad!, 12. c, 13. d, 14. c, 15. d

Trading Post: The memorabilia of the John Wayne Museum
$8 – Shot Glass; $10 – Pillow; $18 – Grill Sauce Set; $20 – Hat; $24 – Golf Shirt; $30 – CD; $30 – Ottoman; $50 – Camp Chair; $75 – Belt Buckle; $145 – Jacket

The Women: The great movie heroines
1. Katharine Hepburn, 2. Greta Garbo, 3. Marlene Dietrich, 4. Ginger Rogers, 5. Barbara Stanwyck, 6. Betty Grable, 7. Ava Gardner, 8. Joan Crawford, 9. Marilyn Monroe, 10. Rita Hayworth, 11. Barbra Streisand, 12. Veronica Lake, 13. Halle Berry, 14. Hedy Lamarr, 15. Bette Davis

The Big Man: Orson Welles
1. c, 2. d, 3. a, 4. a, 5. b, 6. c, 7. c, 8. d, 9. c, 10. a, 11. c, 12. a, 13. d (Fire it up on your phone NOW!), 14. c, 15. b

Make 'Em Laugh: Comic capers
1. Gummo, 2. *Starship Troopers*, 3. Preston Sturges, 4. *Duck Soup*, 5. *It Happened One Night*, 6. Fox terrier (terrier is acceptable; bonus point if you specified wirehair fox terrier), 7. Leopard, 8. Scout leader, 9. Cary Grant and Katharine Hepburn, 10. 250 (it's actually 240), 11. Snakes, 12. *O Brother, Where Art Thou?*, 13. *To Be or Not To Be*, 14. *Adam's Rib*, 15. *Bringing Up Baby* (*Baby* was #14, closely followed by *Philadelphia* at #15 and *Friday* at #19, with *Godfrey* further back at #44)

After the Golden Age: Notable B-pictures
1. Oliver Reed, 2. *The Magnificent Ambersons*, 3. Howard Hughes, 4. A kettle, 5. Steve McQueen, 6. He wired the cinema seats up to the mains, 7. He was her chiropractor, 8. Jack Nicholson, 9. *Carnival of Souls*, 10. Jonathan Demme

ANSWERS

5

Performance
ART

On actors
and acting.

FIRST CONTACT

Stars' unusual early roles

1. In which of the following films did Clint Eastwood NOT appear before he got his big-screen break playing the Man With No Name in 1964's *A Fistful of Dollars*?

A) *Operation Cummerbund*

B) *Lady Godiva of Coventry*

C) *Lafayette Escadrille*

D) *The First Traveling Saleslady*

2. Which Expendable is to be found flexing a different kind of muscle in 1970's softcore opus *The Party at Kitty and Stud's*?

A) Harrison Ford

B) Arnold Schwarzenegger

C) Sylvester Stallone

D) Bruce Willis

3. What fate befalls Johnny Depp in 1984's *A Nightmare on Elm Street*?

A) He is sucked into his own bed

B) He is electrocuted by his Sony Walkman

C) Believing he is in a dream, he jumps off the roof of his school

D) He is stuffed into the freezer compartment of the family refrigerator and dispensed as ice cubes

4. As what can a pre-fame Kevin Costner briefly be spotted in 1983's *The Big Chill*?

A) A street corner mime

B) A life-size cardboard cut-out in an ad agency office

C) A reporter on a TV news show

D) A corpse in a coffin

5. Which of the following starlets did NOT make an early appearance in 1983's *Grizzly II: The Concert*?

A) George Clooney

B) Julia Roberts

C) Charlie Sheen

D) Laura Dern

6. Michael Keaton made an early showing in the 1978 comedy *Rabbit Test*. Who was his director?

A) Johnny Carson

B) Joan Rivers

C) Carrie Fisher

D) Richard Pryor

7. Sandra Bullock starred in a 1989 TV movie that was intended to reboot which character?

A) She-Hulk

B) The Bionic Woman

C) Morticia Addams

D) Catwoman

8. Who rocks up in the guise of an Elvis impersonator in a 1988 episode of *The Golden Girls*?

A) Matt LeBlanc

B) Patricia Arquette

C) Ray Romano

D) Quentin Tarantino

9. Which star-to-be played Billy Crystal's son in 1991's cattle-prodding crowdpleaser *City Slickers*?

A) Seth Green

B) Zac Efron

C) Jake Gyllenhaal

D) Sean Astin

10. Which of the following performers did NOT make an early appearance on TV's *Baywatch*?

A) Michelle Williams

B) Mila Kunis

C) Bryan Cranston

D) Dwayne 'The Rock' Johnson

11. In a 1993 pop video, Meatloaf throws a protective arm around a soon-to-be-stellar teenage runaway and promises that 'Rock and Roll Dreams Come Through'. For who though?

A) Courtney Cox

B) Juliette Lewis

C) Angelina Jolie

D) Liv Tyler

12. La Bullock again! What fate befalls poor Sandy in the opening moments of 1993's *The Vanishing*?

A) She is smothered with a chloroform-soaked handkerchief

B) She drives off a cliff

C) She falls into a manhole

D) She volunteers to be part of a magic trick at her niece's bat mitzvah

13. What do we find Jennifer Aniston doing in the parking lot of a McDonald's in 1988's feeblest *E.T.* rip-off *Mac and Me*?

A) Vomiting

B) Having her ear pierced

C) Thumb wrestling

D) Competing in an impromptu dance-off

14. 1994's bloody *Texas Chainsaw Massacre: The Next Generation* drew fresh blood from future romcom standbys Renée Zellweger and Matthew McConaughey. What was its tagline?

A) 'Who Wants a Second Helping?'

B) 'He Wants You to Stay ... For Dinner.'

C) 'If Looks Could Kill, He Wouldn't Need a Chainsaw.'

D) 'Ol' Buzzkill is Back!'

15. Jennifer Lawrence's first screen credit was as a basketball mascot harassing Tony Shalhoub in a 2007 episode of TV crime dramedy *Monk*. What was Monk's defining detective schtick?

A) He was a reforming shopaholic

B) He suffered from an obsessive compulsive disorder

C) He was a policeman – and a priest

D) He could predict crimes before they happened

SELF-PORTRAITS

Actors/personalities play themselves

1. Who plays himself as a jobbing American actor in Cold War Berlin in Wim Wenders' 1987 existential meditation *Wings of Desire*?

A) Peter Fonda
B) Ernest Borgnine
C) Peter Falk
D) Jerry Lewis

2. Who does Woody Allen magically pull out of thin air to to help him win an argument in 1977's *Annie Hall*?

A) Noam Chomsky
B) Marshall McLuhan
C) Tom Wolfe
D) John Lennon

3. In 1990's eminently self-referential *Gremlins 2: The New Batch*, which American film critic meets a nasty end while taping a negative review of the first movie?

A) Roger Ebert
B) Gene Shalit
C) Leonard Maltin
D) Pauline Kael

4. In 1992's *Wayne's World*, Alice Cooper/ Vincent Furnier helpfully expounds upon the etymology of the name Milwaukee. What does he claim the city's name means in the native Algonquin tongue?

A) 'The good land'
B) 'Where the buffalo roam'
C) 'The devil's outhouse'
D) 'Land of the unworthy'

5. John Malkovich plays various versions of himself in 1999's *Being John Malkovich*. In one of Malkovich's realities the actor has which celeb for a best pal?

A) Cyndi Lauper
B) Adam Sandler
C) Charlie Sheen
D) Kermit the Frog

6. Which music legend gives John Cusack some sage life advice in 2000's record-store romcom *High Fidelity*?

A) Sting
B) Keith Richards
C) Stevie Nicks
D) Bruce Springsteen

7. And which member of rock royalty lays down the rules before the climactic runway 'walk-off' in 2001's *Zoolander*?

A) Cher
B) David Bowie
C) Annie Lennox
D) Elton John

8. 2003 curio *Pauly Shore is Dead* finds Nineties comedian Shore attempting

to make a career comeback. Which heavyweight actor can be witnessed in a bar scene, blearily trying to recall the stars of Shore's 1996 vehicle *Bio-Dome*?

A) Susan Sarandon

B) Cameron Diaz

C) Sean Penn

D) Ed Harris

9. Which actor played both themself and their own sleazebag 'cousin' in John Turturro's 2003 caffeine and nicotine anthology *Coffee and Cigarettes*?

A) Charlotte Gainsbourg

B) James Gandolfini

C) Cate Blanchett

D) Viggo Mortensen

10. David Hasselhoff makes a strangely affecting appearance as a version of himself who is also somehow the lead character's father in which Marvel superhero movie?

A) *Doctor Strange*

B) *Thor: Ragnarok*

C) *Ant-Man*

D) *Guardians of the Galaxy Vol. 2*

11. During his death scene in 2009's *Zombieland*, Bill Murray is asked whether he has any regrets. He responds with which typically oblique Murray-esque answer ...?

A) 'Global warming.'

B) 'Disco.'

C) 'Never understood soccer.'

D) '*Garfield*, maybe ...'

12. The same year's *I Love You, Man* finds realtor Peter Klaven (Paul Rudd) struggling to sell which TV star's house?

A) Erik (*CHiPs*) Estrada

B) Paul Michael (*Starsky & Hutch*) Glaser

C) Lou (*The Incredible Hulk*) Ferrigno

D) Farrah (*Charlie's Angels*) Fawcett

13. Which fellow thespian directed Joaquin Phoenix in the 2010 hoax-doc *I'm Still Here*, in which the actor attempted to convince the world that he had traded the big screen for a career in hip-hop?

A) Shia LaBeouf

B) Seth Rogan

C) Casey Affleck

D) Jack Black

14. Which Oscar-winning actor makes something of a spectacle of themself by shamelessly shilling for Dunkin' Donuts during a dance routine in the 2011 Adam Sandler comedy *Jack and Jill*?

A) Colin Firth

B) Dustin Hoffman

C) Al Pacino

D) Helen Mirren

15. According to the 2012 Sacha Baron Cohen comedy *The Dictator*, which actor is alleged to sell sexual favours to the highest bidder?

A) Sir Ben Kinglsey

B) Daniel Craig

C) Kristen Bell

D) Megan Fox

GET CARTER

The career of Helena Bonham Carter

True or false?

1. HBC is the great-granddaughter of former British prime minister Herbert Asquith.

2. She made her TV debut with a love-interest role on Nineties mainstay *Baywatch*.

3. HBC's one-time husband Tim Burton claims to have fallen for her when he spotted her eating lipstick at a bar mitzvah in San Francisco.

4. She played the wife of JFK shooter Lee Harvey Oswald in 1993's Sixties-set TV movie *Fatal Deception*.

5. She has spoken publicly about her fondness for cream crackers, though has rebuffed numerous approaches by cracker brands for her official endorsement.

6. After a 1996 *Time Out* interview in which HBC proposed that acting was easier for actors who weren't posh and pretty, fellow Equity member Kathy Burke wrote in with a curt response: 'Shut up, you stupid c**t.'

7. Bonham Carter reportedly based the role of Marla Singer in 1999's *Fight Club* on a mix of Sammy Davis Jr and a kindly coffee barista she met en route to the set.

8. In 2005's *The Curse of the Were-Rabbit* she provides the voice of a cockney greengrocer called Doreen.

9. Bonham Carter designs patchwork jeans as part of her Pantaloonies fashion line. She describes them as 'a kind of scrapbook on the bum'.

10. In a *Vanity Fair* profile of 2010, Bonham Carter described her style influences as Vivienne Westwood and Clint Eastwood.

11. During her cameo as herself on TV sitcom *Life's Too Short*, HBC insists that distracting co-star Warwick Davis be replaced by a bin with a face drawn on it.

12. In 2009, HBC herself replaced Tilda Swinton to make an unexpected appearance in summer blockbuster *Transformers: Dark of the Moon*.

13. In 2013, Bonham Carter played Elizabeth Taylor in the BBC TV movie *Burton and Taylor* opposite Dominic West as Richard Burton.

14. In 2015, HBC appeared in the promo for 'Brand New Day', a non-charting single for North American rocker Bryan Adams.

15. She received Golden Globe nominations for her roles in the following films: *Howards End*, *The Wings of a Dove*, *Sweeney Todd* and *The King's Speech*.

BRIEF ENCOUNTER

The best and worst screen cameos

1. Robert De Niro made a memorably manic cameo as Archibald Tuttle in Terry Gilliam's sweeping 1985 sci-fi classic *Brazil*. What was his vocation?

A) Paramedic

B) Taxi driver

C) Heating engineer

D) Bicycle repairman

2. Which acting powerhouse makes a rare early comic diversion to play the blind priest in Mel Brooks' loving 1974 spoof *Young Frankenstein*?

A) Gene Hackman

B) James Caan

C) Jon Voight

D) Robert Duvall

3. In which horror remake does the star of the original movie show up in a cameo appearance to warn of terrible events to come?

A) *The Thing*

B) *Carrie*

C) *Invasion of the Body Snatchers*

D) *The Fly*

4. To which informed source does Rodney Dangerfield's Thornton Melon turn for help with a crucial term paper in 1986's *Back to School*?

A) Carl Sagan

B) Kurt Vonnegut

C) Lenny Bruce

D) Hunter S. Thompson

5. Michael Imperioli, who played the mouthy young bartender who gets his toes shot off by Joe Pesci in 1990's *Goodfellas*, went on to land a plum role in which hit TV show?

A) *Sons of Anarchy*

B) *Breaking Bad*

C) *The Sopranos*

D) *Entourage*

6. Who played himself in a biopic of his own life in 1997's *Private Parts*?

A) David Letterman

B) Chris Rock

C) Howard Stern

D) Garry Shandling

7. Which native New Yorker can be seen giving young Kevin McCallister (Macaulay Culkin) directions in 1992's *Home Alone 2: Lost in New York*?

A) Mayor Rudy Giuliani

B) Sylvester Stallone

C) Donald Trump

D) Jerry Seinfeld

8. 1992's cameo-studded Hollywood satire *The Player* features a film-within-a-film that climaxes with 'Bruce Willis' rescuing 'Julia Roberts' from death row. What's it called?

A) *Prognosis Negative*

B) *The Other Side of Darkness*

C) *Rochelle, Rochelle*

D) *Habeas Corpus*

9. The Spielberg-directed film-within-a-film that wraps up 2002's *Austin Powers in Goldmember* casts Tom Cruise as Powers, Kevin Spacey as Dr Evil and Danny DeVito as Mini-Me. Who plays the suggestively monikered female lead, Dixie Normous?

A) Kim Basinger

B) Sharon Stone

C) Naomi Watts

D) Gwyneth Paltrow

10. The singer of which British band pops up in the Leaky Cauldron pub in 2004's *Harry Potter and the Prisoner of Azkaban*?

A) Liam Gallagher of Oasis

B) Thom Yorke of Radiohead

C) Geri Halliwell of the Spice Girls

D) Ian Brown of the Stone Roses

11. Which Oscar winner is all but unrecognizable beneath a chemical suit and mask as the forensics specialist jilted by Simon Pegg's Nicholas Angel in 2007's *Hot Fuzz*?

A) Cate Blanchett

B) Rachel Weisz

C) Hilary Swank

D) Anna Paquin

12. 2008's *Tropic Thunder* opens with a fake trailer for *Satan's Alley*, a drama about forbidden love between two monks. One is played by Robert Downey Jr. Who plays the other?

A) Mark Wahlberg

B) Tobey Maguire

C) Luke Wilson

D) Sam Rockwell

13. In 2013's all-star apocalypse comedy *This Is the End*, which A-lister fills the unenviable position of Danny McBride's personal sex slave?

A) Charlize Theron

B) Joseph Gordon-Levitt

C) Channing Tatum

D) Isla Fisher

14. The news team fight finale in 2013's *Anchorman 2: The Legend Continues* serves up cameo after cameo – including one from John C. Reilly, playing the ghost of ...?

A) Wyatt Earp

B) Abraham Lincoln

C) General Thomas 'Stonewall' Jackson

D) Sitting Bull

15. If you wanted to sit down and enjoy a film without seeing Piers Morgan's face, which of the following titles would ensure painless viewing?

A) *Flight*

B) *Entourage*

C) *Sex and the City 2*

D) *Snowden*

UNCAGED

—

Nic Cage's weirder roles

How much do you know about the magnificent Method man? Test your wits with these true or false questions.

1. In the landmark Eighties teen movie *Fast Times at Ridgemont High*, Cage can briefly be seen flipping burgers behind the counter of a fast food establishment.

-

2. As part of his committed preparations for 1984's Vietnam war-trauma saga *Birdy*, Cage had several teeth removed.

-

3. Cage swallowed a diamond wedding ring for real while filming 1988's *Vampire's Kiss*.

-

4. Little Junior Brown, the villain Cage plays in the 1995 remake of *Kiss of Death*, has a phobia of cutlery.

-

5. Cage's Cameron Poe makes vigorous efforts to transport home a fully primed Nintendo GameCube for his young daughter in 1997's *Con Air*.

-

6. Cage was all set to play Spider-Man for Tim Burton before the studio got cold feet and pulled the plug.

-

7. Cage earned an Academy Award nomination for 2002's *Adaptation*, playing agonized screenwriter Charlie Kaufman and his twin brother Donald.

8. In the very same year, Cage completed work on his sole directorial credit to date – a dark psychological drama, *Sonny*, which brought together the diverse talents of James Franco and Brenda Blethyn.

-

9. Bees take their revenge on Cage's character in 2006's remake of *The Wicker Man*.

-

10. Cage crops up as Fu Manchu in one of the fake trailers for Quentin Tarantino and Robert Rodriguez's double feature spectacular, *Grindhouse*.

-

11. Sometimes it's good to know when to hold back. Cage snorted self-raising flour in place of cocaine while playing corrupt copper Terence McDonagh in 2009's *Bad Lieutenant: Port of Call New Orleans*.

-

12. Cage lent his voice to haughty peacock Speckles in Disney's spy-themed 2009 animation caper *G-Force*.

-

13. In 2009's sci-fi *Knowing*, Cage apparently amassed a library of some 7,000 books on the subject of the apocalypse as part of his research. When shooting finished, he donated them all to a local kindergarten.

-

14. In 2011's neo-exploitationer *Drive Angry*, Cage plays a cigar-chomping, waitress-tupping badass named T.S. Eliot.

-

15. In 2016's based-on-a-true-story *Army of One*, Cage's construction worker Gary Faulkner sets out to take down film actor Richard Gere.

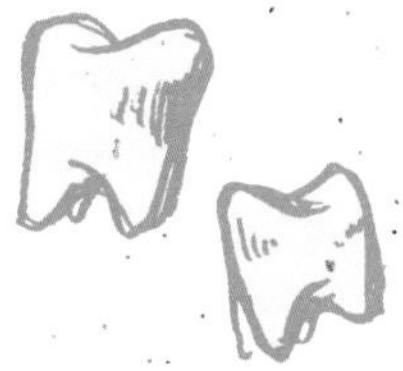

PITT BITS

Key props from the films of Brad Pitt

Connect the image to the film:

Inglourious Basterds, Burn After Reading, Ocean's Eleven, Snatch, Fight Club, Meet Joe Black, 12 Monkeys, Seven, Johnny Suede, A River Runs Through It

1

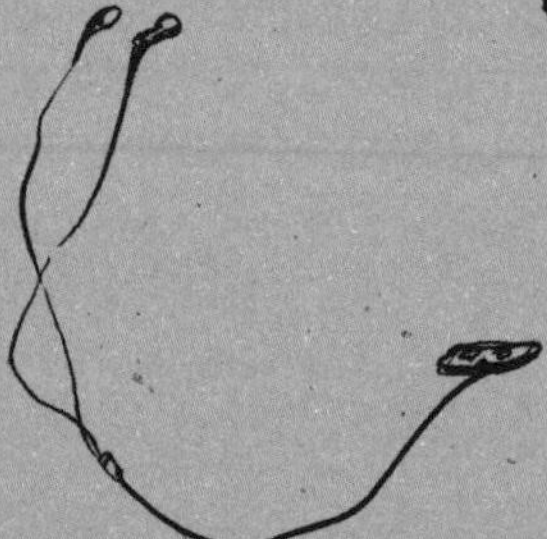

2

3

4

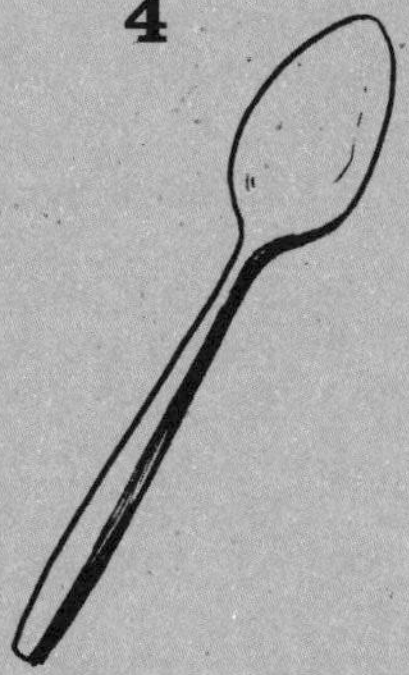

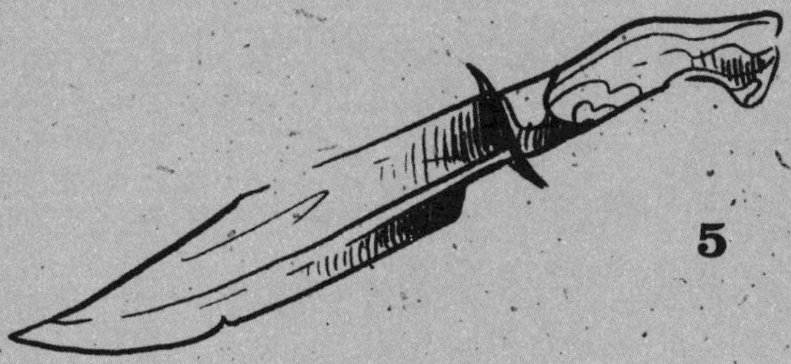

5

7

6

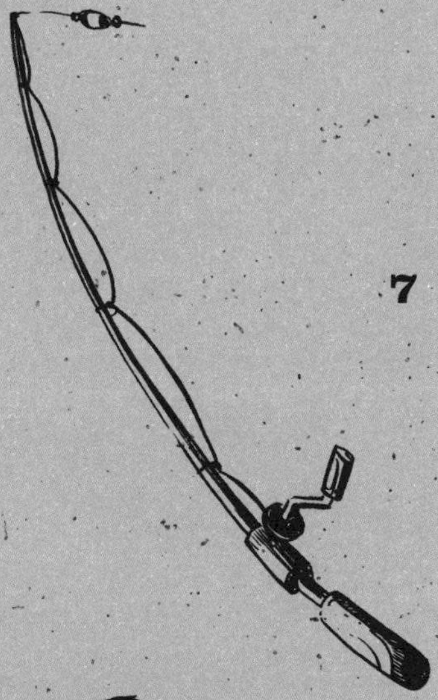

8

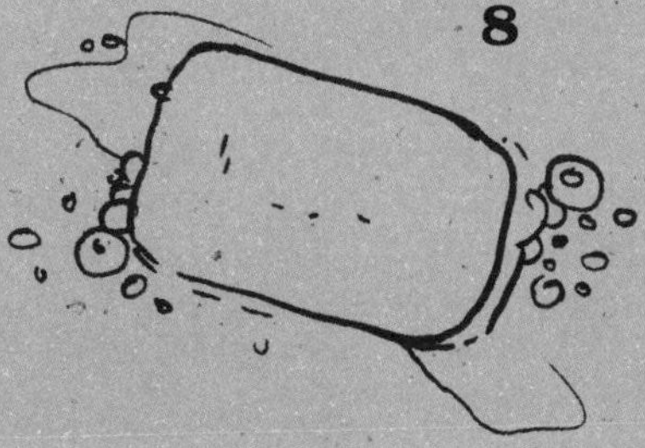

9

10

BACKUP

Notable supporting players

1. Bug-eyed sideman Peter Lorre stole both *The Maltese Falcon* and *Casablanca* from under Humphrey Bogart's nose, but all good runs come to an end. What was the title of Lorre's final screen credit in 1964 – in which he co-starred with Stevie Wonder, Don Rickles and Dick Dale?

A) *Freddie the Freeloader's Christmas Dinner*
B) *Muscle Beach Party*
C) *Dr. Goldfoot and the Bikini Machine*
D) *Cucumber Castle*

2. Much-loved character actor Allison Janney – of TV's *The West Wing* and so much more – won the 2018 Best Supporting Actress Oscar for which film?

A) *I, Tonya*
B) *Lady Bird*
C) *Phantom Thread*
D) *Three Billboards Outside Ebbing, Missouri*

3. Warren Oates' racist deputy Sam Wood in 1967's *In the Heat of the Night* is revealed to have a particular sexual peccadillo. What is it?

A) He likes to dress up as Uncle Sam
B) He can only get excited on Christmas Eve
C) He is obsessed with extremely tall women
D) He likes having sex on gravestones

4. Character actor Mercedes McCambridge won a Supporting Actress Oscar for 1949's *All the King's Men* and would go on to provide the voice of the demon in 1973's *The Exorcist*. What was it called?

A) Chemosh
B) Pazuzu
C) Azazel
D) Babadook

5. John Cazale, who played Fredo in *The Godfather* and its sequel, passed away in 1978 at the age 42, having appeared in only five films. Which of these classics did NOT benefit from his brilliance?

A) *The Conversation*
B) *Dog Day Afternoon*
C) *The French Connection*
D) *The Deer Hunter*

6. Which modern comedy great is found bloated, out of their mind, semi-clothed and surrounded by outsize bunny heads in the most bonkers scene of bonkers 2006 Vegas crime caper *Smokin' Aces*?

A) Dave Chappelle
B) Will Arnett
C) Jason Bateman
D) Amy Poehler

7. Which member of the cast of 1979's *Alien* was way ahead of their co-stars in their preparation for their role, claiming

'I was having extraterrestrial experiences from the time I was 10 years old. Weird experiences.'?

A) Tom Skerritt

B) Veronica Cartwright

C) Yaphet Kotto

D) John Hurt

8. Scuzzbag private eye M. Emmet Walsh lies dying on a dirty bathroom floor, watching a water droplet condense on the pipes on the underside of a sink, in the Coen brothers' 1984 debut *Blood Simple*. The drop falls ... The credits come up ... What song plays?

A) 'It's the Same Old Song' by the Four Tops

B) 'Sweet Caroline' by Neil Diamond

C) 'Heart of Gold' by Neil Young

D) 'Build Me Up Buttercup' by the Foundations

9. Judy Greer has appeared in *Jurassic World*, *Ant-Man and The Wasp* and *Halloween* in recent times, but is perhaps still best known for her role as Kitty Sanchez in which TV sitcom?

A) *The Office*

B) *30 Rock*

C) *Parks and Recreation*

D) *Arrested Development*

10. Which actor was Tim Burton's second choice to play the Joker in 1989's *Batman*, and was later replaced as the voice of the Joker in *Batman: The Animated Series* for being 'too scary'?

A) Crispin Glover

B) Christopher Walken

C) Tim Curry

D) Michael Keaton

11. Silver-maned screen heavy Frank Vincent – Billy Batts in *Goodfellas*, Jennifer Aniston's dad in *She's the One*, Phil Leotardo on TV's *The Sopranos* – penned a self-help book for wannabe players in 2007. What was it called?

A) *A Guy's Guide to Being a Man's Man*

B) *A Word to the Wiseguy*

C) *How to Be a Real Goodfella*

D) *So You Wanna Be a Gangster ...?*

12. To the memory of which consummate second banana did Jack Nicholson dedicate his 1998 Best Actor Oscar for *As Good As it Gets*?

A) Jack Palance

B) Raul Julia

C) Jack Warden

D) J.T. Walsh

13. Which bad boy broke the fourth wall with an ill-advised, self-congratulatory 2007 mockumentary that was, alas, more *Curb Your Enthusiasm* than *Being John Malkovich*? Was it ...?

A) *Being Denis Leary*

B) *Being Stephen Baldwin*

C) *Being Tom Sizemore*

D) *Being Michael Madsen*

14. Imprisoned in a Russian 're-education' camp in 1984's *Red Dawn*, what is Harry Dean Stanton's final rallying cry to his renegade sons?

A) 'Avenge me!'

B) 'The South will rise again!'

C) 'Communism is bullshit!'

D) 'Stay gold, my ponyboys!'

15. Which of the following wingmen does NOT turn up in the character actor cavalcade of 1995's *Heat*?

A) Danny Trejo

B) Jeremy Piven

C) Hank Azaria

D) Chazz Palminteri

CROSSING OVER II

Directors who act

1. Which prominent figure in American independent film played Mia Farrow's husband in 1968's horror blockbuster *Rosemary's Baby*?

2. What is the name of the grave top-hatted loon played by the Brazilian writer-director-star José Mojica Marins in a run of horror movies from the 1960s onwards?

3. Golden Age legend John Huston twice played obsessively protective sorts named Noah – once in his own 1966 film of *The Bible*, and then again in which Oscar-winning 1974 production?

4. Which French New Waver played the role of UFOlogist Claude Lacombe in 1977's *Close Encounters of the Third Kind*?

5. Name the director who also played the role of the diminutive Half-Pint in his 1988 film *School Daze*?

6. Which Canadian body horror maestro turns up to kill Nicole Kidman's ladder-climbing weather girl character in Gus Van Sant's 1995 satire *To Die For*?

7. Which Eighties blockbuster does Quentin Tarantino claim has a major homoerotic subtext during his party-sequence cameo in 1994's *Sleep with Me*? [Hint: 'You can ride my tail anytime.']

8. In which vital school role can Wes Craven be seen, clad in a Freddy Krueger-style striped jumper, during 1996's *Scream*?

9. The role of Victor Ziegler, the shady millionaire luring Tom Cruise into the erotic conspiracies of 1999's *Eyes Wide Shut*, was played by which American actor and director?

10. What's the name of the character that filmmaker Tyler Perry has repeatedly dragged up in the run of profitable comedies that began in 2005? (Bonus point for the character's full name.)

11. In 2006's scabrous political comedy *The Caiman*, writer-director-star Nanni Moretti took a dual role, playing himself and which other notable Italian public figure?

12. Which Kiwi director stabs Simon Pegg in the hand during a blink-and-you'll-miss-it cameo appearance as an unhinged Santa Claus in 2007's *Hot Fuzz*?

13. 2014's animated sequel *Penguins of Madagascar* featured an unlikely voice cameo from which usually ultra-serious German filmmaker?

14. M. Night Shyamalan has appeared, to good and ill effect, in all his directorial outings. Of which adult-themed American fast-food chain was his character in his 2017 comeback *Split* an enthusiast?

15. Which of the following roles has John Waters not filled on screen over the course of his fifty-year acting career – 'Flasher', Ed Wood, 'Pervert on Phone' or Jesus Christ?

BEAT THE DEVIL

Beyond *Friends* ... Rachel, Ross and co. flex their acting muscles

1. Prior to his casting as Joey in *Friends* (and later, spin-off sitcom *Joey*), actor Matt LeBlanc featured in a footwear-referencing TV serial based around erotic clinches. Name that serial.

2. Four years into his *Friends* tenure, David Schwimmer (Ross) directed a light comic feature which ended up playing on TV rather than in cinemas. Name the film, whose title name-checks a classic single by British poodle rockers, Rainbow.

3. Jennifer Aniston starred in a cheapo horror movie in 1993 whose antagonist is a perennial figure of Irish folklore. Name the film.

4. Launching his attack on the world of feature films, Matthew Perry (Chandler Bing) snagged the role of the nervy neighbour to a noted gangster in *The Whole Nine Yards* (2000). Who played that gangster?

5. Lisa Kudrow, who played loveable ditz Phoebe, starred in a 1997 high-school comedy (and latter-day cult classic) revolving around a reunion. Whose reunion?

6. Perhaps the biggest big-screen breakout of the entire *Friends* crew was Courteney Cox, who scored a recurring role in the wildly popular *Scream* franchise. But what was the name of her tenacious news anchor?

7. In the 1996 sports comedy *Ed*, Matt LeBlanc strikes up a rapport with the titular baseball team mascot. Which animal plays that mascot?

8. David Schwimmer played Dr Kevin Saunders – one of the inventors of silicone breast implants – in which 1997 film?

9. What was the name of the yellow Labrador retriever mentioned in the title of a 2008 family hit which stars Jennifer Aniston and Owen Wilson?

10. Matthew Perry's screen debut came in 1988 in the teen comedy *A Night in the Life of Jimmy Reardon*. Perry didn't play Jimmy Reardon, but which tragic teen heartthrob did?

First Contact: Stars' unusual early roles
1. a, 2. c, 3. a, 4. d, 5. b, 6. b (a film about the world's first pregnant man, played by Billy Crystal), 7. b (in *Bionic Showdown: The Six Million Dollar Man and the Bionic Woman*), 8. d, 9. c, 10. d, 11. c, 12. a, 13. d, 14. c, 15. b

Self-Portraits: Actors/personalities play themselves
1. c, 2. b, 3. c, 4. a, 5. c, 6. d, 7. b, 8. c, 9. c, 10. d, 11. d, 12. c, 13. c, 14. c, 15. d

Get Carter: The career of Helena Bonham Carter
1. True, 2. False – it was *Miami Vice*, 3. False, 4. True, 5. False, 6. True, 7. False – it was Judy Garland, 8. False – she voices an aristocrat, 9. True, 10. False – it's Vivienne Westwood and Marie Antoinette, 11. True, 12. False – it was *Terminator: Salvation*, 13. True, 14. True, 15. False – she didn't receive one for *Howards End*

Brief Encounter: The best and worst screen cameos
1. c, 2. a, 3. c (Kevin McCarthy, star of the 1956 version, warns Donald Sutherland's 1978 incarnation that 'They're coming!'), 4. b, 5. c, 6. c, 7. c, 8. d, 9. d, 10. d, 11. a, 12. b, 13. c, 14. c, 15. c

Uncaged: Nic Cage's weirder roles
1. True, 2. True, 3. False – it was a cockroach, 4. True, 5. False – it was a stuffed rabbit, 6. False – it was Superman, 7. True, 8. True, 9. True, 10. True, 11. False – it was baby powder, 12. False – Speckles was a mole, 13. False, 14. False – his character is named John Milton, 15. False – it was Osama bin Laden

Pitt Bits
1. *12 Monkeys*, 2. *Ocean's Eleven*, 3. *Seven*, 4. *Burn After Reading*, 5. *Inglourious Basterds*, 6. *Johnny Suede*, 7. *A River Runs Through It*, 8. *Fight Club*, 9. *Snatch*, 10. *Meet Joe Black*

Backup: Notable supporting players
1. b, 2. a, 3. d, 4. b, 5. c, 6. c, 7. c, 8. a, 9. d, 10. c, 11. a, 12. d, 13. d (Madsen later described it as being 'probably the worst film I've been involved in in my entire life. I actually despise it.'), 14. a, 15. d

Crossing Over II: Directors who act
1. John Cassavetes, 2. Coffin Joe, 3. *Chinatown*, 4. François Truffaut, 5. Spike Lee, 6. David Cronenberg, 7. *Top Gun*, 8. Janitor, 9. Sydney Pollack, 10. Madea, full name Mabel Simmons, 11. Silvio Berlusconi, 12. Peter Jackson, 13. Werner Herzog, 14. Hooters, 15. Ed Wood

Beyond *Friends* ...
1. *Red Shoe Diaries*, 2. *Since You've Been Gone*, 3. *Leprechaun*, 4. Bruce Willis, 5. Romy and Michele, 6. Gale Weathers, 7. A chimpanzee, 8. *Breast Men*, 9. Marley (in the film *Marley & Me*), 10. River Phoenix

ANSWERS

6

Pot LUCK

Eight rounds of blind chance

ROLE PLAY

Five characters in search of a film

Identify the film from the characters listed below:

1. Juror 1, Juror 2, Juror 3, Juror 4, Juror 5 (1957)

2. Squire Jöns, Death, Antonius Block, The Monk, Blacksmith Plog (1957)

3. The Cooler King, The Scrounger, Big X, The SBO, Tunnel King (1963)

4. Joker, Animal Mother, Pyle, Payback, Doorgunner (1987)

5. Westley, Miracle Max, Prince Humperdinck, Vizzini, The Impressive Clergyman (1987)

6. Grant, Sattler, Malcolm, Hammond, Muldoon (1993)

7. Phil, Rita, Larry, Ned, Buster (1993)

8. Detective William Somerset, Detective David Mills, Detective Taylor, Tracy, John Doe (1995)

9. McManus, Keaton, Fenster, Hockney, Kint (1995)

10. Ripley, Call, Vriess, Johner, Christie (1997)

11. Tom, Soap, Eddy, Bacon, Barry the Baptist (1998)

12. Cobb, Arthur, Ariadne, Eames, Saito (2010)

13. Major Marquis Warren, John Ruth, Daisy Domergue, Sheriff Chris Mannix, Bob (2015)

14. Nux, Immortan Joe, The Splendid Angharad, The People Eater, Imperator Furiosa (2015)

15. Joy, Sadness, Fear, Anger, Disgust (2015)

THE INCREDIBLES

Pixar's amazing voice artists

Pixar have long benefitted from the pick of thespian talent (and Jeremy Clarkson) when it comes to voicing their animated crowdpleasers. But can you match the following performers to the characters they voiced?

Frozone (*The Incredibles/The Incredibles 2*)
Momma (*The Good Dinosaur*)
Jessie the Yodelling Cowgirl (*Toy Story* 2–4)
Queen (*A Bug's Life*)
Randall (*Monsters, Inc./Monsters University*)
Harv (*Cars* [UK version])
Dory (*Finding Nemo/Finding Dory*)
Ken (*Toy Story 3*)
Anton Ego (*Ratatouille*)
The Witch (*Brave*)
Doc Hudson (*Cars*)
Butch (*The Good Dinosaur*)
Ship's Computer (*WALL-E*)
Finn McMissile (*Cars 2*)
Buzz Lightyear (*Toy Story* 1–4)

Tim Allen

Steve Buscemi

Michael Caine

Jeremy Clarkson

Joan Cusack

Ellen DeGeneres

Phyllis Diller

Sam Elliott

Samuel L. Jackson

Michael Keaton

Frances McDormand

Paul Newman

Peter O'Toole

Julie Walters

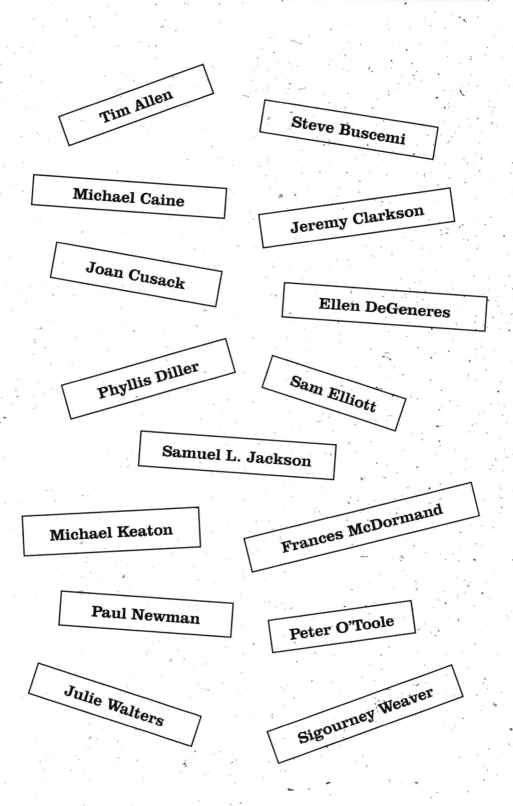

Sigourney Weaver

CHARACTER STUDIES

Match the silhouettes to the following characters:

Amphibian Man (*The Shape of Water*), The Babadook (*The Babadook*), Boonsong (*Uncle Boonmee Who Can Recall His Past Lives*), Carol (*Where the Wild Things Are*), Death (*The Seventh Seal*), Dick Tracy (*Dick Tracy*), Frank (*Donnie Darko*), The Goblin King (*Labyrinth*), The Kukeri (*Toni Erdmann*), Lulu (*Pandora's Box*), Nosferatu (*Nosferatu*), Toothless (*How to Train Your Dragon*), Totoro (*My Neighbour Totoro*), Travis Bickle (*Taxi Driver*), Yoda (*Star Wars*)

1

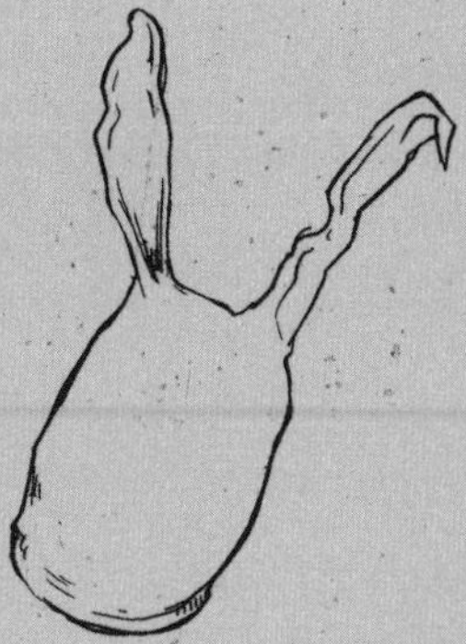

2

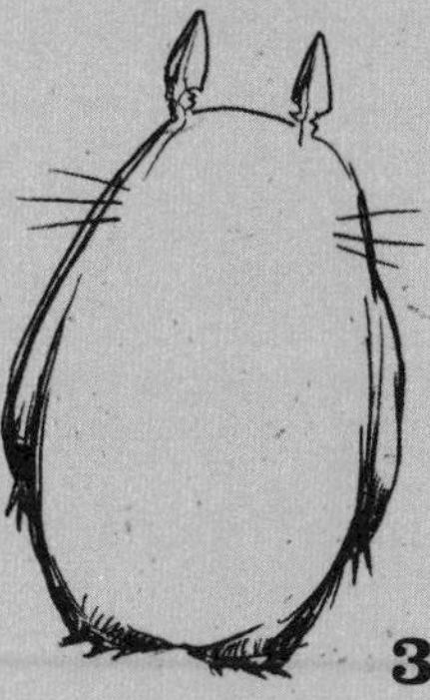

3

4

5

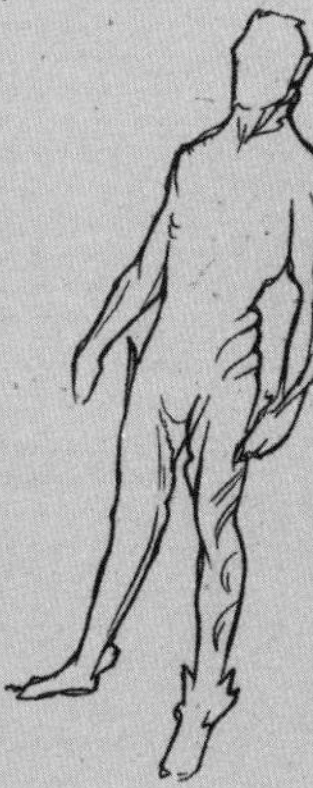

6

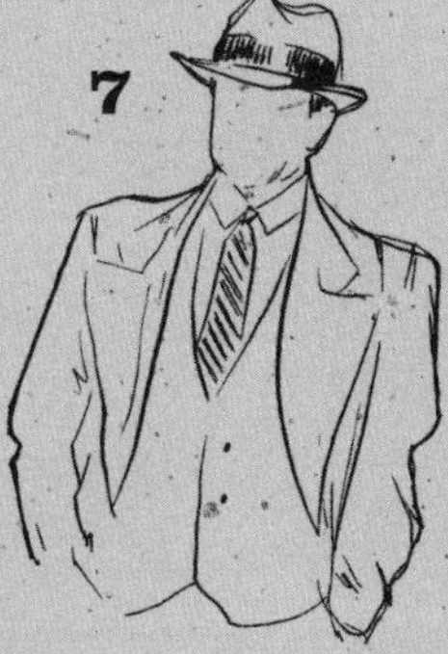

7

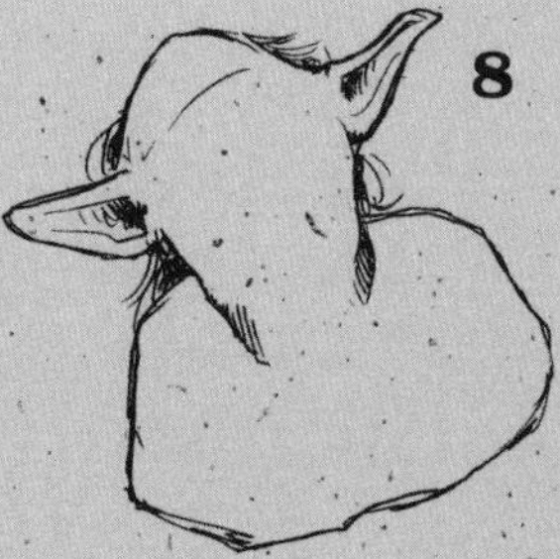

8

9

10

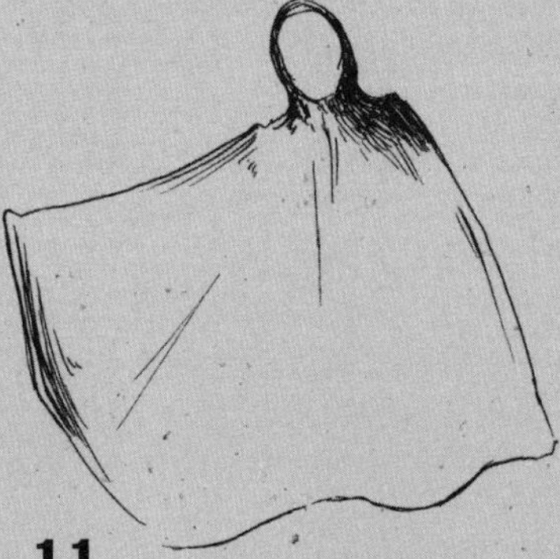

11

12

13

14

15

METHOD MAYHEM

A history of extreme acting

1. Complete the title of the 1936 book by Konstantin Stanislavski, the Russian actor-director who laid the foundations for Method acting and the Actor's Studio in New York: *An Actor* _______?

A) *Acts*

B) *Exists*

C) *Prepares*

D) *Suffers*

2. Which of the following performers did NOT pass through the doors of the Actors Studio?

A) Julia Roberts

B) Kevin Spacey

C) Hayden Christensen

D) Steve Buscemi

3. How did Marlon Brando, Godfather of the Method, prepare for his role as an injured Army veteran in his 1950 film debut *The Men*?

A) He had both of his legs put in plaster

B) He got a friend to run over his foot with his car

C) He dosed himself with morphine

D) He confined himself to bed for a month

4. Al Pacino has been known to immerse himself into his roles. He would, however, have been ill advised to do too much Method research for 1977 oddity *Bobby Deerfield*, in which he played ...?

A) An astronaut

B) A big-game hunter

C) An IRA gun-runner

D) A Formula 1 driver

5. Who wrote an NYU graduate thesis on Al Pacino's acting methods before going on to co-star with the great man?

A) John Cusack

B) Michelle Pfeiffer

C) Alec Baldwin

D) Bridget Fonda

6. What was the advice famously offered by stage and screen great Laurence Olivier upon witnessing Dustin Hoffman struggle to get into his character's mindset while filming 1976's *Marathon Man*?

A) 'Simply ask yourself: how would Larry do it?'

B) 'Have you tried acting, dear boy?'

C) 'Imagine a conifer ...'

D) 'Just get sloshed, turn up on time and try not to make a fool of yourself.'

7. On which animal did Robert de Niro base his *Taxi Driver* character Travis Bickle's movements?

A) The narwhal

B) The shark

C) The meerkat

D) The crab

8. Robert De Niro famously put on 60 pounds for 1980's *Raging Bull*. Which committed performer piled on a similar amount of poundage for Stanley Kubrick's 1987 Vietnam War epic, *Full Metal Jacket*?

A) James Woods
B) Willem Dafoe
C) Vincent D'Onofrio
D) Kevin Kline

9. How did Halle Berry prepare for her role as a crack addict in Spike Lee's 1991 drama *Jungle Fever*?

A) She slept on a bench in Central Park
B) She worked for a week as a nurse in a rehab centre
C) She went without bathing
D) She watched the 1971 Al Pacino film *Panic in Needle Park* on a loop

10. Charlize Theron glammed down for her Oscar-winning turn as a serial killer in Patty Jenkins' 2003 film *Monster*. What was her character's name?

A) Jelena Kazlowski
B) Aileen Wuornos
C) Brenda van den Camp
D) Nichole Breithaupt

11. Christian Bale dropped 65 pounds for his role in 2004's *The Machinist* by subsisting for four months on only water, coffee and what?

A) An apple a day
B) A peeled radish every six hours
C) A handful of Lucky Charms every morning
D) A Big Mac the night before the start of filming

12. Sometimes all this effort goes unnoticed. 2007's little-seen *Chapter 27* saw the elfin Jared Leto gain a full 67 pounds to play the assassin of which historical figure?

A) Abraham Lincoln
B) John F. Kennedy
C) Martin Luther King
D) John Lennon

13. The beats dropped by Joaquin Phoenix in his ill-fated hip-hop diversion in 2010's mockumentary *I'm Still Here* eventually found their way into a track by which real-life rapper?

A) The Game
B) Lil Wayne
C) Eminem
D) Pusha T

14. To what lengths has Method man Daniel Day-Lewis NOT gone while preparing for a role?

A) Join a street gang (for *Gangs of New York*)
B) Learn to build canoes (for *Last of the Mohicans*)
C) Learn to speak Czech (for *The Unbearable Lightness of Being*)
D) Confine himself to a wheelchair (for *My Left Foot*)

15. The 2017 documentary *The Great Beyond* presents alarming footage of Jim Carrey going Full Method during the filming of 1999 Andy Kaufman biopic *Man on the Moon*. What does Carrey/Kaufman demand after storming into Steven Spielberg's office?

A) Freedom for the *Jurassic Park* dinosaurs
B) That the director shave off his trademark beard
C) A meeting with the shark from *Jaws*
D) That E.T. come back to Earth and 'explain himself'

NEAT EATS

Foodie faves

1. Behind which fine establishment do our smitten canine leads share a plate of spaghetti in 1955's *Lady and the Tramp*?

A) Vesuvio's

B) Sloppy Giuseppe's

C) Tony's Restaurant

D) Hernando's Hideaway

2. What fate befalls poor Augustus Gloop in both the 1971 and 2005 adaptations of Roald Dahl's *Charlie and the Chocolate Factory*?

A) He chokes on a gobstopper

B) He floats away while chewing bubble gum

C) He turns into an Oompa Loompa

D) He falls into a river of chocolate

3. Which big-name director dialled back the bangs and the bucks to make lo-fi 2014 street food parable *Chef*?

A) Jon Favreau

B) Michael Bay

C) Kathryn Bigelow

D) Peter Jackson

4. What tasty morsel tips Terry Jones's Mr Creosote so explosively over the edge in 1983's *The Meaning of Life*?

A) A grape

B) A salted peanut

C) A mint

D) A profiterole

5. Which of the following dishes is NOT on the menu during the ethnically dubious banquet scene in 1984's *Indiana Jones and the Temple of Doom*?

A) Snake Surprise

B) Panther paws

C) Eyeball soup

D) Chilled monkey brains

6. 1985's Japanese import *Tampopo* concerns the quest to find the perfect ...?

A) Dumpling

B) Menu

C) Soy sauce

D) Noodle

7. What was the name of the 2008 Brittany Murphy vehicle that *Tampopo* inspired?

A) *American Sushi*

B) *The Ramen Girl*

C) *Miso & Me*

D) *My Wasabi Nights*

8. Amid the heat of cinema's sexiest refrigerator scene in 1986's *9½ Weeks*, Mickey Rourke feeds Kim Basinger a spoonful of what substance?

A) Cough syrup

B) Castor oil

C) Mustard powder

D) Cat food

9. Which of the following movies does NOT involve the big foodie taboo – cannibalism?

A) *How Tasty Was My Little Frenchman*

B) *Delicatessen*

C) *Let Me Eat Your Pancreas*

D) *Ravenous*

10. 1996's *Big Night* builds towards the unveiling of a vast, intricate baked pasta timballo, but a palate-cleansing coda finds chef Secondo (Stanley Tucci) whipping up an altogether simpler dish for himself and his brother Primo (Tony Shalhoub). What?

A) A grilled cheese sandwich

B) An omelette

C) A green salad

D) A hamburger

11. *Eat Drink Man Woman*, Ang Lee's 1994 Taiwanese heartwarmer, was reworked in 2001 with a decidedly Mexican flavour. What was it called?

A) *Taco Belles*

B) *Burrito, Burrito!*

C) *Enchilada Combo*

D) *Tortilla Soup*

12. What was the title of the 2017 sequel to Morgan Spurlock's hit 2004 documentary *Super Size Me*?

A) *Hot Dog!: How the Sausage is Made*

B) *Pizza: The Motion Picture*

C) *Super Size Me 2: Holy Chicken!*

D) *Going Underground: The Subway Diet*

13. Which dessert plays a major supporting role during the terse confrontation between Shoshanna (Mélanie Laurent) and Colonel Landa (Christoph Waltz) in 2009's *Inglourious Basterds*?

A) Arctic roll

B) Black Forest gateau

C) Spotted dick

D) Strudel

14. What's unusual about the high-end sushi restaurant owned by Jiro Ono in the 2011 documentary *Jiro Dreams of Sushi*?

A) It only has ten seats

B) It is located in a cable car on the slopes of Mount Fuji

C) Patrons eat in the nude

D) It is open for only one day a year

15. In which film would you find yourself dining at Le Hollandais?

A) *Ratatouille*

B) *Babette's Feast*

C) *The Cook, the Thief, His Wife and Her Lover*

D) *Eat the Rich*

NEW RULES

The Dogme films

1. How long, according to Thomas Vinterberg, did it take for him and fellow director Lars von Trier to pen the official Dogme manifesto?

A) Less than a minute

B) 45 minutes

C) The time it takes to eat two bananas

D) 38 years

2. Which of the following is not one of that manifesto's core tenets?

A) The film must not contain superficial action

B) Genre movies are not acceptable

C) Each film must contain a shot of a person scooping the seeds from a melon

D) The director must not be credited

3. How did Vinterberg contravene his own manifesto while shooting 1998's *Festen*, the first Dogme title?

A) He decided to kill off the entire cast

B) He covered a window for better lighting

C) He included a CGI zeppelin in the film's climactic scene

D) He exploited the on-set interns as a way to get around not using a tripod

4. Which phrase, vociferously shouted at the screen in broken French, saw the usually cool-headed British critic Mark Kermode ejected from the Cannes screening of von Trier's *The Idiots*?

A) 'Neuf à la banque!'

B) 'J'adore les champignons!'

C) 'Il est merde!'

D) 'Où est la salle de bains, s'il vous plaît?'

5. Jean-Marc Barr, the first non-Danish director to shoot an officially certified Dogme movie (*Lovers* from 1999), has a small but important place in Britpop history. What is it?

A) He egged on Jarvis Cocker to sabotage Michael Jackson's performance at the Brit Awards

B) The Gallagher brothers claimed his eyebrows inspired their own

C) He once roadied for Lawrence from Felt

D) He played the Charmless Man in Blur's 'Charmless Man' video

6. 1999's *Julien Donkey-Boy,* the first US Dogme movie, finds Werner Herzog utilizing an unusual method of ingesting cough syrup. What is it?

A) He spreads it on a sandwich

B) He splashes it into his armpits

C) He tries to sip it from a shoe

D) He takes it rectally

7. 2000's *The King Is Alive* features an impromptu staging of *King Lear* in which setting?

A) A penguin colony in Antarctica

B) A Berlin gabba club

C) A derelict motorway service station in northern France
D) The Namibian desert

8. Director Lone Scherfig counts films like *An Education* and *Their Finest* on her CV. But she also kicked off her career with a Dogme film adapted from a Maeve Binchy novel which is set in a language class. What was it called?
A) *Italian for Beginners*
B) *Italian for Imbeciles*
C) *Italian for People Who Eat Road Gritting*
D) *Justa Learna To Talka Likea Thisa*

9. Leif Tilden, the Boston-born co-director of Dogme #17 (2001's *Reunion*), is better known for playing which staff-wielding Teenage Mutant Ninja Turtle?
A) Leonardo
B) Donatello
C) Michelangelo
D) Raphael

10. 2002's *Shoot or Be Shot!* is an alleged spoof of all things Dogme and centres on a man played by William Shatner who holds a film crew hostage and obliges them to realize his deranged vision. What quirk does Shatner's character possess?
A) He's an escaped psychiatric patient
B) He suffers from Tourette's syndrome
C) He has no short-term memory and so remembers things with the aid of tattoos and photographs
D) He's playing Captain Kirk

11. 2005's *Gypo*, the first British Dogme production, offered a rare dramatic lead role for Pauline McLynn, better known as a mainstay of which British sitcom?
A) *The Office*
B) *I'm Alan Partridge*
C) *'Allo 'Allo*
D) *Father Ted*

12. The acclaimed English-language theatre adaptation of *Festen* reached Melbourne in 2006. Which local actor assumed the role played by Ulrich Thomsen in the original film?
A) Guy Pearce
B) Jason Donovan
C) Geoffrey Rush
D) Stefan Dennis

13. A later von Trier-engineered project, aiming to generate three films from first-time directors, gave rise to 2006's *Red Road* and 2010's *Donkeys*. What was this project's name?
A) Debutante's Ball
B) New New Wave
C) Advance Party
D) New Grit

14. How many Dogme films were certified in total?
A) Fewer than 20
B) Between 20 and 40
C) Between 40 and 60
D) 60 or above

15. At the time of publication, which Dogme film has the highest rating on critical aggregator site Metacritic?
A) *The Idiots*
B) *Julien Donkey-Boy*
C) *Festen*
D) *Mifune*

HACK ATTACK

Writers on film

1. 1981's *Tales of Ordinary Madness*, 1987's *Barfly* and 2005's *Factotum* all mine their source material from the boozy misadventures of which legendary scribbler?

A) Ernest Hemingway
B) F. Scott Fitzgerald
C) Charles Bukowski
D) Dylan Thomas

2. Celebrated Kiwi writer Janet Frame is the subject of which 1990 drama, directed by Jane Campion?

A) *The Lovely Bones*
B) *The Unexpected Virtue of Ignorance*
C) *Top of the Lake*
D) *An Angel at My Table*

3. John Turturro's zealous, pretentious man-of-the-people playwright Barton Fink is wooed by Hollywood in the Coen brothers' 1991 Palme d'Or-winning satire of the same name, and immediately set to work on the script for ...?

A) A jungle adventure
B) A wrestling movie
C) A film about a talking yak
D) A Shirley Temple musical

4. The verses Janet Jackson's aspirant poet arrived at in 1993's *Poetic Justice* were provided by ...?

A) Maya Angelou
B) Nina Simone
C) Alice Walker
D) Toni Morrison

5. And the words of which Latin American writer helped the humble hero of 1994's *Il Postino* woo the object of his affections?

A) Jorge Luis Borges
B) Isabelle Allende
C) Pablo Neruda
D) Gabriel García Márquez

6. Which actor struggles to balance his writerly ambitions with his humdrum day job in Steven Soderbergh's 1991 expressionistic offering *Kafka*?

A) Geoffrey Rush
B) Jeremy Irons
C) Harvey Keitel
D) Jonathan Pryce

7. Which emerging heartthrob put in a fine shift as French poet Arthur Rimbaud in 1995's *Total Eclipse*?

A) Brendan Fraser
B) Stephen Dorff
C) Johnny Depp
D) Leonardo DiCaprio

8. *All the President's Men* follows Bob Woodward and Carl Bernstein, the *Washington Post* journos who brought down the Nixon administration. Who plays their editor?

A) John Huston

B) Angela Lansbury

C) Jason Robards

D) Katharine Hepburn

9. Nicolas Cage plays twin scriptwriters in which 2002 film?

A) *The Orchid Thief*

B) *Stuck on You*

C) *Adaptation*

D) *Double Jeopardy*

10. Which novel links three generations – including a fictional version of the author – in 2002's *The Hours*?

A) *Mrs Dalloway* by Virginia Woolf

B) *The Heather Blazing* by Colm Tóibín

C) *Postcards* by E. Annie Proulx

D) *The Tartan Bride* by Edna O'Lacey

11. In 2004's *Before Sunset* we learn that Jesse (Ethan Hawke) has written a book about his Viennese experiences with Céline (Julie Delpy) in 1995's *Before Sunrise*. What is the book's title?

A) *One Crazy Summer*

B) *This Time*

C) *You Will Know Me By My Name*

D) *All Tomorrow's Parties*

12. Philip Seymour Hoffman took home the plaudits (and the Oscar) for playing the title role in the 2005 biopic *Capote*. But which British actor played Capote all over again in the following year's *Infamous*?

A) Christian Bale

B) Toby Jones

C) Michael Sheen

D) Ewan McGregor

13. Which actress has, in recent years, played gossip columnist Hedda Hopper, *Shadow of a Doubt* screenwriter Alma Reville and *The Fountainhead* novelist Ayn Rand?

A) Joan Allen

B) Emma Thompson

C) Helen Mirren

D) Laura Linney

14. Which of the following actors has NOT played Beat poet Allen Ginsberg on the big screen since the turn of the millennium?

A) Daniel Radcliffe

B) James Franco

C) William H. Macy

D) David Cross

15. 2015's Oscar-winning *Spotlight* centred on the journalists of which American publication?

A) *Wisconsin Seed Bulletin*

B) *Baltimore Sun*

C) *National Inquirer*

D) *Boston Globe*

BEAT THE DEVIL

Version Original: Foreign-language titles

1. You've arrived at a cinema in Stockholm ahead of a major Ingmar Bergman retrospective. Unfortunately, none of the showtimes have been translated into English. Which of the following is NOT part of Bergmania – *Smultronstället*, *Tillsammans*, *Ansiktet* or *Vargtimmen*? (Bonus point if you can name that film's director.)

2. *L'uccello dalle Piume di Cristallo. Il Gatto a Nove Code. Profondo Rosso.* Which key horror director?

3. The original German title of 1974's Werner Herzog offering *Jeder für sich und Gott gegen Alle* translates literally as *Every Man for Himself and God Against All*. How is that film better known in English-speaking markets?

4. *C'est Arrivé Près de Chez Vous* was the original title for which censor-troubling film of the 1990s?

5. When translated into English, the title of 1995's blockbusting Hindi romance *Dilwale Dulhania Le Jayenge* features the name of a prominent Oscar Best Picture winner from the same decade. Which film?

6. *Hip Hip Hora!*, a Swedish coming-of-age saga from 2004, is better known in English-speaking markets by which condiment-related title?

7. The original Swedish title for 2009's first screen adaptation of *The Girl with the Dragon Tattoo*, *Män Som Hatar Kvinnor*, translates as what?

8. The 1968-themed drama released in France in 2012 as *Après Mai* drew its English-language title from a countercultural pop anthem of 1969. Which one?

9. 2013's Japanese drama *Yurusarezaru Mono* is a samurai-themed remake of which Oscar-winning American feature of the Nineties?

10. Which of the following made the top ten of *Sight & Sound*'s 2012 list of the greatest movies of all time (albeit under its Anglicized title) – *Chelovek s Kino-Apparatom*, *Bronenosets Potemkin*, *À Bout de Souffle* or *Shichinin no Samurai*?

ANSWERS

Role Play

1. *12 Angry Men*, 2. *The Seventh Seal*, 3. *The Great Escape*, 4. *Full Metal Jacket*, 5. *The Princess Bride*, 6. *Jurassic Park*, 7. *Groundhog Day*, 8. *Seven*, 9. *The Usual Suspects*, 10. *Alien: Resurrection*, 11. *Lock, Stock and Two Smoking Barrels*, 12. *Inception*, 13. *The Hateful Eight*, 14. *Mad Max: Fury Road*, 15. *Inside Out*

The Incredibles: Pixar's amazing voice artists

Tim Allen = Buzz Lightyear (*Toy Story* 1–4); Steve Buscemi = Randall (*Monsters, Inc./ Monsters University*); Michael Caine = Finn McMissile (*Cars 2*); Jeremy Clarkson = Harv (*Cars* [UK version]); Joan Cusack = Jessie the Yodelling Cowgirl (*Toy Story* 2–4); Ellen DeGeneres = Dory (*Finding Nemo/Finding Dory*); Phyllis Diller = Queen (*A Bug's Life*); Sam Elliott = Butch (*The Good Dinosaur*); Samuel L. Jackson = Frozone (*The Incredibles/The Incredibles 2*); Michael Keaton = Ken (*Toy Story 3*); Frances McDormand = Momma (*The Good Dinosaur*); Paul Newman = Doc Hudson (*Cars*); Peter O'Toole = Anton Ego (*Ratatouille*); Julie Walters = The Witch (*Brave*); Sigourney Weaver = Ship's Computer (*WALL-E*)

Character Studies

1. Toothless, 2. Frank, 3. Totoro, 4. Nosferatu, 5. Carol, 6. Amphibian Man, 7. Dick Tracy, 8. Yoda, 9. The Goblin King, 10. The Kukeri, 11. Death, 12. The Babadook, 13. Lulu, 14. Travis Bickle, 15. Boonsong

Method Mayhem: A history of extreme acting

1. c, 2. d, 3. d, 4. d, 5. c, 6. b, 7. d, 8. c (as Private Pyle), 9. c, 10. b, 11. a, 12. d, 13. d, 14. a, 15. c

Neat Eats: Foodie faves

1. c, 2. d, 3. a, 4. c (a 'wafer-thin' one, to be precise), 5. b, 6. d, 7. b, 8. a, 9. c, 10. b, 11. d, 12. c, 13. d, 14. a, 15. c

New Rules: The Dogme films

1. b, 2. c, 3. b, 4. c, 5. d, 6. c, 7. d, 8. a, 9. b, 10. a, 11. d, 12. b, 13. c, 14. b (35), 15. c (which scores a fulsome 82; *Mifune* lands an iffy 57, *Julien Donkey-Boy* has 52, and *The Idiots* an iffier 47)

Hack Attack: Writers on film

1. c, 2. d, 3. b, 4. a, 5. c, 6. b, 7. d, 8. c, 9. c, 10. a, 11. b, 12. b, 13. c (in *Trumbo*, *Hitchcock* and *The Passion of Ayn Rand* respectively), 14. c (Radcliffe in *Kill Your Darlings*, Franco in *Howl*, Cross in *I'm Not There*), 15. d

Version Original: Foreign-language titles

1. *Tillsammans* (that's Lukas Moodysson's *Together*, from 2000; the others are *Wild Strawberries*, *The Face* and *Hour of the Wolf*), 2. Dario Argento, 3. *The Enigma of Kaspar Hauser*, 4. *Man Bites Dog*, 5. *Braveheart* (full translation would be *The Brave Heart Will Take the Bride*), 6. *The Ketchup Effect*, 7. *Men Who Hate Women*, 8. 'Something in the Air', 9. *Unforgiven*, 10. *Chelovek s kino-apparatom* (it's *Man with a Movie Camera*, #8 on the *S&S* list; the others are *Battleship Potemkin* at #11, *Breathless* at #13 and *The Seven Samurai* at #17)

7

New
HORIZONS

The best of world cinema

FOREIGN FACES

Match the fifteen world cinema directors listed below to the corresponding portrait

Pedro Almodóvar, Roberto Benigni, Jane Campion, Guillermo del Toro, Federico Fellini, Jean-Luc Godard, Mia Hansen-Løve, Takeshi Kitano, Akira Kurosawa, Nanni Moretti, Gaspar Noé, Marjane Satrapi, François Truffaut, Agnès Varda, Lars von Trier

1

2

3

4

5

6

7

8

9

10

11

12

13

14

15

BREATHLESS

The French New Wave

1. For which magazine did the bulk of the New Wave directors originally write?

A) *Vogue*
B) *Positif*
C) *Cahiers du Cinéma*
D) *TV Quick*

2. François Truffaut cited the 1953 film *Little Fugitive* as the biggest influence on the New Wave directors. To what does the title of the film refer?

A) A ginger kitten lost in a covered market
B) A toddler who runs off to Coney Island
C) A miniature version of Dr Richard Kimble, aka TV's *The Fugitive*
D) A talking guitar

3. The one-two of 1958's *Le Beau Serge* and 1959's *Les Cousins* were written and directed by which New Wave lynchpin?

A) Claude Chabrol
B) Jean-Luc Godard
C) Agnès Varda
D) Chris Columbus

4. Which Disney film did the suspense-minded Chabrol claim had a huge impact on his filmmaking?

A) *Snow White and the Seven Dwarfs*
B) *Herbie Goes Bananas*
C) *Dumbo*
D) *Planes: Fire and Rescue*

5. What was unusual about the scene in 1959's *The 400 Blows* in which troubled schoolboy protagonist Antoine Doinel (Jean-Pierre Léaud) is questioned by a psychiatrist?

A) It was filmed with a real psychiatrist
B) Léaud was unavailable for filming, so a lookalike was used
C) It led to the actor being placed in care
D) It was made up of footage from Léaud's screen test

6. Which towering director did the usually equanimous Truffaut declare, 'the only important director I have nothing good to say about. He bores me; he's so solemn and humourless'?

A) Jean-Luc Godard
B) Ingmar Bergman
C) Michelangelo Antonioni
D) Zack Snyder

7. Famed novelist and playwright Marguerite Duras provided the screenplay for a 1959 romantic classic by director Alain Resnais. What was it called?

A) *Tokyo Tickle Time*
B) *Night Flight to Osaka*
C) *Hiroshima Mon Amour*
D) *Okinawa or Bust*

8. Which newspaper do we find street vendor Patricia (Jean Seberg) selling in Jean-Luc Godard's 1960 breakthrough À *Bout de Souffle*?

A) *Le Parisien*

B) *Le Figaro*

C) The *New York Herald Tribune*

D) The *Sunday Sport*

9. In 1960's *À Bout de Souffle*, the gangster character played by Jean-Paul Belmondo is named Michel Poiccard, but his alias is László Kovács. Who was the real László Kovács?

A) A racist milliner based on the Parisian Left Bank

B) A disgraced military general known for his giant blond beard

C) The man who invented Grenadine

D) The Hungarian cinematographer behind *Easy Rider*, *Five Easy Pieces* and *Ghostbusters*

10. What's odd about the trees in the gardens of the hotel at the centre of Alain Resnais's eternally discombobulating 1961 mystery *Last Year at Marienbad*?

A) They're played by human performers

B) They stand upside down

C) They cast no shadows

D) They play Charles Aznavour songs whenever someone passes

11. Georges Delerue, the composer whose music played such a memorable part in Truffaut's *Jules et Jim* and Godard's *Le Mépris*, went on to score prolifically on both sides of the Atlantic. Which of the following Arnold Schwarzenegger comedies did he later work on?

A) *Kindergarten Cop*

B) *Jingle All the Way*

C) *Twins*

D) *Junior*

12. The director Éric Rohmer loved to make films which were part of a wider series. Which of the following was the name of his first series, which included (among others) *Claire's Knee*, *Suzanne's Career* and *My Night with Maud*?

A) *Six Kinky Yarns*

B) *Six Sexy Stories*

C) *Raising Your Child in the Global Village: A Taxonomy*

D) *Six Moral Tales*

13. Chris Marker's influential 1962 short *La Jetée* comprises 28 minutes of photographic stills, punctuated by one image that appears to move. But what does this image depict?

A) A sleeping woman

B) A man being shot

C) A young Bruce Willis

D) A flag ruffling in the wind

14. Agnès Varda became the first director to do what in 1965?

A) Film while abseiling down the Eiffel Tower

B) Cast the young Gérard Depardieu

C) Win the French Academy's Best Director César

D) Get into a fistfight at a Cannes press conference

15. What is extraordinary about Jacques Rivette's improvised 1971 experimental film *Out 1*?

A) The entire film takes place under a snooker table in the Pigalle

B) It's over 12 hours long

C) Rivette made the film to be projected on the moon

D) The film doesn't actually exist

THE TWO BERGMANS

Ingrid and Ingmar

For each of the following questions, answer either 'Ingrid', 'Ingmar' or 'both'.

Which Bergman ...

1. Spent time working at Stockholm's Royal Dramatic Theatre?

2. Sparked controversy after leaving their partner to run off with a prominent Italian?

3. Inspired a key sequence in 1991's *Bill and Ted's Bogus Journey*?

4. Can boast no fewer than three films with the word 'summer' in their title on their CV?

5. Lost out on a 1959 Oscar to representatives of the Rock Hudson/ Doris Day comedy *Pillow Talk*?

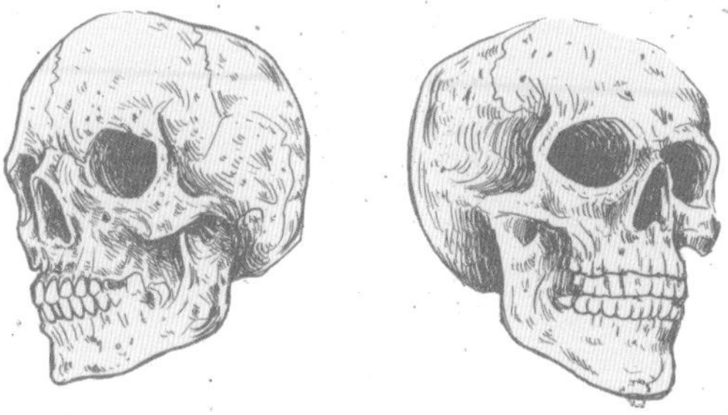

6. Was an avowed inspiration on a key early work in the Wes Craven filmography?

7. Performed a spoken-word rendition of the theme to *Chitty Chitty Bang Bang* at the 1969 Oscar ceremony?

8. Was arrested (but later cleared) on a charge of tax evasion?

9. Went into retreat on the island of Fårö?

10. Counts Isabella Rossellini among their offspring?

11. Inspired track 8 on *Mermaid Avenue*, a 1998 album of lyrics by Woody Guthrie recorded by Billy Bragg and Wilco?

12. Factored their experiences of adultery into writing the 2000 film *Faithless*?

13. Took a prominent credit on 1978's *Autumn Sonata*?

14. Died on the same day as Michelangelo Antonioni?

15. Counted crime writer Henning Mankell as a son-in-law?

THUNDER DOWN UNDER

Ozploitation

True or false?

1. The bespectacled nerd hero Stork gave his name to the title of this 1971 coming-of-age comedy.

2. Ted Kotcheff, the Canadian director of 1971's recently rediscovered Outback shocker *Wake in Fright*, went on to direct comic disasterpiece *Weekend at Bernie's*.

3. Urbane TV pundit Clive James shows up in an altogether well-refreshed state in 1972's *The Adventures of Barry McKenzie* and 1974's sequel *Barry McKenzie Holds His Own*.

4. A cop infiltrates a club known as the Grave Diggers in 1974's thriller *Stone*. It's a club in which all members profess to have murdered someone.

5. David Gulpilil, star of 1971's *Walkabout*, went walkabout during the production of 1976's *Mad Dog Morgan* to ask the trees what they thought of the film's hard-drinking American star Dennis Hopper. The trees' reported response? 'He's a very fine chap actually.'

6. The surname Rockatansky belonged to the character of Mad Max, played three times by Mel Gibson (in 1979, 1981 and 1985) and once (in 2015) by Tom Hardy.

7. The helmet-wearing foe in 1981's *Mad Max 2: The Road Warrior* is named Louisiana Joe.

8. In the same year *Halloween II* was released (1981), Jamie Lee Curtis played a hitchhiker pursued by a serial killer in *Road Games*.

9. A pre-fame Nicole Kidman can be seen as the frizzy-haired young heroine of 1983's push-bike fun aria *BMX Bandits*.

10. The animal that stalks the residents of the Outback in 1984's Russell Mulcahy-directed *Razorback* is a massive crocodile.

11. 1986's *Dead End Drive-In* was based on a short story by Peter Carey, a Booker Prize winner two years later.

12. Joan Rivers cameoed as the US President in 1987's *Les Patterson Saves the World*.

13. In the 1993 gore shocker *Body Melt*, it's a new brand of fast food which causes people's bodies to melt.

14. Peter Jackson's no-budget splatter debut feature, *Bad Taste*, about aliens invading Wellington, New Zealand, was expanded from a short feature called *Chainsaw Afterbirth*.

15. Brian Trenchard-Smith's 1982 film *Turkey Shoot* was described by the renowned Australian critic David Stratton as 'a catalogue of sickening horrors'.

BOLLYWOOD AND BEYOND

Indian cinema

1. 1913's *Raja Harishchandra*, the first feature-length Indian film, was advertised as 'a performance with 57,000 photographs ... a picture _________ in length'. How long?

A) 57 minutes, 32 seconds
B) Two miles
C) Four furlongs
D) Too long

2. What was the nickname of Raj Kapoor, the actor who became an audience favourite after playing a Chaplinesque itinerant in such titles as 1951's *Awaara* and 1955's *Shree 420*?

A) The Showman of Bollywood
B) The Hobo of Hearts
C) The Poor Man's Tramp
D) The Hero of Hindustan

3. The legendary star Nargis met her husband Sunil Dutt on the set of 1957's *Mother India*, where he played her son – and wound up saving her life. How?

A) He rescued her after a haystack fire got out of control
B) He performed the Heimlich manoeuvre after she choked on a whelk
C) He gave blood after she collapsed with anaemia
D) He gave her the kiss of life following a hovercraft pile-up

4. The same year's *Naya Daur* climaxes with a thrilling race between which two means of transportation?

A) A horse and a hot rod
B) A tank and a tuk-tuk
C) A Maglev and a Segway
D) A horse-drawn cart and a bus

5. In *Kagaaz Ke Phool*, the 1959 masterpiece of the brooding, Welles-like writer-director-star Guru Dutt, a film director struggles to bring which text to the screen?

A) *The Dictionary*
B) *Romeo and Juliet*
C) *Bridge to Terabithia*
D) *Devdas*

6. One of Indian cinema's most prolific comic actors took his stage name from a popular beverage. What was that name?

A) Stella Artois
B) Dr Pepper
C) Harvey Wallbanger
D) Johnny Walker

7. Which of the following is not the title of a film directed by the great Satyajit Ray?

A) *Aparajito*
B) *Charulata*
C) *Clown Car*
D) *Jalsaghar*

8. Current Hindi megastar Aamir Khan played a villainous role in Deepa Mehta's 1998 Partition drama *Earth* – but how was his character Dil Navaz better known, a nickname born of his profitable popsicle-selling sideline?

A) The Rocket Man

B) The Ice Candy Man

C) The Calippo Cowboy

D) Mr Freeze

9. Which cricket team does megastar Shah Rukh Khan own?

A) Chennai Super Kings

B) Delhi Daredevils

C) Kolkata Knight Riders

D) Bombay Bashers

10. Karan Johar, the director of such massive hits as 2001's *Kabhi Khushi Kabhie Gham ...* and 2010's *My Name Is Khan*, hosts a talk show on Indian TV. What's it called?

A) *Jawing with Johar*

B) *Kavorting with Karan*

C) *The Karan Johar Solution*

D) *Koffee with Karan*

11. Bollywood often remakes films from other industries. Of which Nineties American film is 2002's *Kaante* a rehash?

A) *The Silence of the Lambs*

B) *Reservoir Dogs*

C) *Bill and Ted's Bogus Journey*

D) *Forrest Gump*

12. Who landed the plum role of Becky Sharp in Mira Nair's 2004 adaptation of *Vanity Fair*?

A) Natasha Lyonne

B) Priyanka Chopra

C) Jessica Biel

D) Reese Witherspoon

13. Deepika Padukone, the star of 2007's *Om Shanti Om*, 2015's *Piku* and 2017's *xXx: Return of Xander Cage* in the States, spent her teenage years playing which sport to national level?

A) Lacrosse

B) Badminton

C) Underwater hockey

D) Competitive hot-dog eating

14. With which object does Sylvester Stallone see off a gang of ne'er-do-wells during his brief cameo in 2009's *Kambakkht Ishq*?

A) A toffee apple

B) A golden broadsword

C) A parking meter

D) A grain of rice

15. What was especially out-of-the-box about Baz Luhrmann's casting of Amitabh Bachchan, angry young man-turned-towering patriarch of Hindi cinema, in 2013's *The Great Gatsby*?

A) He was playing a character 50 years his junior

B) He was playing a character identified as Jewish in the book

C) He was playing a 1930s flapper

D) He was obliged to bust several moves to a Jay-Z track

SOUTH OF THE BORDER

Latin American pin-ups

True or false?

1. A commemorative plaque outside the Durango, the Mexico property where glamourpuss Dolores del Río was born, claims there have only been two perfect faces in the history of photography – del Rio's own, and that belonging to Greta Garbo.

2. Nicknamed 'the Brazilian Bombshell', Carmen Miranda was renowned for wearing a recently caught sea bream on her head in a run of films from the 1940s onwards.

3. Dominican star Maria Montez starred in 1944's *Cobra Woman*, so-called because of the infamous 'snake dance' she performs in the film.

4. Alfonso Cuarón has won plaudits for his monochrome epic *Roma*, starring newcomer Yalitza Aparicio. The title is a reference to Fellini's 1972 semi-autobiographical film of the same name.

5. Al Pacino's melancholic Mafia don Michael Corleone is grandfather to Andy Garcia's Vincent in 1990's *The Godfather Part III*.

6. Santanico Pandemonium was the altogether spectacular stage name of the exotic dancer played by Jennifer Lopez in 1996's *From Dusk till Dawn*.

7. Lopez played Selena Quintanilla-Pérez, the biggest-selling female artist in Latin music history, in a 1997 biopic entitled *Have You Selena Yet*?

8. Jimmy Smits played Bail Organa, a minor member of Alderaan's royal family, in the *Star Wars* prequels.

9. *Nine Queens*, a twisty Argentinian arthouse hit of 2000, was remade in Hollywood four years later as *Criminal*. Doughy American actor (and Paul Thomas Anderson favourite) John C. Reilly played the con man played in the original by Ricardo Darín.

10. In the Oscar-nominated, financially themed 2015 comedy-drama *The Big Short*, actress Selena Gomez is brought on to help explain the complexities of 'synthetic CDOs'.

11. Screen idol Oscar Isaac was born in Patagonia.

12. Jessica Alba has twice been cited by the Alliance of Women Film Journalists in their annual award category Most Egregious Age Difference Between the Leading Man and the Love Interest. The first time was for her pairing with Danny Trejo – 37 years her senior – in 2010's *Machete*. The second was an instance she was paired with a 104-year-old ex-Army colonel in 2005's *Into the Blue*.

13. The astrological sign Cancer provided the title of an acclaimed 2016 drama that saw Sônia Braga holding out against developers in latter-day Brazil.

14. Actress Sofia Vergara, currently most prominent on TV, had the honour of voicing the Poo avatar in 2017's *The Emoji Movie*.

15. All of the following actors have played screen versions of Ernesto Che Guevara – Michael Palin, Benicio del Toro, Gael García Bernal.

BEAT THE DEVIL

Abbas ABC: All things Kiarostami

True or false?

1. The young Abbas Kiarostami majored in two subjects during his time at the University of Tehran. One was painting, the other was egg painting.

2. Kiarostami's 1990 documentary-fiction hybrid film *Close-Up* features a lengthy shot in which the camera tracks a can as it rolls down a street.

3. Kiarostami's 1997 film *Taste of Cherry* – which won the Palme d'Or at the Cannes Film Festival – has a place alongside the Demi Moore version of *The Scarlet Letter* and *Deuce Bigalow: European Gigolo* on critic Roger Ebert's Most Hated list.

4. The 2001 digital documentary *ABC Africa* found Kiarostami meeting orphans in the African republic of Uganda.

5. After September 2001, Kiarostami was refused a visa to appear at the New York Film Festival.

6. Kiarostami produced a poetry anthology which was published by the Harvard Film Archive in 2002. Its title is *Snorting Live Ants*.

7. 2005's *Tickets*, a portmanteau movie organized around the twin themes of trains and refugees, was a joint enterprise by Kiarostami, Ken Loach and Tom Six (director of the *Human Centipede* films).

8. *Where is My Romeo?* – Kiarostami's contribution to 2007's portmanteau *Chacun son Cinéma*, and a dry run for the following year's *Shirin* – features close-ups of Iranian women reacting, often tearfully, to the final moments of Franco Zeffirelli's 1968 version of *Romeo & Juliet*.

9. The original, altogether more definitive title of 2012's *Like Someone in Love* was *End of Days*.

10. Kiarostami entered into an intellectual correspondence with the filmmaker Ron Howard for a 2016 essay film named *Correspondences*.

Foreign Faces
1. Roberto Benigni, 2. Nanni Moretti, 3. Mia Hansen-Løve, 4. Takeshi Kitano, 5. Gaspar Noé, 6. Agnès Varda 7. Lars von Trier, 8. Guillermo del Toro, 9. Marjane Satrapi, 10. Pedro Almodóvar, 11. François Truffaut, 12. Jean-Luc Godard, 13. Jane Campion, 14. Federico Fellini, 15. Akira Kurosawa

Breathless: The French New Wave
1. c, 2. b, 3. a, 4. a, 5. d, 6. c, 7. c, 8. c, 9. d, 10. c, 11. c, 12. d, 13. a, 14. b (in an aborted short film project), 15. b

The Two Bergmans: Ingrid and Ingmar
1. Both, 2. Ingrid, 3. Ingmar, 4. Ingmar, 5. Ingmar, 6. Ingmar (1972's *The Last House on the Left*, freely adapted from 1960's *The Virgin Spring*), 7. Ingrid, 8. Ingmar, 9. Ingmar, 10. Ingrid, 11. Ingrid, 12. Ingmar, 13. Both (directed by Ingmar, starring Ingrid), 14. Ingmar, 15. Ingmar

Thunder Down Under: Ozploitation
1. True, 2. True, 3. True, 4. False – it's a biker club, 5. False – the trees said 'He's crazy', 6. True, 7. False – it's the Humungus, 8. True, 9. True, 10. False – it's a wild boar, 11. True, 12. True, 13. False – it's diet pills, 14. False – the short was called *Roast of the Day*, 15. True

Bollywood and Beyond: Indian cinema
1. b, 2. a, 3. a, 4. d, 5. d, 6. d, 7. c, 8. b, 9. c, 10. d, 11. b, 12. d, 13. b, 14. c, 15. b

South of the Border: Latin American pin-ups
1. True, 2. False – it was a selection of fruit, 3. True, 4. False – Roma is the name of the neighbourhood featured in the film, 5. False – Al is Andy's uncle, 6. False – she was played by Salma Hayek, 7. False – it's just called *Selena*, 8. True, 9. True, 10. True, 11. False – he was born in Guatemala, 12. False – the second was a pairing with Jason Statham in *The Transporter* 2, 13. False – it was Aquarius, 14. False – she voiced the flamenco dancer, while Patrick Stewart voiced Poo, 15. True

Abbas ABC: All things Kiarostami
1. False – the other was graphic design, 2. True, 3. True, 4. True, 5. True, 6. False – it's called *Walking with the Wind*, 7. False – Kiarostami, Loach and Ermanno Olmi made the film together, 8. True, 9. False – it was *The End*, 10. False – it was Víctor Erice

ANSWERS

8

The Gong SHOW

Cinema's award winners

TROPHY HUNT

Guess the award

Academy Award (commonly known as Oscar), BAFTA, Bodil Award (Denmark), Cannes Palme d'Or, César (France), Costume Designers Guild, Fangoria Best Film, Filmfare Award (India's Oscar), Genie (Canada), Golden Horse (China), Golden Kela (India's Razzie), Golden Lion (Venice Film Festival), Guldbagge (Sweden), MTV Movie Award, NAFCA (Africa)

2

1

3

4

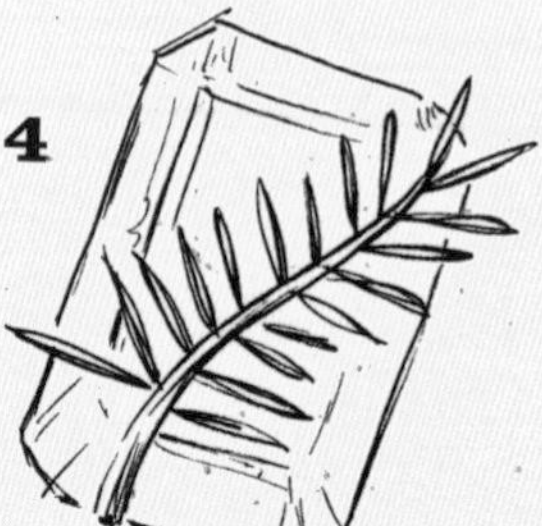

5

6

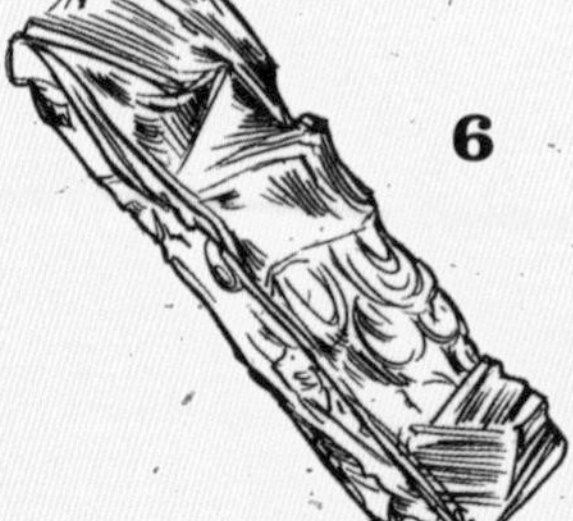

7

8

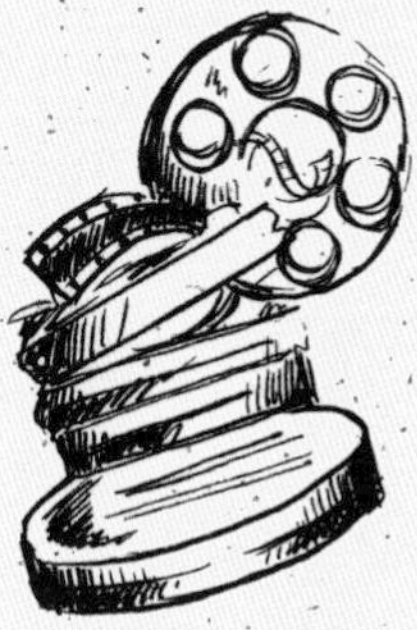

9

10

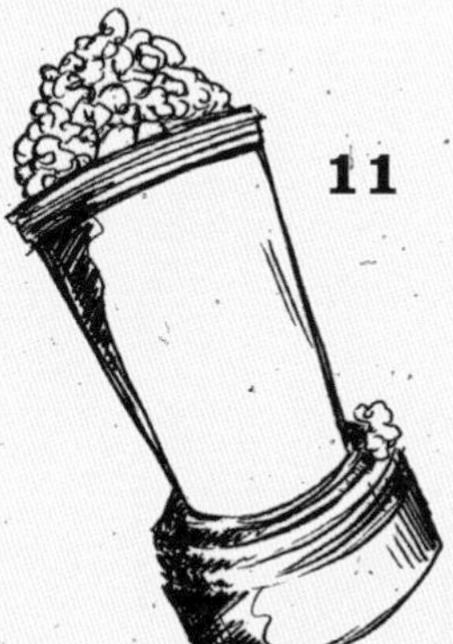

11

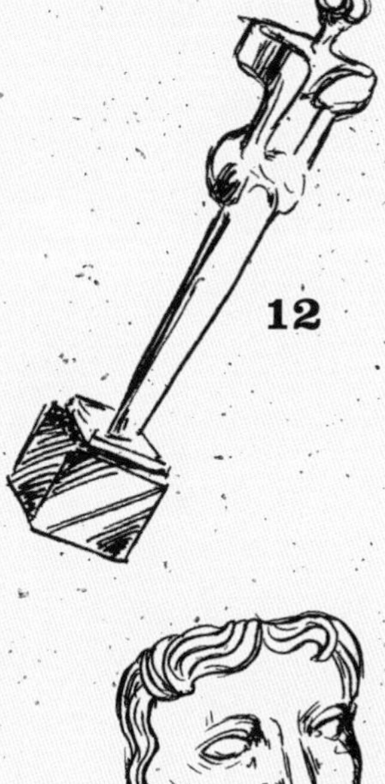

12

13

14

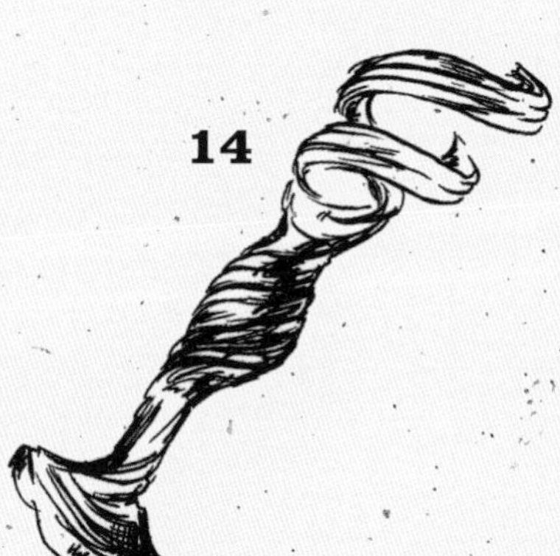

15

OSCAR ODDITIES

Award-winning surprises

1. Grace Kelly won her only Oscar in 1954. But when the film she won it for was released on VHS in Canada in the 1980s it was slapped with an 'Adults Only' rating after censors mistook it for a pornographic film of the same name. What title caused all the ruckus?

A) *A Tight Spot*
B) *Interrupted Melody*
C) *Young at Heart*
D) *The Country Girl*

2. What 1969 film became the first X-rated title to win the Oscar for Best Picture?

A) *Carnal Knowledge*
B) *Back Seat Cabbie*
C) *Midnight Cowboy*
D) *Last Tango in Paris*

3. *Chinatown* scribe Robert Towne was so distraught at the changes made to which of his scripts that he had his name removed and replaced with that of his dog, P.H. Vazak – who was subsequently nominated for the 1985 Adapted Screenplay Oscar?

A) *Prizzi's Honor*
B) *Greystoke: The Legend of Tarzan, Lord of the Apes*
C) *Platoon*
D) *Kiss of the Spider Woman*

4. The 1987 Best Actor line-up of Paul Newman, William Hurt, James Woods and Bob Hoskins was completed by which jazz great?

A) Miles Davis
B) Lester Corncrake
C) Wynton Marsalis
D) Dexter Gordon

5. What was unprecedented about the nominees for the 1988 Best Director category?

A) They were all female
B) It was the first time the nominees had all been non-American
C) It was the first time the nominees were all under 40 years of age
D) There were only three, as two of the directors were nominated twice

6. What was unique about Liza Minnelli's Best Actress Oscar win for 1972's *Cabaret*?

A) It was the first acting Oscar awarded to a character who had no spoken dialogue
B) It was the first Oscar to be given to a character who had dropped the 'F'-bomb
C) It was the first Oscar to be declined (beating Brando's *Godfather* diss of the same year by dint of her award being presented before his)
D) She was the first Oscar winner whose parents had also both won Oscars.

7. Which of these bands has NOT seen one or more of its members win an Oscar for Best Original Score?

A) Radiohead

B) Art of Noise

C) Nine Inch Nails

D) Talking Heads

8. Only one Doctor Who has ever won an Oscar. Who?

A) Tom Baker

B) David Tennant

C) Paul McGann

D) Peter Capaldi

9. Grumpy old George Bernard Shaw – Adapted Screenplay Oscar winner in 1939 for *Pygmalion* – is reported to have put his statuette to what practical use?

A) As a hatstand

B) As a toilet roll holder

C) He had it melted down for scrap metal and sold

D) As a doorstop

10. Only three films have won the 'Big Five' – the Oscar for Best Picture, Director, Screenplay, Actress and Actor. Which of the following is NOT one of the gang?

A) *The English Patient*

B) *The Silence of the Lambs*

C) *It Happened One Night*

D) *One Flew Over the Cuckoo's Nest*

11. Three of the following films are all tied in having won a record eleven Oscars each. Which one is the black sheep, clocking up a measly six?

A) *Ben-Hur*

B) *The Lord of the Rings: The Return of the King*

C) *Titanic*

D) *The Godfather Part II*

12. What is the lowest budgeted film (allowing for inflation) ever to have won Best Picture?

A) *Room*

B) *Rocky*

C) *Whiplash*

D) *Moonlight*

13. Former ranch hand, stuntman and *Gone with the Wind* bit player Richard Farnsworth became, at 79, the oldest nominee for Best Actor in 1999. For which film?

A) *The Straight Story*

B) *Bringing Out the Dead*

C) *The Cider House Rules*

D) *The Green Mile*

14. Rap collective Three 6 Mafia snagged a Best Song Oscar in 2006 with their contribution to the *Hustle & Flow* soundtrack. For which song?

A) 'Carbon 15s, A.K.s & Mac 11s'

B) 'Sippin' on Some Syrup'

C) 'It's Hard Out Here for a Pimp'

D) 'Shake dat Jelly'

15. But which of these musical legends has NOT won an Oscar for Best Original Song?

A) Phil Collins

B) Lionel Richie

C) David Bowie

C) Eminem

RIVIERA DAYS

Cannes memories

Match the year with the prize winner

1. Queer Palm/Todd Haynes/*Carol*
2. Best Actress/Björk/*Dancer in the Dark*
3. Camera d'Or for Best First Film/Jim Jarmusch/*Stranger Than Paradise*
4. Best Actress/Cher/*Mask*
5. Best Actor/Marlon Brando/*Viva Zapata!*
6. Special Jury Prize/David Cronenberg/*Crash*
7. Grand Prix/Terry Jones/*Monty Python's The Meaning of Life*
8. Palm Dog for Best Dog/Uggie/*The Artist*
9. Best Screenplay/Steven Spielberg, Hal Barwood and Matthew Robbins/*The Sugarland Express*
10. Best Actor/John Turturro/*Barton Fink*

1952

1974

1983

1984

1985

1991

1996

2000

2011

2015

THANKSGIVING

Memorable awards speeches

1. At the 1969 Oscars, Ruth Gordon picked up the Best Supporting Actress award for *Rosemary's Baby* with the comment, 'I can't tell you how encouraging a thing like this is.' To the nearest three years, how old was Gordon at the time of the ceremony?

2. Who famously sent an activist (concerned with portrayals of Native Americans on film) to pick up his Best Actor Oscar for *The Godfather* in 1973?

3. Which actress picked up her Oscar in 1984 for *Places in the Heart* with the immortal (if often misremembered) words, 'You like me! Right now, you like me!'

4. Sometimes actions speak louder than words. Veteran tough guy Jack Palance performed one-armed push-ups upon accepting his Best Supporting Actor Oscar for which 1991 cowboy comedy?

5. Tom Hanks made a rare PR blunder at the 1994 Oscars, accidentally outing his high-school drama teacher as gay while accepting his Best Actor award for *Philadelphia*. The incident provided the inspiration for which later comedy starring Kevin Kline?

6. Hilary Swank pointedly failed to thank husband Chad Lowe in her acceptance speech for Best Actress in 2000, an oversight she addressed at the 2004 ceremony. In which year did the couple divorce: 2007; 2016; or are they still happily married?

7. Which calming prescription drug did Jack Nicholson confess to having ingested during his acceptance speech at the 2003 Golden Globes?

8. At the 2005 Oscars, awards presenter Sean Penn had a flinty onstage difference of opinion with host Chris Rock about which then-ubiquitous British actor?

9. To which off-the-radar performer (and brother to the female star of *Pretty Woman*) did *The Wrestler*'s comeback kid Mickey Rourke give a shoutout and hopeful leg-up in his acceptance speech at the 2009 Golden Globes?

10. Upon accepting the Best Actress award for *Certified Copy* at the 2010 Cannes Festival, which lauded French actress held up a placard bearing the name of the housebound director Jafar Panahi?

11. Who evidently realized a dream upon winning a Supporting Actress Oscar for Tom Hooper's *Les Misérables* at the 2013 Oscars, opening her speech with the line: 'It came true'?

12. Which pressing industry issue did Patricia Arquette address while accepting her Best Supporting Actress Oscar for *Boyhood* in 2015?

13. At the same ceremony, J.K. Simmons told audiences to call their mum and dad while he picked up a Best Supporting Actor gong for playing a sadistic drumming teacher in which film?

14. Frances McDormand flummoxed journalists by name-dropping the legal term 'inclusion rider' while picking up her second Best Actress Oscar in 2018 for *Three Billboards Outside Ebbing, Missouri*. For which 1996 film did she win her first?

15. At the same Oscars, Jimmy Kimmel offered a bonus prize to the winner who gave the shortest acceptance speech. Costume designer Mark Bridges (*Phantom Thread*) was the winner of winners. But what did he take home, besides his Oscar?

MTV MOVIE AWARDS

Highlights from the awards show

1. Which comedian was the somewhat unlikely host of the inaugural MTV Movie Awards in 1992?

A) George Carlin

B) Bill Hicks

C) Dennis Miller

D) Billy Connolly

2. For which (very) short-lived category did Pierce Brosnan's 007 debut *GoldenEye*, comedy anthology *Four Rooms* and Wayne Wang and Paul Auster's *Smoke* compete in 1996?

A) Unlikeliest Sexual Position

B) Cutest Dog Moment

C) Best Sandwich

D) Coolest Sunglasses

3. And in what category did thespian heavyweights Brad Pitt, Jessica Chastain, Ethan Hawke and Vera Farmiga face off in 2014?

A) Swearer of the Year

B) Fugliest Makeup

C) Worst Accent

D) Best Scared-As-S**t Performance

4. In 2012 the Best Villain award was – for some reason – renamed Best On-Screen Dirt Bag. Who was that year's dirtiest bag?

A) Mila Kunis in *Oz the Great and Powerful*

B) Adam Driver in *Star Wars: The Force Awakens*

C) Jennifer Aniston in *Horrible Bosses*

D) Tom Hiddleston in *The Avengers*

5. In 2005 and 2006 respectively, *The Breakfast Club* and *Do the Right Thing* picked up special awards for having 'made lasting impact on moviegoers and the MTV audience'. What was this august award called?

A) The MTV Masterworks Prize

B) The Top of the Popcorn Award

C) The Silver Bucket of Excellence

D) The Golden Clapperboard

6. Which of the following figures did NOT scoop one of the bizarre 'Lifetime Achievement' awards that were dished out between 1992 and 1998?

A) Godzilla

B) Clint Howard

C) Chewbacca

D) Pee-wee Herman

7. What Paramount Pictures film received the dubious honour of winning the freshly minted Best Summer Movie You Haven't Seen Yet award in 2007? (Note: Paramount and MTV are both owned by the same company.)

A) *300*

B) *Pirates of the Caribbean: Dead Man's Chest*

C) *Transformers*

D) *Borat*

8. Who took on the roles originally played by Brad Pitt, Morgan Freeman and Kevin Spacey in the spoof of *Seven* that played during the 1996 awards show?

A) Betty White

B) William Shatner

C) Ben Stiller

D) Mike Myers

9. For what award did Kanye West, Tina Fey, Robert De Niro, Joan Rivers and Rihanna battle it out in 2014?

A) Sickest Burn

B) Most Outrageous Hair

C) Best Cameo

D) Jaw Droppingest Moment

10. Who both presented the show and won the Breakout Star award in 2013?

A) Melissa McCarthy

B) Rebel Wilson

C) Margot Robbie

D) Andrew Garfield

11. Jon Heder won the 2005 Best Musical Sequence award for the epic dance routine that caps *Napoleon Dynamite*. What song was he grooving to?

A) 'Super Freak' by Rick James

B) 'Maneater' by Hall & Oates

C) 'Canned Heat' by Jamiroquai

D) 'We Don't Need Another Hero' by Tina Turner

12. Which of the following nominees won 1992's inaugural Most Desirable Female award?

A) Linda Hamilton for *Terminator 2: Judgment Day*

B) Christina Applegate for *Don't Tell Mom the Babysitter's Dead*

C) Tia Carrere for *Wayne's World*

D) Julia Roberts for *Dying Young*

13. Jack Nicholson scooped the 2007 Best Villain award for *The Departed*. What was his character's name in the film?

A) Colin Sullivan

B) Frank Costello

C) Eddie Dane

D) Peaches McCann

14. Which of the following has NOT been a short-lived MTV Movie Awards category?

A) Slickest Cellphone Move

B) Sexiest Performance

C) Biggest Badass Star

D) Best Shirtless Performance

15. The 35-year-old George Clooney won his 1996 Best Breakthrough Performance for which movie?

A) *Batman & Robin*

B) *Out of Sight*

C) *Return of the Killer Tomatoes!*

D) *From Dusk till Dawn*

BREAKOUTS

Film folk who have won honours in other fields

1. Writer and adventurer Sir Compton Mackenzie – Order of the British Empire, French Legion of Honour, Serbian Order of the White Eagle and Greek Order of the Redeemer – played a crucial role in the making of which classic British film?

A) *The Wicker Man*

B) *Dr. No*

C) *Whisky Galore!*

D) *Trainspotting*

2. Audie Murphy, one of the most decorated soldiers in US military history, played himself in which 1955 recreation of his own wartime heroics?

A) *The Red Badge of Courage*

B) *To Hell and Back*

C) *Murphy's Marauders*

D) *Bastard Battalion*

3. Which actress, in 1962, became the first woman to win the Grammy for Album of the Year?

A) Marilyn Monroe

B) Doris Day

C) Lucille Ball

D) Judy Garland

4. Which was the first soundtrack recording to win the Grammy for Album of the Year?

A) *Saturday Night Fever*

B) *The Bodyguard*

C) *The Way We Were*

D) *Jonathan Livingston Seagull*

5. Which of the following movie stars has never won a Tony – Broadway's equivalent of an Oscar?

A) Susan Sarandon

B) Laurence Fishburne

C) Hugh Jackman

D) Scarlett Johansson

6. In 1997 the late Jay Silverheels, best known for playing Tonto in the 1950s serial *The Lone Ranger*, was inducted into the Canadian Hall of Fame for which sport?

A) Archery

B) Ice hockey

C) Billiards

D) Lacrosse

7. Three musicals share the record for the most nominations at the Tonys. One of them is the all-conquering *Hamilton*. The remaining two were adapted from which big-screen hits?

A) *The Lion King* and *Jersey Boys*

B) *Billy Elliot* and *The Producers*

C) *Once* and *Hairspray*

D) *Spamalot* and *Matilda*

8. Which of the following film directors has a black belt in Brazilian jiu-jitsu?

A) John Carpenter

B) Jodie Foster

C) Guy Ritchie

D) Zack Snyder

9. Which of these filmmakers has NOT won a Grammy?

A) David Fincher

B) Peter Bogdanovich

C) Zach Braff

D) Greta Gerwig

10. Only two people have won a Tony as both writer and performer – Harvey Fierstein and Tracy Letts. Which foodstuff is put to dubious erotic use in the latter's darkly comic 1993 play *Killer Joe*, which was adapted into a 2011 film by William Friedkin?

A) Trifle

B) Tabasco sauce

C) A chicken drumstick

D) A walnut

11. A small group of individuals have won what's known as an EGOT – the grand slam of an Emmy (TV), a Grammy (music), an Oscar (movies) and a Tony (theatre). Who is the only film producer on this elite list?

A) Harvey Weinstein

B) James Cameron

C) Jerry Bruckheimer

D) Scott Rudin

12. For what film did EGOT gold member Whoopi Goldberg win her Oscar?

A) *Ghost*

B) *The Color Purple*

C) *Sister Act*

D) *Theodore Rex*

13. Which of the following Hollywood greats has NOT received the Légion d'Honneur, France's highest decoration?

A) Jerry Lewis

B) Robert Redford

C) Orson Welles

D) Mickey Rourke

14. Which American actor was awarded an honorary OBE (Order of the British Empire) in 2011 for their work with children with special needs?

A) Kelsey Grammer

B) Henry Winkler

C) Laura Dern

D) Jamie Lee Curtis

15. Finally, which of these action stars holds a master's degree in chemical engineering?

A) Milla Jovovich

B) Jet Li

C) Gerard Butler

D) Dolph Lundgren

BEAT THE DEVIL

The Golden Raspberry Awards

1. In which decade did the very first Golden Raspberry Awards – dished out for the worst films and performances of the year – take place?

2. The first film to 'win' the Worst Picture award was *Can't Stop the Music*, the fictionalized biography of which disco group?

3. Michael Douglas won a Best Actor Oscar and Daryl Hannah won a Worst Supporting Actress Raspberry for which 1987 film (making it the only movie to win both an Oscar and a 'Razzie')?

4. Most recipients don't actually bother to collect their award in person, but in 2005 Halle Berry played the good egg by turning up to pick up her Worst Actress Razzie. For which film?

5. Five years later Sandra Bullock also razzed up in person to collect the Worst Screen Couple award for wacky stalker comedy *All About Steve*. Who was the other half of the couple?

6. The Razzies just love to razz on Sylvester Stallone, who among many, many other gongs won the 1984 Worst Original Song award for 'Drinkenstein' ('Budweiser, you created a monster, and they call him ... Drinkenstein!'). From which film does the song come?

7. Gore Verbinski's update of *The Lone Ranger* won the 2013 Worst Prequel, Remake, Rip-off or Sequel Razzie. Johnny Depp wore one of his trademark silly hats to play Tonto in the film, but who was behind the Lone Ranger's black mask?

8. Which Nicolas Cage film won the 1997-only award for Worst Reckless Disregard for Human Life and Public Property?

9. In 2009, schlock director Uwe Boll joined Ronald Reagan, Linda Blair and the shark from *Jaws* as one of the select recipients of the Razzies' Worst Career Achievement award. From which country does Boll hail?

10. For which 2013 film did Will Smith and son Jaden win the Worst Supporting Actor and Worst Actor respectively?

Trophy Hunt: Guess the award

1. Golden Horse, 2. Bodil Award, 3. Fangoria Best Film, 4. Cannes Palme d'Or, 5. Golden Kela, 6. César 7. Golden Lion, 8. Academy Award, 9. NAFCA, 10. Guldbagge, 11. MTV Movie Award, 12. Genie, 13. Filmfare Award , 14. Costume Designers Guild, 15. BAFTA

Oscar Oddities: Award-winning surprises

1. d, 2. c, 3. b, 4. d (for *Round Midnight*; Newman won for *The Color of Money*), 5. b, 6. d (Judy Garland for *The Wizard of Oz/Babes in Arms*, and Vincente Minnelli for *Gigi*), 7. a (Anne Dudley for *The Full Monty*, Trent Reznor for *The Social Network* and David Byrne for *The Last Emperor* respectively. Radiohead's Jonny Greenwood was nominated for *Phantom Thread*, but did not win), 8. d (for 1995's Best Live Action Short Film *Franz Kafka's It's a Wonderful Life*), 9. d, 10. a, 11. d, 12. d (source: IMDb Pro/Business Insider), 13. a, 14. c, 15. c (Collins for 'You'll Be in My Heart' from *Tarzan*, Richie for 'Say You, Say Me' from *White Knights* and Eminem for 'Lose Yourself' from *8 Mile*)

Riviera Days: Cannes memories

1. 2015 Queer Palm/Todd Haynes/*Carol*, 2. 2000 Best Actress/Björk/*Dancer in the Dark*, 3. 1984 Camera d'Or for Best First Film/Jim Jarmusch/*Stranger Than Paradise*, 4. 1985 Best Actress/Cher/*Mask*, 5. 1952 Best Actor/Marlon Brando/*Viva Zapata!*, 6. 1996 Special Jury Prize/David Cronenberg/*Crash*, 7. 1983 Grand Prix/Terry Jones/*Monty Python's The Meaning of Life*, 8. 2011 Palm Dog for Best Dog/Uggie/*The Artist*, 9. 1974 Best Screenplay/Steven Spielberg, Hal Barwood and Matthew Robbins/*The Sugarland Express*, 10. 1991 Best Actor/John Turturro/*Barton Fink*

Thanksgiving: Memorable awards speeches

1. 72 (so anywhere between 69 and 75 gets you the point), 2. Marlon Brando, 3. Sally Field, 4. *City Slickers*, 5. *In & Out*, 6. 2007, 7. Valium, 8. Jude Law, 9. Eric Roberts, 10. Juliette Binoche, 11. Anne Hathaway, 12. The gender pay gap, 13. *Whiplash*, 14. *Fargo*, 15. A jet ski

MTV Movie Awards: Highlights from the awards show

1. c, 2. c (*Smoke* won with a classic ham & cheese), 3. d (Pitt won for *World War Z*), 4. c (the award hastily reverted back to Best Villain the next year), 5. c, 6. d, 7. c, 8. b (find it online – it's actually quite good), 9. c (Rihanna won for *This Is the End*), 10. b (for *Pitch Perfect*), 11. c, 12. a, 13. b, 14. a, 15. d

Breakouts: Film folk who have won honours in other fields

1. c (he wrote the source novel, and played the role of Captain Buncher), 2. b, 3. d, 4. a, 5. a, 6. d, 7. b, 8. c, 9. d (the other three won for the Rolling Stones' video for 'Love is Strong'; for Tom Petty doc *Runnin' Down a Dream*; and for Best Compilation Soundtrack for *Garden State* respectively), 10. c, 11. d (for kids' show *He Makes Me Feel Like Dancin'*, *The Book of Mormon* cast recording, *No Country For Old Men* and any number of Tonys respectively), 12. a, 13. d, 14. b, 15. d

The Golden Raspberry Awards

1. The 1980s (1981, to be exact), 2. The Village People (the film co-starred Steve Guttenberg and Bruce Jenner), 3. *Wall Street*, 4. *Catwoman*, 5. Bradley Cooper (Sandy would scoop her Best Actress Oscar for *The Blind Side* the very next night), 6. *Rhinestone* (the song was written by co-star Dolly Parton), 7. Armie Hammer, 8. *Con Air*, 9. Germany, 10. *After Earth*

ANSWERS

9

Music and
LYRICS

The sound of film

ON THE QT

Tarantino's soundtracks

You've just compiled a mixtape of essential Quentin Tarantino jams for a cinephile friend. Can you match the tracks to the following films: *Reservoir Dogs*, *Pulp Fiction*, *Jackie Brown*, *Kill Bill*, *The Hateful Eight*? (Hint: there are three tracks per film.)

1. George Baker Selection, 'Little Green Bag'
2. Chuck Berry, 'You Never Can Tell'
3. Randy Crawford, 'Street Life'
4. Dick Dale and His Del-Tones, 'Misirlou'
5. Delfonics, 'Didn't I (Blow Your Mind This Time)'
6. The 5.6.7.8.s, 'Woo Hoo'

7. Ennio Morricone, 'Regan's Theme (Floating Sound)'

8. Harry Nilsson, 'Coconut'

9. Santa Esmeralda, 'Don't Let Me Be Misunderstood'

10. Nancy Sinatra, 'Bang Bang'

11. Stealers Wheel, 'Stuck in the Middle with You'

12. Urge Overkill, 'Girl, You'll Be a Woman Soon'

13. Roy Orbison, 'There Won't Be Many Coming Home'

14. The White Stripes, 'Apple Blossom'

15. Bobby Womack and Peace, 'Across 110th Street'

MOVIES TAKE THE MIC

Cinema's one-hit wonders

1. Which of the following is NOT one of the life lessons passed down by Australian director Baz Luhrmann in 'Everybody's Free (To Wear Sunscreen)', his 1999 global chart-topper?

A) 'Do not read beauty magazines. They will only make you feel ugly.'

B) 'Don't mess with your hair or by the time you're 40, it will look 85.'

C) 'Try to visit Australia at least once a year. For the vibe.'

D) 'Be kind to your knees. You'll miss them when they're gone.'

2. A surprise chart-topper in both the UK and Ireland, Lee Marvin's 'Wand'rin' Star' came from the soundtrack of which film?

A) *Point Blank*

B) *Cat Ballou*

C) *The Dirty Dozen*

D) *Paint Your Wagon*

3. Which of the following is NOT a line from Richard Harris's 1968 hippie-lite hit 'MacArthur Park'?

A) 'We followed in the dance between the parted pages and were pressed in love's hot, fevered iron like a striped pair of pants.'

B) 'I don't think that I can take it, 'cause it took so long to bake it, and I'll never have that recipe again. Oh no!'

C) 'I looked to the sky, where an elephant's eye was looking at me from a bubblegum tree.'

D) 'I recall the yellow cotton dress foaming like a wave on the ground around your knees.'

4. What was the full name of Harris's *Gladiator* co-star Russell Crowe's band, which was often shortened to TOFOG?

A) Too Old For Oven Gloves

B) Thirty Odd Foot of Grunts

C) These Ockers Fight Over Gallantry

D) Tangy Odours From Overdue Gasses

5. Which legendary comic had a middling hit with 1983's 'The Hitler Rap' (opening line: 'Well, hi there people, you know me – I used to run a little joint called Germany!')?

A) George Burns

B) Mel Brooks

C) Robin Williams

D) Chevy Chase

6. Between 2013 and 2018 Macaulay Culkin fronted a band whose schtick consisted solely of ...?

A) Pizza-themed spoofs of Velvet Underground tracks

B) Reggae versions of Seventies TV theme tunes

C) Thrash metal takes on nursery rhymes

D) Bluegrass Bowie covers

7. Which member of the *Pitch Perfect* cast reached number 6 on the Billboard Hot 100 with soundtrack song 'Cups'?

A) Rebel Wilson

B) Elizabeth Banks

C) Anna Kendrick

D) Brittany Snow

8. What is the name of Juliette Lewis's hard-rocking backing band?

A) Trash Panda

B) The Mallorys

C) The Licks

D) Fingerbox

9. As the Blues Brothers, *Saturday Night Live* stars Dan Aykroyd and John Belushi carved out a bona fide second career as musicians. Who directed the 1980 film that cemented their legend?

A) Joe Dante

B) John Landis

C) Ivan Reitman

D) Dan Aykroyd

10. Fellow *SNL*-ers Andy Samberg, Akiva Schaffer and Jorma Taccone – aka The Lonely Island – hit number 69 on the Billboard Hot 100 (and #2 in Norway!) with the song 'Jack Sparrow'. Who guest-vocaled as a movie trivia-obsessed Captain Jack?

A) Keith Richards

B) David Hasselhoff

C) Michael Bolton

D) Iggy Pop

11. Which of the following is, sadly, not a real album?

A) Jeff Daniels: *Live and Unplugged*

B) *Little Joe Sure Can Sing!* by Joe Pesci

C) Lisa Kudrow: *Coffee and Cats*

D) *A Heavy Metal Christmas* by Christopher Lee

12. Scarlett Johansson's 2008 debut album *Anywhere I Lay My Head* is a collection of songs by which artist?

A) Loretta Lynn

B) Charles Manson

C) Joni Mitchell

D) Tom Waits

13. Jeff Bridges has released a clutch of well-regarded country-tinged albums, but for which music-based film did he win his Best Actor Oscar?

A) *The Fabulous Baker Boys*

B) *Crazy Heart*

C) *Tender Mercies*

D) *Country Strong*

14. Steve Martin hit number 17 on the Billboard charts in 1978 with a novelty song based on what real-life events?

A) The bad-tempered gas station queues that formed during the 1973 oil crisis

B) The 'Treasures of Tutankhamun' exhibit that toured the US the previous year

C) The rumours that Elvis Presley died on the toilet

D) The mania that surrounded the release of *Star Wars*

15. In 1991 Brent Spiner – Data from *Star Trek: The Next Generation* – released an album of swing classics and pop standards. What was it titled?

A) *Hits from the Holodeck*

B) *Ol' Yellow Eyes Is Back*

C) *Set Phasers for Swing*

D) *Fly Me to the Moon!*

KEY THEMES

Songs from motion pictures

1. The song 'Otto Titsling', immortalized by Bette Midler in 1988's *Beaches*, celebrates the inventor of what item?

2. Who sang 'Everybody's Talkin'', the hit song from 1969's *Midnight Cowboy* soundtrack?

3. Bing Crosby initially called for his best-known recording to be cut from 1942's *Holiday Inn* on the grounds that it might commercialize the song's subject. What was the song?

4. 'His palms are sweaty, knees weak, arms are heavy. There's vomit on his sweater already – mom's spaghetti. He's nervous, but on the surface he looks calm and ready.' The first lines of which 2002 hit?

5. The Best Original Song of the 1976 Golden Globes and Academy Awards was 'I'm Easy' from Robert Altman's *Nashville*. Which member of that film's grand and illustrious cast wrote and performed it?

6. The success of some songs outstrips the films they soundtrack. Phil Collins's power ballad 'Against All Odds' hit the top of the US charts in 1984. But who was the star of the largely forgotten film of the same name that it sprang from?

7. Pharrell Williams's 2013 mega-earworm 'Happy' came from the soundtrack for which animated movie?

8. What is the name of the character who pumps Public Enemy's 'Fight the Power' out through his ever-present boombox in Spike Lee's 1989 polemic *Do the Right Thing*?

9. What was the title of the hit single spawned by 1970's *M*A*S*H*?

10. Carly Simon's 1977 smash 'Nobody Does it Better' was the theme song for which James Bond film?

11. 'Someday we'll find it, the rainbow connection – the lovers, the dreamers and me ...' To which beloved 1979 film does Oscar-nominated chart hit 'Rainbow Connection' belong?

12. Which American girl group had a worldwide hit with their version of 'Jai Ho', the Oscar-winning theme to 2008's *Slumdog Millionaire*?

13. What is the actual title of Bill Conti's 'Theme from Rocky', which reached the top of the US charts in 1977?

14. 'Do Not Forsake Me, O My Darlin'' is the Oscar-winning theme to which classic Western?

15. Which latter-day troubadour penned the Oscar-nominated 'Mystery of Love' – a hit in Portugal, Hungary, France and Scotland – for 2017's *Call Me by Your Name*?

ROLL OVER BEETHOVEN

Tuneful biopics

Fifteen musical figures. Fifteen actors who've played them on screen. Can you match them up?

June Carter Cash
Tupac Shakur
Glenn Miller
James Brown
Serge Gainsbourg
Chas Hodges (Chas 'n' Dave)
Joan Jett
Bob Dylan
Glenn Gould
Brian Wilson
John Lennon
Wolfgang Amadeus Mozart
Etta James
Elvis Presley
Keith Richards

Chadwick Boseman (2014's *Get on Up*)
Reece Witherspoon (2005's *Walk the Line*)
Cate Blanchett (2007's *I'm Not There*)
Éric Elmosnino (2010's *Gainsbourg: A Heroic Life*)
Colm Feore (1993's *Thirty-Two Short Films About Glenn Gould*)
Ralf Little (2008's *Telstar: The Joe Meek Story*)
Beyoncé Knowles (2008's *Cadillac Records*)
Kristen Stewart (2010's *The Runaways*)
Ian Hart (1991's *The Hours and Times* and 1994's *Backbeat*)
James Stewart (1954's *The Glenn Miller Story*)
Tom Hulce (1984's *Amadeus*)
Kurt Russell (1979's *Elvis: The Movie*)
Ben Whishaw (2005's *Stoned*)
Anthony Mackie (2009's *Notorious*)
John Cusack (2014's *Love & Mercy*)

VÉRITÉ VIRTUOSOS

Pop documentaries

1. Which Nineties comedy finds a politician copying Bob Dylan's card-carrying moves from the 'Subterranean Homesick Blues' sequence that kicks off D.A. Pennebaker's 1967 Dylan doc *Don't Look Back*?

A) *Wag the Dog*

B) *Bulworth*

C) *Bob Roberts*

D) *Primary Colors*

2. What band is immortalized in Jonathan Demme's celebrated 1984 concert film *Stop Making Sense*?

A) The Police

B) Dire Straits

C) The Cure

D) Talking Heads

3. Why does Madonna mock Kevin Costner after a backstage encounter in 1991's *In Bed with Madonna* (aka *Truth or Dare*)?

A) He uses the word 'neat' to describe her stage show

B) He is carrying his Oscar for *Dances with Wolves* with him

C) He is wearing dungarees

D) He makes an ill-advised attempt to vogue

4. According to Marty DiBergi's warts-and-all 1984 documentary *This is Spinal Tap*, which of the following is NOT the title of an album by hard rock's most seminal of acts?

A) *Shark Sandwich*

B) *The Gospel According to Spinal Tap*

C) *Intravenous de Milo*

D) *Brain Salad Surgery*

5. What act closes Michael Wadleigh's 1970 documentary *Woodstock*?

A) Jimi Hendrix

B) Crosby, Stills, Nash & Young

C) The Who

D) Country Joe and the Fish

6. 2004's *Some Kind of Monster* intercuts footage of Metallica on tour and in the studio with scenes that found them in which unlikely scenario?

A) Building a barn on drummer Lars Ulrich's farm in Denmark

B) In their therapist's office

C) Camping in Yosemite National Park

D) On a UN aid relief mission to Haiti

7. The same year's *Dig!* documented a feud between which two bands?

A) The Hives and the Rembrandts

B) The Dandy Warhols and the Brian Jonestown Massacre

C) Modest Mouse and Death Cab for Cutie

D) Len and Spoon

8. What was the title of the 2009 film that documented Michael Jackson's preparations for the London concerts that were dashed by the singer's death?

A) *LonDONE*

B) *HIStory*

C) *This Is It*

D) *Xscape*

9. 2012's *Shut Up and Play the Hits* documents which band's Madison Square Garden farewell concert?

A) My Chemical Romance

B) LCD Soundsystem

C) REM

D) The White Stripes

10. 2013's *20 Feet from Stardom* – which features interviews with Mick Jagger, Sheryl Crow and Bruce Springsteen – focuses on which breed of unsung hero?

A) Concert photographers

B) Backing singers

C) Bass players

D) Roadies

11. Which anthem does NOT feature on the set list of 2011's *Glee: The 3D Concert Movie*?

A) 'Don't Stop Believin''

B) 'River Deep – Mountain High'

C) 'Bat Out of Hell'

D) 'The Safety Dance'

12. In which country had the mysterious American singer Rodriguez – dragged back into the limelight by 2012's *Searching for Sugar Man* – achieved cult status in the early Seventies?

A) South Africa

B) Japan

C) Greece

D) East Germany

13. Which singer reads Janis Joplin's diaries and letters in 2015's *Janis: Little Girl Blue*?

A) Cat Power

B) Pink

C) St. Vincent

D) Gwen Stefani

14. Director Chris Moukarbel's 2017 Netflix study of Lady Gaga draws its title from what aspect of the singer's appearance?

A) Her tattoos

B) Her height

C) Her hair

D) Her eyes

15. What film is the highest-grossing music documentary or concert film of all time at the US box office?

A) *Justin Bieber: Never Say Never*

B) *The Rolling Stones: Shine a Light*

C) *U2: Rattle and Hum*

D) *Hannah Montana and Miley Cyrus: Best of Both Worlds Concert*

MULTIPLE THREADS

Musicians turned actors

True or false?

1. George Formby's 1939 comedy *Come on George!* takes place against the backdrop of illegal bare-knuckle boxing.

2. Bruce Springsteen has an oddball cameo in Dennis Hopper's generally bizarre 1990 farrago *Catchfire*, playing Artist Painting with Chainsaw.

3. Million-selling chart-topper Bruno Mars made his screen debut aged seven, playing the all-singing, all-dancing, all-righty-ma'am Little Elvis in 1992's *Honeymoon in Vegas*.

4. Genesis drummer and vaunted solo artist Phil Collins boasts credits in such films as Beatles comedy *A Hard Day's Night*, kiddie fable *Chitty Chitty Bang Bang* and Steven Spielberg's *Hook*.

5. Michael Winner's 1998 folly *Parting Shots* saw smoky-voiced singer Chris Rea playing a photographer who turns vigilante after being diagnosed with terminal cancer.

6. Mariah Carey blamed the 9/11 terrorist attacks on the World Trade Centre and the Pentagon for the poor box-office performance of starring vehicle *Glitter*.

7. No Doubt singer Gwen Stefani essayed glamorous golden-aged star Jean Harlow in Martin Scorsese's Howard Hughes biopic *The Aviator*.

8. The White Stripes' main man Jack White has a small role in 2007's *Walk Hard: The Dewey Cox Story*, in which he plays Richard Nixon.

9. Spice Girl Emma Bunton enjoyed a musical cameo during a wedding sequence in 2005's Bollywood comedy *Pyaar Mein Twist*.

10. One of the most jaw-droppingly bizarre pop-star turns of recent years came from Victoria Beckham, who was cast as Jason Statham's Cockney mum in the flashbacks of 2009's *Crank: High Voltage*.

11. OutKast's André 'André 3000' Benjamin starred as Jimi Hendrix in a biopic, which wasn't allowed to feature any of the star's music.

12. In Christopher Nolan's 2006's period drama *The Prestige*, David Bowie has a supporting role as a strange man who pours a cup of water on his wrist and says the word 'pardon' four times.

13. 2011's generally negligible *Mega Python vs. Gatoroid* reunited Eighties teen stars Tiffany and Debbie Gibson.

14. Bette Midler has a small role in *Fast & Furious 6*, in which she drops the flag on a race around London's Piccadilly Circus.

15. Nightclub scenes are a haven for moonlighting singers. The Welsh chanteuse Duffy can be seen entertaining the Kray twins as Italian-American balladeer Timi Yuro in 2015's *Legend*.

VIDEOTHEQUE

Songs inspired by movies and movie stars

1. The debut single by goth rockers Bauhaus reminds us that a beloved horror icon is no longer with us. What is it titled?

A) 'Lon Chaney's Dead'

B) 'Vincent Price is Dead'

C) 'Bela Lugosi's Dead'

D) 'Boris Karloff's Dead'

2. Iron Maiden's 1995 single 'Man on the Edge' – a number 1 hit in Finland – was based on which film?

A) *Falling Down*

B) *Pusher*

C) *Stalker*

D) *The Medusa Touch*

3. Washington D.C. punk legends Fugazi based their song 'Walken's Syndrome' on a Christopher Walken character's urge to crash his car into oncoming traffic in which of his early films?

A) *Brainstorm*

B) *The Anderson Tapes*

C) *Annie Hall*

D) *The Deer Hunter*

4. You'll remember the song but can you remember the band? Who soundtracked 1995 with the Audrey Hepburn-inspired hit 'Breakfast at Tiffany's'?

A) Menswear

B) Smash Mouth

C) The New Radicals

D) Deep Blue Something

5. Which actor is roundly mocked on 'Medicine Ball', a track from Eminem's 2009 album *Relapse*?

A) Christopher Reeve

B) Laurence Olivier

C) Robert De Niro

D) Lindsay Lohan

6. Who did British literature-loving Lloyd Cole's unattainable dream woman look like in the lyrics of 1984 single 'Rattlesnakes'?

A) 'Jean Seberg in *À Bout de Souffle*'

B) 'Eva Marie Saint in *On the Waterfront*'

C) 'Elizabeth Taylor in *Suddenly, Last Summer*.'

D) 'Farrah Fawcett in *The Cannonball Run*.'

7. Which director's entire filmography is comprehensively covered in Big Audio Dynamite's 1985 hit 'E=MC2'?

A) Stanley Kubrick

B) Sergio Leone

C) Nicolas Roeg

D) Federico Fellini

8. 'I've said it before and I'll say it again. Life moves pretty fast. If you don't stop and look around once in a while, you could

miss it.' From which film did hip-hop horrorcore legends Gravediggaz sample this upbeat line for their 1994 self-help aria '1-800 Suicide'?

A) *Say Anything*

B) *Heathers*

C) *Flatliners*

D) *Ferris Bueller's Day Off*

9. Which leading man lent his name to a 1985 Prefab Sprout LP and a 2002 Sheryl Crow single?

A) James Dean

B) Montgomery Clift

C) Marlon Brando

D) Steve McQueen

10. Surrealist 1929 short *Un Chien Andalou* was the basis for the Pixies' 1989 song 'Debaser'. Who directed the original film?

A) Luis Buñuel

B) Jean Cocteau

C) René Magritte

D) Man Ray

11. Kate Bush named her 1993 album after which movie?

A) *Hellzapoppin'*

B) *All That Jazz*

C) *The Red Shoes*

D) *Grease 2*

12. The Kinks' 1967 hit 'Waterloo Sunset' is widely believed to describe the Swinging Sixties romance between Terence Stamp and Julie Christie, who had hit it off on the set of which film that same year?

A) *Doctor Zhivago*

B) *The Knack ... and How to Get It*

C) *Blow Up*

D) *Far from the Madding Crowd*

13. How does the White Stripes' 2001 track 'The Union Forever' relate to the world of cinema?

A) It was co-written with Jeff Bridges

B) It quotes liberally from *Citizen Kane*

C) Its promo video was directed by Wes Anderson

D) It boasts backing vocals from the Soggy Bottom Boys – George Clooney, John Turturro and Tim Blake Nelson – from *O Brother, Where Art Thou?*

14. In 2001 REM hit the charts with a song that shared a title with which romantic movie?

A) *Out of Sight*

B) *Dirty Dancing*

C) *Imitation of Life*

D) *All That Heaven Allows*

15. Sometimes a back-handed compliment is taken the wrong way. Neil Diamond had to fork out $25,000 to Universal Studios in 1982 for having used ideas from which film as the basis of his hit 'Heartlight'?

A) *The Dark Crystal*

B) *Short Circuit*

C) *E.T. the Extra-Terrestrial*

D) *The NeverEnding Story*

BEAT THE DEVIL

Plastic Pop: Fictional bands in films

1. In 1984's mockumentary *This is Spinal Tap*, guitarist Nigel Tufnel (Christopher Guest) reveals his delicate, piano-led number 'Lick My Love Pump' is a hybrid of two composers. Which two?

2. What's the name of Bill and Ted's garage rock band? (And be careful: no marks for the wrong misspelling.)

3. Venus in Furs, the all-star glam act who feature in 1998's *Velvet Goldmine*, were constituted from members of Radiohead, Suede and which 1970s band?

4. Russell Hammond, Jeff Bebe, Ed Vallencourt and Larry Fellows form the classic line-up of which entirely fictional rock band?

5. What's the name of the rock band uber-fan Mark Wahlberg joins as replacement frontman in 2001's *Rock Star*?

6. Which A-lister made an unexpected, shaven-headed appearance as the frontman for 'Scotty Doesn't Know' hitmakers Lustra in 2004's *EuroTrip*?

7. Which British musician plays the frontman of Weird Sisters, the 'Do the Hippogriff' band headlining Hogwarts' Yule Ball in 2005's *Harry Potter and the Goblet of Fire*?

8. Promising youngsters I Can't Go On, I'll Go On receive a major career leg-up from none other than David Bowie at the climax of which Noughties teen movie?

9. Gary Clark, who penned the songs for teen popsters Sing Street in the 2016 film of the same name, was a founder member of which Eighties hitmakers?

10. What's the Nouvelle Vague-inspired name of Timothée Chalamet's band in 2017's *Lady Bird*?

On the QT: Tarantino's soundtracks

1. *Reservoir Dogs* (1992), 2. *Pulp Fiction* (1994), 3. *Jackie Brown* (1997), 4. *Pulp Fiction*, 5. *Jackie Brown*, 6. *Kill Bill* (2003–4), 7. *The Hateful Eight* (2015), 8. *Reservoir Dogs*, 9. *Kill Bill*, 10. *Kill Bill*, 11. *Reservoir Dogs*, 12. *Pulp Fiction*, 13. *The Hateful Eight*, 14. *The Hateful Eight*, 15. *Jackie Brown*

Movies Take the Mic: Cinema's one-hit wonders

1. c, 2. d, 3. c (this acid-tastic line is from 'Hole in My Shoe' by Traffic), 4. b, 5. b, 6. a (they were called The Pizza Underground. Ha.), 7. c, 8. c, 9. b, 10. c, 11. c, 12. d, 13. b, 14. b (The single was 'King Tut': 'Now, if I'd known they'd line up just to see him, I'd have taken all my money and bought me a museum. King Tut!'), 15. b

Key Themes: Songs from motion pictures

1. The brassiere ('Otto Titsling had found his quest: to lift and mold the female breast; to point the small ones to the sky; to keep the big ones high and dry!'), 2. Harry Nilsson, 3. 'White Christmas', 4. 'Lose Yourself' by Eminem, from *8 Mile*, 5. Keith Carradine, 6. Jeff Bridges, 7. *Despicable Me 2*, 8. Radio Raheem, 9. 'Suicide is Painless', 10. *The Spy Who Loved Me*, 11. *The Muppet Movie*, 12. The Pussycat Dolls, 13. 'Gonna Fly Now', 14. *High Noon*, 15. Sufjan Stevens

Roll over Beethoven: Tuneful biopics

James Brown: Chadwick Boseman (2014's *Get on Up*); June Carter Cash: Reese Witherspoon (2005's *Walk the Line*); Bob Dylan: Cate Blanchett (2007's *I'm Not There*); Serge Gainsbourg: Éric Elmosnino (2010's *Gainsbourg: A Heroic Life*); Glenn Gould: Colm Feore (1993's *Thirty-Two Short Films About Glenn Gould*); Chas Hodges (Chas 'n' Dave): Ralf Little (2008's *Telstar: The Joe Meek Story*); Etta James: Beyoncé Knowles (2008's *Cadillac Records*); Joan Jett: Kristen Stewart (2010's *The Runaways*); John Lennon: Ian Hart (1991's *The Hours and Times* and 1994's *Backbeat*); Glenn Miller: James Stewart (1954's *The Glenn Miller Story*); Wolfgang Amadeus Mozart: Tom Hulce (1984's *Amadeus*); Elvis Presley: Kurt Russell (1979's *Elvis: The Movie*); Keith Richards: Ben Whishaw (2005's *Stoned*); Tupac Shakur: Anthony Mackie (2009's *Notorious*); Brian Wilson: John Cusack (2014's *Love & Mercy*)

Vérité Virtuosos: Pop documentaries

1. c, 2. d, 3. a, 4. d (prog supergroup Emerson, Lake & Palmer got there before them in 1973), 5. a, 6. b, 7. b, 8. c, 9. b, 10. b, 11. c, 12. a, 13. a, 14. b (which according to the film is Five Foot Two), 15. a

Multiple Threads: Musicians turned actors

1. False – it's horse racing, 2. False – it's Bob Dylan, 3. True, 4. True, 5. True, 6. True, 7. True, 8. False – he plays Elvis, 9. True, 10. False – it was Geri Halliwell, 11. True – 2013's *Jimi: All Is by My Side,* 12. False – he plays the famed inventor Nikola Tesla, 13. True, 14. False – it's Rita Ora who drops the flag, 15. True

Videotheque: Songs inspired by movies and movie stars

1. c, 2. a, 3. c, 4. d, 5. a, 6. b, 7. c, 8. d, 9. d, 10. a, 11. c, 12. d, 13. b (including a good chunk of the 'Charlie Kane' song), 14. c, 15. c

Plastic Pop: Fictional bands in films

1. Mozart and Bach ('It's a Mach piece'), 2. Wyld Stallyns, 3. Roxy Music, 4. Stillwater, from 2000's *Almost Famous*, 5. Steel Dragon, 6. Matt Damon, 7. Jarvis Cocker, 8. *Bandslam*, 9. Danny Wilson, 10. L'Enfance Nue

ANSWERS

10

Quote me on THAT

Putting the talk into the talkies

WHAT'S MY LINE?

Who said it?

These fifteen characters have temporarily been rendered speechless – but can you match each character to one of the quotes on the opposite page?

Grusinskaya (Greta Garbo), *Grand Hotel*
Margo Channing (Bette Davis), *All About Eve*
President Merkin Muffley (Peter Sellers), *Dr. Strangelove*
Clemenza (Richard Castellano), *The Godfather*
Lt. Col. Bill Kilgore (Robert Duvall), *Apocalypse Now*
Matty Walker (Kathleen Turner), *Body Heat*
Truvy Jones (Dolly Parton), *Steel Magnolias*
Older Woman Customer (Estelle Reiner), *When Harry Met Sally*
Col. Nathan R. Jessep (Jack Nicholson), *A Few Good Men*
Blake (Alec Baldwin), *Glengarry Glen Ross*
Jim Lovell (Tom Hanks), *Apollo 13*
Dorothy Boyd (Renée Zellweger), *Jerry Maguire*
Max Rothman (John Cusack), *Max*
Regina George (Rachel McAdams), *Mean Girls*
Jack Twist (Jake Gyllenhaal), *Brokeback Mountain*

'Gentlemen, you can't fight in here. This is the War Room!'
'I want to be alone.'
'Leave the gun. Take the cannoli.'
'You had me at hello.'
'Fasten your seatbelts, it's going to be a bumpy night.'
'You're not very bright, are you? I like that in a man.'
'Smile! It increases your face value.'
'You're an awfully hard man to like, Hitler.'
'I'll have what she's having.'
'I wish I knew how to quit you.'
'You can't handle the truth!'
'Stop trying to make "fetch" happen.'
'Houston, we have a problem.'
'Always. Be. Closing.'
'I love the smell of napalm in the morning.'

ENTRANCES AND EXITS

Memorable first and last lines

1. Which film gets cooking with the opening lines 'Do you find me sadistic? You know, I bet I could fry an egg on your head right now, if I wanted to.'

A) *The Good, the Bad and the Ugly*

B) *Kill Bill*

C) *Cool Hand Luke*

D) *Ice Cold in Alex*

2. What film closes out with the world-weary lines, 'Ernest Hemingway once wrote, "The world is a fine place and worth fighting for." I agree with the second part.'

A) *Predator*

B) *Shutter Island*

C) *Children of Men*

D) *Seven*

3. Which movie begins with the lines 'I believe in America. America has made my fortune.'?

A) *The Wolf of Wall Street*

B) *The War of the Roses*

C) *The Godfather*

D) *The Big Short*

4. 'Let them see what kind of person I am. I'm not even going to swat that fly. I hope they're watching ... they'll see. They'll see and they'll know, and they'll say, "Why, she wouldn't even harm a fly."' The final lines of which film?

A) *Girl, Interrupted*

B) *Psycho*

C) *Gorillas in the Mist*

D) *Under the Skin*

5. Which of the following films does NOT conclude with its title being spoken?

A) *The Breakfast Club*

B) *Chinatown*

C) *Iron Man*

D) *Days of Thunder*

6. Raucous 1980 golf-club comedy *Caddyshack* ends with which comic declaring 'Hey, everybody, we're all gonna get laid!'?

A) Rodney Dangerfield

B) Bill Murray

C) Chevy Chase

D) Robin Williams

7. What film opens with the line 'We were somewhere around Barstow, on the edge of the desert, when the drugs began to take hold.'?

A) *Natural Born Killers*

B) *The Man Who Fell to Earth*

C) *Fear and Loathing in Las Vegas*

D) *Less Than Zero*

8. Cult Patrick Swayze actioner *Road House* rounds off with what hall-of-fame payoff?

A) 'A polar bear fell on me.'

B) 'Let's go to Reykjavik.'

C) 'Duran Duran?'

D) 'Please welcome to the stage ... Mr John Cougar Mellencamp!'

9. Which film opens by enquiring, 'Did you know there are more people with genius IQs living in China than there are people of any kind living in the United States?'?

A) *Ocean's Thirteen*

B) *Catch Me If You Can*

C) *The Social Network*

D) *Limitless*

10. At the end of 1990's *Goodfellas*, relocated gangster Henry Hill (Ray Liotta) ruefully shrugs that he gets to live the rest of his life 'like a ______'?

A) Schlemiel

B) Schnook

C) Putz

D) Bum

11. 'I was 12 going on 13 the first time I saw a dead human being.' Which film's grisly opening gambit?

A) *The Lovely Bones*

B) *The Hunger Games*

C) *Stand by Me*

D) *The Outsiders*

12. Which cops 'n' robbers film ends with the lines, 'Some men get the world. Others get ex-hookers and a trip to Arizona.'?

A) *Bad Lieutenant*

B) *The Friends of Eddie Coyle*

C) *Bad Lieutenant: Port of Call New Orleans*

D) *L.A. Confidential*

13. What gets rolling with the line, 'When I was lying there in the VA hospital, with a big hole blown through the middle of my life, I started having these dreams of flying.'?

A) *The Grey*

B) *Born on the Fourth of July*

C) *Avatar*

D) *Gattaca*

14. 2000's *Memento*, Christopher Nolan's tricksy backwards-spooling memory-loss thriller, ends with which of the following lines?

A) 'Who are you?'

B) 'Now, where was I?'

C) 'I'm sorry – have we met?'

D) 'You'll have to forgive me, my mind's an absolute sieve today!'

15. 'I'm finished.' Exactly where is Daniel Day-Lewis's character when he delivers the last line of 2007's *There Will Be Blood*?

A) In a bowling alley

B) On an oil rig

C) Sitting on the lavatory

D) In a courtroom

PR EXERCISE

Poster taglines

1. Which 1939 Western was originally sold as 'A Powerful Story of 9 Strange People!'

2. 'When you deal a fast shuffle ... Love is on the cards' was the tagline of which Forties comedy?

3. According to the poster, the title character of a 1949 classic was 'Hunted by men ... Sought by WOMEN!' Who was he?

4. Which of the following was not among the descriptives that found their way on to the hyperventilating poster of 1965's *Cat Ballou* – gasser, swinger, gutbuster or she-bang?

5. The same year's self-explanatory *Orgy of the Dead* trumpeted the fact it was shot 'In gorgeous ASTRAVISION and shocking ____ COLOR'. What?

6. 'They're young ... They're in love ... And they kill people.' Which iconic screen couple?

7. The tagline of 1972's *Deliverance* ('This is the weekend they didn't __________') suggested the film's central quartet had a Plan B if white-water canoeing didn't work out. What was that back-up plan?

8. Complete the tagline of 1984's late-cycle slasher movie *The Mutilator*: 'By sword. By pick. By axe. ___ ___'?

9. According to the tagline of 1988's *Rabid Grannies*, the eponymous old dears 'love their grandchildren ___________' What?

10. Which Nineties sequel bears the tagline 'Here they grow again'?

11. The tagline of 1993's *Jurassic Park* stressed this was an adventure how many years in the making?

12. Early preview posters of which animated film deployed the ace tagline 'Escape or die frying'?

13. 'Great trilogies come in threes', insisted which 2003 release?

14. 2005's *House of Wax*, released at the height of Paris Hilton's overexposure, made cinemagoers a blunt offer: 'On May 6th, see Paris die!' How did the debatably sympathetic heiress cark it within the film?

15. Complete this inspired tagline for 2009's Nazi-themed horror *Dead Snow*: 'Ein, zwei, __________!' What?

Bye bye

The Lady Eve

Gremlins 2: The New Batch

Chicken Run

Bonnie and Clyde

Stagecoach

Gutbuster

SEXI

Well done

Scary Movie 3

Die!

The Third Man

65 million

Play golf

Spike through the head

BARD INFLUENCE

Shakespeare on screen

1. Which of the following Shakespeare texts was NOT reworked by the great Japanese director Akira Kurosawa?

A) *Macbeth*

B) *Othello*

C) *Hamlet*

D) *King Lear*

2. Which Hollywood star slipped on doublet and hose to play the lead in Franco Zeffirelli's 1990 adaptation of *Hamlet*?

A) Val Kilmer

B) Michael Douglas

C) Mel Gibson

D) Sigourney Weaver

3. Richard Loncraine's 1995 take on *Richard III* sets its scene in a Thirties Britain that's gearing up for the Second World War. Who plays King Rich?

A) Anthony Hopkins

B) Patrick Stewart

C) Jeremy Irons

D) Ian McKellen

4. To which track does Harold Perrineau's Mercutio get truly ecstatic during the loved-up party scene in Baz Luhrmann's 1996 *Romeo + Juliet*?

A) Candi Staton's 'Young Hearts Run Free'

B) Gloria Gaynor's 'I Will Survive'

C) Prince's 'Let's Go Crazy'

D) McFadden & Whitehead's 'Ain't No Stoppin' Us Now'

5. Classic 1956 sci-fi *Forbidden Planet* slingshots which of Shakespeare's plays into outer space?

A) *Coriolanus*

B) *The Tempest*

C) *Titus Andronicus*

D) *Cymbeline*

6. Which rocker turned his dulcet tones to narrating Troma Films' 1996 schlock-shocker *Tromeo and Juliet*?

A) Ozzy Osbourne

B) Meatloaf

C) Gene Simmons

D) Lemmy

7. With which song does Heath Ledger serenade Julia Stiles during soccer training in 1999's *Taming of the Shrew* update *10 Things I Hate About You*?

A) 'Nothing Compares 2 U'

B) 'How Deep Is Your Love?'

C) 'Always on My Mind'

D) 'Can't Take My Eyes Off You'

8. Who does NOT appear in Jean-Luc Godard's 1987 'post-Chernobyl science fiction' adaptation of *King Lear*?

A) Molly Ringwald

B) Grace Jones

C) Burgess Meredith

D) Woody Allen

9. In 2001's high-school drama *O* – a retelling of *Othello* that stars Josh Hartnett and Martin Sheen – the lead character is no longer a military commander, but rather ...?

A) President of the Debate Society

B) The Homecoming Queen

C) A basketball star

D) A janitor

10. Which former sportsman played Amanda Bynes's football coach in 2006's tweeny *Twelfth Night* spin *She's the Man*?

A) Dan Marino

B) 'Rowdy' Roddy Piper

C) Dwayne 'The Rock' Johnson

D) Vinnie Jones

11. Rick Moranis, Max von Sydow and the voice of Mel Blanc star in a beloved 1983 Canadian comedy take on *Hamlet* that's set in Toronto's Elsinore Brewery. What's it called?

A) *Strange Brew*

B) *You're Bard!*

C) *To Beer or Not To Beer*

D) *Last Orders*

12. Kenneth Branagh's 2006 adaptation *As You Like It* – starring Bryce Dallas Howard and Kevin Kline – shifted the play's setting from 17th-century France to ...?

A) Caveman times

B) 19th-century Japan

C) Modern-day Las Vegas

D) Post-apocalypse London

13. The 2014 Bollywood release *Haider* relocated which of the Shakespeare's plays to the Kashmir region?

A) *The Winter's Tale*

B) *Henry V*

C) *All's Well That Ends Well*

D) *Hamlet*

14. Steve Coogan played a high-school drama teacher pandering to his students with a youth-centric production of one of the Bard's plays in a 2008 comedy. What was the title of his play – and the film?

A) *M@cbet#*

B) *Two Homies of Verona*

C) *Hamlet 2*

D) *The Merchant of Venice Beach*

15. Who played the young Bard himself in surprise 1998 mega-hit *Shakespeare in Love*?

A) Ralph Fiennes

B) Colin Firth

C) Joseph Fiennes

D) Ben Affleck

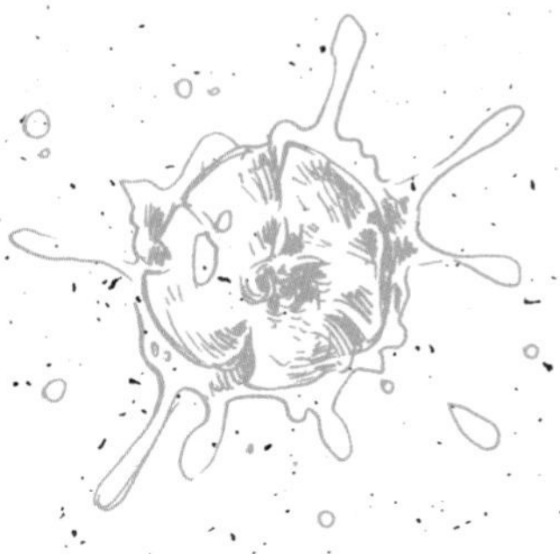

LET'S GET CRITICAL

The best and worst reviews

1. The first published film review – of 1896's *The Kiss* – appeared in American literary magazine *The Chap-Book* on 15 June of that year. What was the verdict?

A) 'Absolutely disgusting.'

B) 'Haunting! A piercing insight into the human condition. Five stars, sirs!'

C) 'Incapacitatingly erotic.'

D) 'Part tone poem, part fever dream, all masterwork.'

2. The world's shortest published review – 'No.' – was Leonard Maltin's response to which film's inquisitive title?

A) 1948's *Isn't It Romantic?*

B) 1969's *Should a Schoolgirl Tell?*

C) 1988's *Casual Sex?*

D) 2005's *Are We There Yet?*

3. What film did Vincent Canby of the *New York Times* describe – somewhat bizarrely – as being 'amusing in fitful patches but you're likely to find more beauty, suspense, discipline, craft and art when watching a New York harbor pilot bring the Queen Elizabeth 2 into her Hudson River berth'?

A) *Starship Troopers*

B) *Rocky IV*

C) *The Empire Strikes Back*

D) *The Dark Knight*

4. What classic did the *Washington Post* decide was 'Pretentious, abysmally slow, amateurishly acted and, above all, wrong'?

A) *The French Connection*

B) *The Godfather*

C) *Apocalypse Now*

D) *2001: A Space Odyssey*

5. Which writer-producer-director was rated by Leslie Halliwell as being 'a man of many talents, all of them minor'?

A) Kevin Smith

B) Francis Ford Coppola

C) Mike Nichols

D) Blake Edwards

6. Critic James Baldwin dissed which biopic for being 'as empty as a banana peel, and as treacherous'?

A) *Bird*

B) *Lady Sings the Blues*

C) *Malcolm X*

D) *Ali*

7. 1971's cult classic *Harold and Maude* was slated by *Variety* as having 'all the fun and gaiety of ...'?

A) Stomach cramps

B) A night in an abattoir

C) A burning orphanage

D) Shit soufflé

8. Rob Reiner's 1994 mis-step *North* inspired the title of one of Roger Ebert's less phlegmatic review collections. What was it called?

A) *This Movie Stinks!*

B) *I Hated, Hated, Hated This Movie*

C) *Burn, Hollywood, Burn!*

D) *So Long, and Thanks for All the Flicks*

9. 'He wears the anxious expression of a man who hasn't had a decent bowel movement in more than a week.' Ever-glum British critic Barry Norman's verdict on which action hero?

A) Steven Seagal

B) Vin Diesel

C) Arnold Schwarzenegger

D) Clint Eastwood

10. *New Yorker* critic Anthony Lane once described Quentin Tarantino as 'less an ironist than a chronic fetishist; he has cooked up a world where ___________ matter, and nothing else.' What?

A) Guns

B) Sharp suits

C) Foul put-downs

D) Hamburgers

11. 'If you want to save yourself the ticket price, go into the kitchen, cue up a male choir singing the music of hell, and get a kid to start banging pots and pans together. Then close your eyes and use your imagination.' Which film elicits the sickest of burns from Roger Ebert?

A) *Man of Steel*

B) *Transformers: Revenge of the Fallen*

C) *Pixels*

D) *Independence Day*

12. In her later years, Pauline Kael declared, 'One of the reasons I retired was so that I'd never have to watch another ___________ movie.' Who filled the gap?

A) Steven Spielberg

B) Ridley Scott

C) Tim Burton

D) Oliver Stone

13. About which film did critic and activist Lindy West write, 'If this is what modern womanhood means, then just fucking veil me and sew up all my holes.'?

A) *Sex and the City 2*

B) *Bride Wars*

C) *The Ugly Truth*

D) *Trainwreck*

14. Which blockbuster was described by the *New Republic* as 'a movie that beats you into submission and makes you wonder if the sun will ever come out again'?

A) *Terminator Genisys*

B) *Suicide Squad*

C) *Batman vs. Superman: Dawn of Justice*

D) *Star Trek Into Darkness*

15. It took time for Channing Tatum's abundant charms to win the critics over. To which of the following was he NOT compared in the press during his early career?

A) Josh Hartnett crossed with an elephant

B) A well-groomed village idiot

C) An orangutan with moves

D) A dinner plate with a frown painted on

KING'S GAME

The films of Stephen King

1. Which was the first of Stephen King's books to be adapted for the screen?

A) *Salem's Lot*
B) *Carrie*
C) *Children of the Corn*
D) *The Shining*

2. Stephen King is famed for his prolific output – so much so that he had to invent the pseudonymous Richard Bachman as an extra outlet for his novels. Which Schwarzenegger film was adapted from a Bachman book?

A) *End of Days*
B) *Junior*
C) *The Running Man*
D) *Total Recall*

3. Other than the film itself, what links the two young male leads of John Carpenter's 1983 killer car flick *Christine*?

A) Neither of them ever acted again
B) They both died before the film was released
C) They both became directors
D) Each of them married one of Carpenter's daughters

4. Christopher Walken was perfectly cast as the haunted psychic in David Cronenberg's 1983 King adaptation *The Dead Zone*. But who was King's choice for the role?

A) Bill Murray
B) Christopher Reeve
C) Gene Hackman
D) Gene Wilder

5. Who plays the knee-high pyromaniac in 1984's *Firestarter*?

A) Bradley Cooper
B) Sara Gilbert
C) Drew Barrymore
D) Jason Sudeikis

6. A militant anti-smoking clinic, an adulterous tennis pro, a killer troll ... What was the title of the 1985 anthology movie that comprised three King stories?

A) *Cat's Eye*
B) *Witch's Brew*
C) *Sweet Dreams*
D) *True Stories*

7. What did King offer as the reason for the failure of his sole directorial effort, 1986's *Maximum Overdrive*?

A) It opened on the same day as *Top Gun* and *Aliens*
B) Emilio Estevez's lead performance
C) He was 'coked out of [his] mind' throughout the shoot
D) 'Black energy' emanating from ley lines under the location where the film was shot

8. What is the name of the fictional town in Maine where so many King books and adaptations are set?

A) Pembroke Dock

B) Castle Rock

C) Cabot Cove

D) Meek's Cutoff

9. In 1990's *Misery*, novelist Paul Sheldon (James Caan) knocks over one of his captor's carefully arranged glass animals and places it back in a different position. When this is discovered it leads to some dire consequences for his ankles... What was the animal?

A) A penguin

B) A poodle

C) A seahorse

D) A unicorn

10. Despite its misleadingly suburban title, 1992's King adaptation *The Lawnmower Man* is mostly concerned with ...?

A) Engineering a race of cyborg monkeys for the US Army

B) Reversing the aging process

C) The mind-expanding possibilities of virtual reality

D) Locating the bones of Judas Iscariot

11. Which natural event connects the plots of 1995's *Dolores Claiborne* and 2017's *Gerald's Game*?

A) An earthquake

B) A solar eclipse

C) A rain of frogs

D) A meteor shower

12. 2007's *1408* was the second time John Cusack had appeared in a King adaptation. 2016's *Cell* would be the third – but what was the first?

A) *Silver Bullet*

B) *Creepshow*

C) *Cujo*

D) *Stand by Me*

13. Sissy Spacek played Carrie White in the 1976 version of *Carrie*, but who gets her prom dress all dirty in the 2013 remake?

A) Maisie Williams

B) Chloë Grace Moretz

C) Elle Fanning

D) Hailee Steinfeld

14. 2017's *It: Chapter One* became the most commercially successful horror film of all time. Which film did it overtake?

A) *The Exorcist*

B) *The Blair Witch Project*

C) *The Sixth Sense*

D) *Paranormal Activity*

15. Which remake did King cite as his all-time favourite film in a 2017 interview?

A) *Sorcerer*

B) *Solaris*

C) *The Departed*

D) *The Thing*

BURN HOLLYWOOD BURN

Actorly disses

1. W.C. Fields described which screen icon as 'a plumber's idea of Cleopatra'?

2. Groucho Marx famously quipped that 1949's Victor Mature/Hedy Lamarr romp *Samson and Delilah* was the 'first film I ever saw where the leading man had bigger _____ than the leading lady'. Bigger what?

3. Which pin-up did Bette Davis dub 'the original good time that was had by all'?

4. Sometimes a self-own is the best own. Which sporadic actor, better known as a flamboyant musician (himself later played by Michael Douglas), was forced to admit, 'I've done my bit for motion pictures. I've stopped making them'?

5. Which cantankerous comic actor was driven to tell Barbra Streisand 'I have more talent in my smallest fart than you do in your entire body'?

6. Which Golden Age director said Peter O'Toole 'looks like he's walking round just to save on the funeral expenses'?

7. Richard Harris, giving a diplomatic assessment of one of his contemporaries: 'An over-fat, flatulent, 62-year-old windbag, a master of inconsequence now passing himself off as a guru, passing off his vast limitations as pious virtues.' Which actor?

8. Which *Monty Python* mainstay wondered 'How difficult can it be to fly a plane? I mean, John Travolta learnt'?

9. Alec Baldwin gruffly described Disney and DreamWorks chief Jeffrey Katzenberg as 'the Eighth Dwarf: ____________.' Who?

10. Nick Nolte on Julia Roberts: 'She's not a nice person. Everybody knows that.' Julia Roberts on Nick Nolte: 'Completely disgusting.' Which was the less-than-smooth production on which the two crossed paths and swords?

11. Quoth Charlie Sheen: 'Rosie Perez's voice would drive me back to _________.' What?

12. What did the infamously gobby Vincent Gallo, in one of his more printable tirades, claim co-star Christina Ricci was on during the filming of 1998's *Buffalo 66*?

13. 'I think he was a fucking idiot.' Harrison Ford, giving a typically sunny account of which young co-star?

14. Which of Ford's co-stars reportedly called him an 'old fart'?

15. Which *Fast & Furious* roadman took to Instagram in 2016 to label unspecified co-stars 'chickenshit candyasses'?

BEAT THE DEVIL

Verbal Gymnastics: Cinema's longest monologues

1. 'Men, all this stuff you've heard about America not wanting to fight, wanting to stay out of the war, is a lot of horse dung. Americans traditionally love to fight. All real Americans love the sting of battle.' Which actor, in which film?

2. Which playwright was responsible for penning newsman Howard Beale's 'I'm mad as hell and I'm not going to take it anymore' rant, first broken into by Peter Finch in 1976's *Network*?

3. On which ship did *Jaws*' Captain Quint (Robert Shaw) serve during the Second World War, as revealed during a memorable mid-film anecdote?

4. Which common household item causes Faye Dunaway's Joan Crawford to enter into her most notorious tirade from 1981's *Mommie Dearest*?

5. In the framing scenes of 1984's *Amadeus*, F. Murray Abraham's Salieri admits to his confessor that he first heard what sounded like 'the voice of God' while listening to which particular Mozart composition?

6. How long does Kevin Costner's Jim Garrison spend summing up his case in court towards the end of 1991's 189-minute drama *JFK*? (A minute either side gets you the point.)

7. Which actress nails a choice rant against unfair beauty standards in 1996's *Beautiful Girls*, signing off with a cautionary, 'And you guys, as a gender, have got to get a grip, otherwise the future of the human race is in jeopardy'?

8. What's the precise shade of the sweater worn by Anne Hathaway's Andy that Meryl Streep's Miranda Priestly singles out for particular scorn in an acidic high point of 2006's *The Devil Wears Prada*?

9. What does Kristen Wiig's Annie wind up demolishing at the end of her baby-shower freakout in 2011's *Bridesmaids*?

10. What's the only line – other than 'Choose life' – from the 'Choose Life' speech in 1996's *Trainspotting* that recurs in the comparable speech in 2017's *T2 Trainspotting*?

What's My Line?: Who said it?
Grusinskaya: 'I want to be alone.'; Margo Channing: 'Fasten your seatbelts, it's going to be a bumpy night.'; President Merkin Muffley: 'Gentlemen, you can't fight in here. This is the War Room!'; Clemenza: 'Leave the gun. Take the cannoli.'; Lt. Col. Bill Kilgore: 'I love the smell of napalm in the morning.'; Matty Walker: 'You're not very bright, are you? I like that in a man.'; Truvy Jones: 'Smile! It increases your face value.'; Older Woman Customer: 'I'll have what she's having.'; Col. Nathan R. Jessep: 'You can't handle the truth!'; Blake: 'Always. Be. Closing.'; Jim Lovell: 'Houston, we have a problem.'; Dorothy Boyd: 'You had me at hello.'; Max Rothman: 'You're an awfully hard man to like, Hitler.'; Regina George: 'Stop trying to make "fetch" happen.'; Jack Twist: 'I wish I knew how to quit you.'

Entrances and Exits: Memorable first and last lines
1. b, 2. d, 3. c, 4. b, 5. d, 6. a, 7. c, 8. a, 9. c, 10. b, 11. c, 12. d, 13. c, 14. b, 15. a

PR Exercise: Poster taglines
1. *Stagecoach*, 2. *The Lady Eve*, 3. *The Third Man*, 4. Gutbuster, 5. SEXI, 6. Bonnie and Clyde, 7. Play golf, 8. Bye bye, 9. Well done, 10. *Gremlins 2: The New Batch*, 11. 65 million, 12. *Chicken Run*, 13. *Scary Movie 3*, 14. Spike through the head, 15. Die!

Bard Influence: Shakespeare on screen
1. b (*Macbeth* provided the raw material for 1957's *Throne of Blood*, *Hamlet* 1960's *The Bad Sleep Well*, and *Lear* 1985's *Ran*), 2. c, 3. d, 4. a, 5. b, 6. d, 7. d, 8. b, 9. c, 10. d, 11. a, 12. b, 13. d, 14. c, 15. c

Let's Get Critical: The best and worst reviews
1. a, 2. a, 3. c, 4. d, 5. d, 6. b, 7. c, 8. b, 9. a, 10. d, 11. b, 12. d, 13. a, 14. c, 15. b

King's Game: The films of Stephen King
1. b (in 1976), 2. c, 3. c (Keith Gordon – *A Midnight Clear*, *Mother Night* – and John Stockwell – *Blue Crush*, *Kickboxer: Vengeance*), 4. a, 5. c, 6. a, 7. c (and he 'really didn't know what [he] was doing'), 8. b, 9. a, 10. c (the film veered from King's story so completely that he successfully sued to have his credit removed), 11. b, 12. d (in a flashback as Wil Wheaton's [dead] older brother), 13. b, 14. c, 15. a

Burn Hollywood Burn: Actorly disses
1. Mae West, 2. 'Tits', 3. Marilyn Monroe, 4. Liberace, 5. Walter Matthau (while filming 1969's *Hello, Dolly!*), 6. John Huston, 7. Michael Caine, 8. Graham Chapman, 9. Greedy, 10. *I Love Trouble*, 11. Heroin, 12. Cough syrup, 13. Shia LaBeouf, 14. Josh Hartnett, 15. Dwayne Johnson

Verbal Gymnastics: Cinema's longest monologues
1. George C. Scott in 1970's *Patton*, 2. Paddy Chayefsky, 3. USS *Indianapolis*, 4. A wire coathanger, 5. Serenade #10, 6. 31 minutes 34 seconds (so anywhere between 30 and 32 will do), 7. Rosie O'Donnell, 8. Cerulean, 9. A giant cookie, 10. 'Choose your future.'

ANSWERS

11

Pot
LUCKIER

Pot luck part two

SEARCH PARTY

IMDb keywords

The Internet Movie Database has a keyword option that breaks films down into easily searchable narrative elements. Which popular films might you find if you typed in the following?

1. Killing an animal, Searching for one's mother, Thumping, Sliding, Talking skunk

2. Advertising executive, United Nations, Biplane, Sex on a train, Mount Rushmore

3. Third Reich, Governess, Widower, Clothes out of curtains, Four-word title

4. Existential crisis, Scuba diving outfit, May–December romance, Wedding ceremony gone awry, Bus ride

5. Transgender protagonist, Accidental cannibalism, Singing, Dancing, Audience participation

6. Tough guy, Philadelphia, Sweat, Pet store, Lead character played by screenwriter

7. Alien contact, Christ allegory, Cardiopulmonary resuscitation, Full moon, Character name in title

8. Paranormal, Firehouse, Receptionist, Budweiser, Marshmallow

9. Flying, Male objectification, Kawasaki, Volleyball, Famous song

10. Christmas, Precocious child, Booby trap, Aftershave, Scene based on painting

11. Chocolate, Innocence, Telling someone to run, Disabled veteran, Shrimp boat

12. American woman, Reading a poem, British renaissance, Hiding in a closet, Rainstorm

13. Steel worker, Thatcherism, Lawn gnome, Reference to Tony Adams, Penis size

14. Two-word title, Africa, Loss of father, Hooton plan, Surprise after end credits

15. Based on a true story, Circus, Interracial love, Australian actor playing American character, Song

FESTIVE FUN

Movie Christmases

1. In which Los Angeles skyscraper does John McClane enjoy an eventful Christmas party in 1988's *Die Hard*?

2. Who plays the mob boss that sends hitmen Colin Farrell and Brendan Gleeson off to Belgium for one last magical Christmas in *In Bruges*?

3. There are only three simple rules: never feed Gremlins after midnight, never get them wet, and ...?

4. The characters Louis Winthorpe III and Billy Ray Valentine team up in which enduring Christmas classic?

5. Who does dowdy Chicago Transit Authority employee Sandra Bullock find herself falling for in 1995's *While You Were Sleeping*?

6. Some filmmakers just love Christmas. Who directed Xmas-set flicks *Kiss Kiss Bang Bang* and *Iron Man 3*, and also wrote the scripts for the Yule-centric *Lethal Weapon 2* and *The Long Kiss Goodnight*?

7. Eliot Loudermilk plots to murder Frank Cross with a shotgun in which super-jolly Eighties Charles Dickens update?

8. A cherubic kid sporting a t-shirt that bears the legend 'Shit Happens When You Party Naked' flips the camera his middle finger and cycles away. The last shot of which modern festive fave?

9. Which idyllic snowglobe hamlet does James Stewart's George Bailey call home in Frank Capra's 1946 tearjerker *It's a Wonderful Life*?

10. More Jimmy Stewart: 1940's *The Shop Around the Corner* – in which he and Margaret Sullavan fall in love behind the counter of a leather goods store – is set in which European city?

11. More geography: 2010's *Rare Exports: A Christmas Tale*, a gruesome reimagining of the Santa Claus legend, was an import from which northerly country?

12. Vince Vaughn, Paul Giamatti, Rachel Weisz, Elizabeth Banks, Ludacris, Frank Stallone, Stephen Baldwin and Jeffrey Dean Morgan ... Which Christmas comedy?

13. After being raised as Santa's biggest little helper, Will Ferrell journeys from the North Pole to New York in order to find his real father in 2003's *Elf*. Who plays said pater?

14. A modern Yuletide classic or a gaudy hellride through the depths of the 'uncanny valley'? Who directed a dead-eyed, motion-captured Tom Hanks in 2004 3D CGI flick *The Polar Express*?

15. By what name are Joe Pesci and Daniel Stern's hapless housebreaking duo known to the police in 1990's *Home Alone*?

BOX KICKER

The world's first Jean-Claude Van Damme wordsearch

Can you find the fifteen JCVD titles in the box below?

R	Y	H	Y	D	J	W	C	Q	Z	B	H	R	R	K
R	E	U	A	C	T	E	R	K	K	S	Z	E	E	I
I	R	V	V	R	E	S	I	Z	E	X	P	T	T	C
A	N	D	E	W	D	L	E	L	S	O	E	L	H	K
W	H	H	I	R	L	T	F	U	C	Y	Z	E	G	B
O	S	S	E	E	O	F	A	E	Q	F	K	W	I	O
L	B	Y	M	L	O	F	M	R	Y	E	F	S	F	X
Y	S	A	I	D	L	I	O	X	G	N	H	H	T	E
D	L	G	N	K	T	E	Y	C	Q	E	C	T	E	R
L	Q	U	C	Y	B	O	R	G	A	J	T	E	E	H
Y	O	F	F	O	K	C	O	N	K	N	X	L	R	W
P	D	S	D	B	L	O	O	D	S	P	O	R	T	U
Z	T	J	G	G	F	S	M	Z	B	F	F	M	S	K
B	P	Y	S	W	B	A	K	K	Y	F	Q	M	U	O
Y	S	W	H	G	R	N	B	B	G	D	O	V	I	D

A.W.O.L.
Bloodsport
Cyborg
Hard Target
In Hell
JCVD
Kickboxer
Kill 'Em All
Knock Off
Monaco Forever
Pound of Flesh
The Quest
Street Fighter
Swelter
Timecop

OUR KANSAS

The Wizard of Oz

1. Which popular comedian was originally lined up to play the title role in MGM's 1939 classic *The Wizard of Oz*?

A) Groucho Marx

B) Bob Hope

C) W.C. Fields

D) Charlie Chaplin

2. In early Technicolor tests, what colour did the Yellow Brick Road show up as?

A) Magenta

B) Green

C) Cyan

D) Tartan

3. What was notable about Dorothy's dog Toto's contract?

A) It required his pawprint as a signature

B) It stipulated he was allowed to relieve himself anywhere on set

C) He earned more than the Munchkin actors

D) It contained a clause that required all his food be prepared by his own personal chef

4. And what was remarkable about the Wizard's shabby dress coat, plucked from the racks of a second-hand store in LA?

A) 1,000 Australian dollars were found sewn into its lining

B) It had been made by Judy Garland's tailor father

C) It had previously been used in the 1914 adaptation *The Patchwork Girl of Oz*

D) It had once belonged to the book's author, L. Frank Baum

5. *The Wizard of Oz* was a famously tumultuous production. Which of these legendary directors was NOT at one point at the helm?

A) George Cukor

B) King Vidor

C) Val Windsor

D) Victor Fleming

6. Meinhardt Raabe, who played the Coroner of Munchkinland, also held which distinction?

A) He was eleventh in line to the throne of Sweden

B) He was the subject of Pablo Picasso's 'Portrait of M. Raabe'

C) He was reputedly the shortest licensed pilot in the US

D) He was the youngest recipient of the Purple Heart

7. Who was the somewhat unlikely director of the Wizard's belated 2013 prequel, *Oz the Great and Powerful*?

A) Eli Roth

B) Spike Lee

C) Rob Zombie

D) Sam Raimi

8. And who starred as Dorothy in the 1985 sequel, *Return to Oz*?

A) Fairuza Balk
B) Elizabeth Shue
C) Christina Applegate
D) Jennifer Connelly

9. In a 1991 interview, Buddy Ebsen – originally cast as the Tin Man, only to be replaced after health problems – revealed his costume almost severed which of his body parts?

A) Earlobes
B) Thumbs
C) Testicles
D) Kneecaps

10. Which ultimately iconic aspect of the film was very nearly cut out altogether by producer Mervyn LeRoy?

A) Toto
B) The Straw Man
C) The flying monkeys
D) The song 'Over the Rainbow'

11. Diana Ross is Dorothy and Michael Jackson is the Tin Man. But who plays the Wizard in 1978's modern-day, New York-set Oz reimagining, *The Wiz*?

A) James Earl Jones
B) Billy Dee Williams
C) Richard Pryor
D) Bill Cosby

12. According to many stoners, which classic album syncs up perfectly with the film's images?

A) *The Lamb Lies Down on Broadway* by Genesis
B) *Goodbye Yellow Brick Road* by Elton John
C) *Dark Side of the Moon* by Pink Floyd
D) *Tales of Topographic Oceans* by Yes

13. We all love *The Wizard of Oz*, don't we? Well, perhaps. But which of the following has NOT been said about the film down the years?

A) 'Any kid tall enough to reach up to a ticket window will be found at the *Tarzan* film down the street.'
B) 'Transported to a surreal landscape, a young girl kills the first person she meets and then teams up with three strangers to kill again.'
C) 'Her companions, the Scarecrow, the Tin Woodman and the Cowardly Lion, each seeks fulfilment of desire. Dorothy wishes only to return home. The plot is as thin as all that.'
D) 'Shrill, gaudy, mawkish, manipulative, horrific, silly and long – there's something for everyone in *The Wizard of Oz*!'

14. What does the title of the 1971 Turkish Oz adaptation *Ayşecik ve Sihirli Cüceler Rüyalar Ülkesinde* translate as?

A) *Sihirli and Her Dog Are Swallowed By a Backyard Typhoon*
B) *Little Ayse and the Magic Dwarfs in the Land of Dreams*
C) *A Cowardly Wizard Tricks His Defective Visitors*
D) *The Yellow Road is More Perilous Than the Viper's Fang*

15. Why was the song 'Ding Dong! The Witch Is Dead' dusted off in 2013?

A) To celebrate the centenary of Judy Garland's birth
B) To mark the death of former British prime minister Margaret Thatcher
C) It was a chart-topper across much of Eastern Europe for speed-metal band Impaled Cradle
D) It was the chant repeated by members of the Blue Harvest cult that invaded a meeting of the Russian Federal Assembly

MONEY SPINNERS

Art versus commerce

In November 2017, Leonardo da Vinci's painting *Salvator Mundi* was bought for $450m, setting a world record for any work of art sold at auction. Below are fifteen of the most profitable films at the global box office. Your task is to evaluate whether the film in question took more or less money during its theatrical lifetime than the Da Vinci painting.

1. *Avatar* (2009)

2. *Batman* (1989)

3. *The Exorcist* (1973)

4. *Ghost* (1990)

5. *Gone with the Wind* (1939)

6. *Independence Day* (1996)

7. *Jaws* (1975)

8. *Minions* (2015)

9. *The Passion of the Christ* (2004)

10. *Pretty Woman* (1990)

11. *Suicide Squad* (2016)

12. *Teenage Mutant Ninja Turtles* (2014)

13. *Terminator 2: Judgment Day* (1991)

14. *Thor* (2011)

15. *Wolf Warrior 2* (2017)

MONSTER MASH

Movie ghouls and ghosts

1. What is Kurt Russell doing when we first meet him in 1982 John Carpenter chiller *The Thing*?

A) Rollerskating

B) Watching the 1951 film *The Thing From Another World* on VHS

C) Playing computer chess

D) Shampooing a dog

2. Whichever way you slice it, 1988's *Beetlejuice* is a fairly odd release for a major studio – but the proposed sequel was to have been even weirder. What was the title of the script Tim Burton commissioned from playwright Jonathan Gems?

A) *Biblejuice*

B) *Space Station Beetlejuice*

C) *Beetlejuice and the Undersea Kingdom*

D) *Beetlejuice Goes Hawaiian*

3. Jeff Goldblum's most famous role might be the over-eager hipster scientist Seth Brundle in the 1986 body-horror classic *The Fly*. But who played the telepod-crazy boffin in the original 1958 version?

A) Peter Lorre

B) Vincent Price

C) Bela Lugosi

D) Leslie Nielsen

4. 1998's Japanese horror *Ring* and its 2002 Hollywood remake *The Ring* (starring Naomi Watts) both revolve around which haunted piece of outdated household kit?

A) A VHS cassette

B) A George Foreman Grill

C) An LP

D) An answering machine

5. And in the spirit of everyday items having a life of their own, complete the title of MGM's 1970 live-action/animated oddity *The Phantom_____*.

A) *Fire Hydrant*

B) *See-Saw*

C) *Tollbooth*

D) *Goalpost*

6. Which of the following is NOT the title of a Godzilla movie produced by Japan's Toho Studios?

A) *Ebirah, Horror of the Deep*

B) *Mothra: Manhattan Overlord*

C) *Destroy All Monsters*

D) *Terror of Mechagodzilla*

7. In which New York location does the demon Zuul set up shop in 1984's *Ghostbusters*?

A) Yankee Stadium

B) Under the ice rink in Central Park

C) Inside Sigourney Weaver's refrigerator

D) In a Korean bodega on Union Square

8. The town of Perfection, Nevada, was besieged by giant mutations of what kind of creature in 1990's *Tremors*?

A) Termites

B) Beetles

C) Rattlesnakes

D) Worms

9. Just before he hit the big time with the *Lord of the Rings* franchise, Peter Jackson directed Michael J. Fox in which 1996 horror-comedy?

A) *The Relic*

B) *The Craft*

C) *The Faculty*

D) *The Frighteners*

10. And what was the name of Sauron's crib in Jackson's *Lord of the Rings* films?

A) Barad-dûr

B) Amon Hen

C) Minas Morgul

D) Isengard

11. What was the name of the British studio that produced such lurid shockers as *To the Devil a Daughter*, *Blood from the Mummy's Tomb* and *Dracula Has Risen from the Grave* that starred the likes of Christopher Lee and Peter Cushing during the Sixties and Seventies?

A) Tower Bridge Studios

B) Blackfriars Productions

C) Hammer Films

D) Red Lion Studios

12. What was the hit song from the soundtrack of surprise 1990 Patrick Swayze/Demi Moore smash *Ghost*?

A) 'Take My Breath Away'

B) 'Wind Beneath My Wings'

C) 'I've Had the Time of My Life'

D) 'Unchained Melody'

13. What's the name of the real-life exorcists played by Patrick Wilson and Vera Farmiga in the *Conjuring* franchise?

A) The Crundales

B) The Warrens

C) The Timpsons

D) The Granvilles

14. Otherworldly Kaiju fight robotic Jaegers in which epic 2013 monster mash, directed by Guillermo del Toro?

A) *Atlantic Ridge*

B) *Battleship*

C) *Pacific Rim*

D) *Robot Jox*

15. Which actor spends 99.9% of his time peering through eye-holes cut out of a bedsheet in 2017's *A Ghost Story*?

A) Edward Norton

B) Tom Hardy

C) Casey Affleck

D) Michael Pitt

RITTER TAINMENT

Is it a John Ritter film?

Sometimes you just want to sit down with a film starring the reassuringly ordinary form of the late comic performer John Ritter. Of the fifteen titles listed opposite, ten are fully fledged Ritter-tainments, and five are not. Can you identify the films that would allow you to do the Ritt thing? Answer 'Ritt' or 'Wrong'.

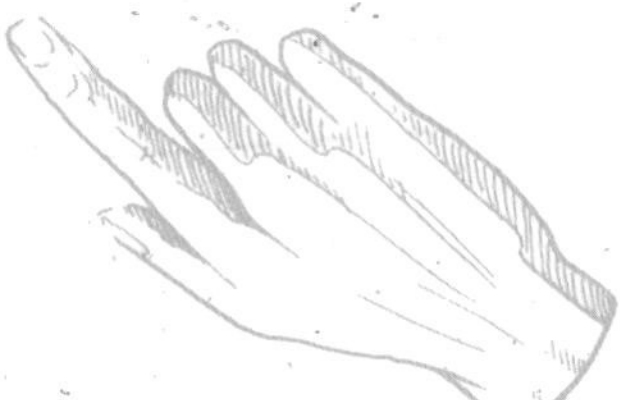

1. *Bride of Chucky* (1998)

2. *Don't Tell Mom the Babysitter's Dead* (1991)

3. *In Love with an Older Woman* (1982)

4. *I Woke Up Early the Day I Died* (1998)

5. *Nuncrackers* (2001)

6. *Problem Child* (1990)

7. *Problem Child 2* (1991)

8. *Problem Child 3: Junior in Love* (1995)

9. *Real Men* (1987)

10. *Der Ritter* (2014)

11. *Santa with Muscles* (1996)

12. *Sling Blade* (1996)

13. *S.O.B.* (1981)

14. *Stanley's Dinosaur Round-Up* (2006)

15. *Stay Tuned* (1992)

FADEOUTS

Memorable closing shots

Name the films from their closing moments

1. After a conversation with a young boy, a bloodied cowboy saddles up and rides away. The boy's calls, shouting the cowboy's name and imploring him to turn back, echo around the valley, but go unheeded.

2. A gangster runs down a Parisian street after being shot in the back. His lover chases after him; finding him lying in the road, the two have a brief, unhappy conversation before he passes. The woman turns to the camera, and repeats a familiar gesture.

3. A steam train pulls along the railroad and into a Western town under construction, just as a cowboy is riding out. A flame-haired woman emerges from her homestead to offer the construction workers water, and the camera pulls back, back, and away ...

4. A heavily aged old man wakes up in a lavishly appointed yet oddly sterile bedroom to find an unusual black object at the foot of his bed. As he reaches towards it, he is reborn, and the camera transcends the black object to reveal the outer reaches of the solar system.

5. A horse carrying a man and woman trots along a beach before pulling up in front of a fallen monument. Struck by something, the man dismounts, drops to his knees, and beats the sand with his fists. The camera pans back to reveal the scene in its entirety.

6. While the residents of a Western town scurry to extinguish a fire

at a church, a wounded man dies in a snowdrift. His former lover, meanwhile, drifts off into blissful oblivion in an opium den.

7. After a terse conversation, a suspect in a major crime shoos the lieutenant questioning him out of his tatty apartment. Just as the door is about to close, the suspect lets slip an incriminatory sneeze. The door opens once more, to reveal the lieutenant's face. Gotcha!

8. Two beardy, semi-frozen men huddle round the fiery remains of their former workplace, sipping from a bottle of whiskey. They make a pact to stay put and see what happens.

9. After driving through a nondescript suburban neighbourhood, the camera alights on one front driveway, where a dark-haired man emerges, clad in a white dressing gown, to pick up the morning paper. He eyes the camera ruefully, before a cutaway shows a former associate of the man firing a gun directly at the camera.

10. A man steps off the deck of his sailing boat and mounts a sky-blue staircase, stopping only to respond to a disembodied voice, then addresses a crowd of onlookers. The man disappears through a doorway; the onlookers wonder what else they might now watch.

11. A bloodied man and a dishevelled woman stand, hands intertwined, on a skyscraper's upper floors, looking on – to the strains of the Pixies' 'Where Is My Mind?' – as a series of detonations reduce several adjacent buildings to rubble.

12. For fully thirty seconds, a young deaf boy stands before the camera, signing in unsubtitled French about birds and fish.

13. Two young women sit in a drab hotel restaurant, where a waiter brings one of them a plate of assorted meats. The other asks the waiter for a glass and she pours herself some water. Cars can be heard passing by. The woman with the water looks helplessly towards the camera.

14. A haunted, grizzled figure sits at a breakfast table in a lovingly appointed Texan home. After his wife fixes him a cup of coffee, he proceeds to recount the details of the disturbing dream he had the previous night about a figure on horseback.

15. A smartly dressed man returns home, where he sets a small top spinning on the breakfast table. Spying his children in the garden, he heads outside to greet them; the top, meanwhile, continues to spin.

BEAT THE DEVIL

Toytown Teasers: Transformers, GoBots, Digimon and Pokémon

1. 1986's *The Transformers: The Movie* is most remembered, if at all, as Orson Welles's sorry final screen credit. But in which critically acclaimed late Nineties movie did one of its none-more-Eighties montage tracks, 'The Touch', recur as a major character's breakout single?

2. The GoBots quickly followed in their pricier robotic pals' clanking footsteps with the same year's feature-length *Battle of the Rock Lords*. Which acclaimed Shakespearean actor could be heard enunciating the words of Nuggit?

3. *Pokémon: The First Movie* briefly held the record of the highest opening weekend for an animated film in the US – only to be toppled two weeks later by what?

4. *Pokémon: The Movie 2000*, rather confusingly issued in 1999, featured a sequence that paid sincere and unironic homage to which then-recent Disney live-action feature?

5. Which now-acclaimed Japanese animator, best known for 2006's *The Girl Who Leapt Through Time*, got his big break helming 2000's *Digimon: The Movie*?

6. Which cast member paid the producers for the privilege of appearing in 2007's first *Transformers*?

7. How did 2009's *Transformers: Revenge of the Fallen* make it into the Guinness Book of World Records?

8. In 2011's *Transformers: Dark of the Moon*, Frances McDormand introduces Optimum Prime to a special celebrity walk-on. Who was the out-of-this-world guest star?

9. Michael Bay was physically threatened on set by a member of a Hong Kong extortion gang while filming 2014's *Age of Extinction*. Which unusual domestic item did the would-be heavy wield?

10. There were audience gasps when Pikachu spoke his first words in comprehensible English during a dream sequence in 2017's *Pokémon the Movie: I Choose You!* Complete his/her/its first sentence: 'It's because I always want ___________'

Search Party: IMDb keywords

1. *Bambi* (1942), 2. *North by Northwest* (1959), 3. The Sound of Music (1965), 4. *The Graduate* (1967), 5. *The Rocky Horror Picture Show* (1975), 6. *Rocky* (1976), 7. *E.T. The Extra-Terrestrial* (1982), 8. *Ghostbusters* (1984), 9. *Top Gun* (1986), 10. *Home Alone* (1990), 11. *Forrest Gump* (1994), 12. *Four Weddings & A Funeral* (1994), 13. *The Full Monty* (1997), 14. *Black Panther* (2018), 15. *The Greatest Showman* (2017)

Festive Fun: Movie Christmases

1. Nakatomi Tower/Plaza, 2. Ralph Fiennes, 3. Never expose them to bright light, 4. *Trading Places*, 5. Bill Pullman, 6. Shane Black, 7. *Scrooged*, 8. *Bad Santa*, 9. Bedford Falls, 10. Budapest, 11. Finland, 12. *Fred Claus*, 13. James Caan, 14. Robert Zemeckis, 15. The 'Wet Bandits'

Our Kansas: *The Wizard of Oz*

1. c (perhaps unwisely, he pulled out in order to devote himself to ventriloquism comedy *You Can't Cheat an Honest Man*), 2. b, 3. c, 4. d, 5. c, 6. c, 7. d, 8. a, 9. c, 10. d (he was concerned that the song 'slowed the picture down'), 11. c, 12. c, 13. d ([a] and [b] come from contemporary reviews by *The New Republic* and *Variety* respectively. [c] was a listing for the film on the Turner Classic Movies website), 14. b, 15. b

Money Spinners: Art versus commerce

1. More ($2,788m), 2. Less ($411m), 3. Less ($441m), 4. More ($505m), 5. Less ($400m), 6. More ($817m), 7. More ($470m), 8. More ($1,159m), 9. More ($611m), 10. More ($463m), 11. More ($746m), 12. More ($493m), 13. More ($520m), 14. Less ($449m), 15. More ($870m)

Monster Mash: Movie ghouls and ghosts

1. c, 2. d, 3. b, 4. a, 5. c, 6. b, 7. c, 8. d, 9. d, 10. a, 11. c, 12. d, 13. b, 14. c, 15. c

Rittertainment: Is it a John Ritter film?

1. Ritt, 2. Wrong, 3. Ritt, 4. Ritt, 5. Ritt, 6. Ritt, 7. Ritt, 8. Wrong, 9. Ritt, 10. Wrong, 11. Wrong, 12. Ritt, 13. Wrong, 14. Ritt, 15. Ritt

Fadeouts: Memorable closing shots

1. *Shane* (1953), 2. *À Bout de Souffle* (1960), 3. *Once Upon a Time in the West* (1968), 4. *2001: A Space Odyssey* (1968), 5. *Planet of the Apes* (1968), 6. *McCabe and Mrs. Miller* (1971), 7. *The Taking of Pelham 1-2-3* (1974), 8. *The Thing* (1982), 9. *Goodfellas* (1990), 10. *The Truman Show* (1998), 11. *Fight Club* (1999), 12. *Code Unknown* (2000), 13. *4 Months, 3 Weeks and 2 Days* (2007), 14. *No Country for Old Men* (2007), 15. *Inception* (2010)

Toytown Teasers: Transformers, GoBots, Digimon and Pokémon

1. *Boogie Nights*, 2. Roddy McDowall, 3. *Toy Story 2*, 4. *Jungle 2 Jungle*, 5. Mamoru Hosoda, 6. Tyrese Gibson, 7. With the Biggest On-Set Detonation, 8. Buzz Aldrin, 9. An air conditioning unit, 10. 'to be with you'

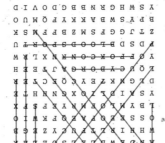

Boxkicker

R	Y	H	Y	D	J	W	C	Q	Z	B	H	R	R	K
R	E	U	A	C	T	E	R	K	K	S	Z	E	E	I
I	R	V	V	R	E	S	I	Z	E	X	P	T	T	C
A	N	D	E	W	D	L	E	L	S	Ø	E	L	H	K
W	H	H	I	R	L	T	F	U	C	Y	Z	E	G	B
O	S	S	E	E	O	F	A	E	Q	F	K	W	I	O
L	B	Y	M	L	Ø	F	M	R	Y	E	F	S	F	X
Y	S	A	I	D	L	I	O	X	G	N	H	H	T	E
D	L	G	N	K	T	E	Y	C	Q	E	C	T	E	R
L	Q	U	C	Y	B	O	R	G	A	J	T	E	E	H
Y	Ø	F	F	O	K	C	O	N	K	N	X	L	R	W
P	D	S	D	B	L	O	O	D	S	P	O	R	T	U
Z	T	J	G	G	F	S	M	Z	B	F	F	M	S	K
B	P	Y	S	W	B	A	K	K	Y	F	Q	M	U	O
Y	S	W	H	G	R	N	B	B	G	D	O	V	I	D

ANSWERS

12

Films in FOCUS

Seven rounds on notable titles

and one on Bula Quo!

ROAD TO MOROCCO

Casablanca

1. What was the title of the unproduced stage play upon which Michael Curtiz' 1942 classic *Casablanca* was based?

A) *A White House in Africa*

B) *You, Me and a Hill of Beans*

C) *Everybody Comes to Rick's*

D) *Never Give a Nazi an Even Break*

2. Other than the film, what links star Humphrey Bogart to the city of Casablanca?

A) He and hard-drinking director John Huston both once lived it up there for two weeks, having 'accidentally' arrived in Africa too early for the shoot of *The African Queen*

B) He entertained troops there during the war as a member of the United Service Organizations

C) He is buried there

D) He traced his ancestral name of Beauregard to a family of French slave owners who had once controlled the neighbouring port of Souira Kedima

3. Director-to-be Don Siegel (*Dirty Harry*) played a small hand in the film. What was it?

A) He helped edit the opening *Indiana Jones*-style map montage

B) He was Bogart's stunt double

C) He was the pilot (and owner) of the plane that carries Ingrid Bergman away in the final scene

D) He was the uncredited script editor who suggested they change the film's last line, which originally ran 'This would make the beginning of a beautiful movie ...'

4. When we first meet Humphrey Bogart's saloonkeeper Rick Blaine he's drowning his sorrows with a tipple that he once shared in Paris with his lost love Ilsa (Ingrid Bergman). What was their Parisian poison?

A) Absinthe

B) Brandy

C) Champagne

D) Lager

5. Director Michael Curtiz boasts an incredibly varied filmography. On which of the following classics did he NOT call the shots?

A) *The Adventures of Robin Hood*

B) *Mildred Pierce*

C) *King Creole*

D) *Gigi*

6. What is the name of the rival drinking den operated by Sydney Greenstreet's shady Signor Ferrari?

A) The Blue Cat

B) The Green Parrot

C) The Yellow Monkey

D) The Pink Flamingo

7. With which song do Rick's patrons drown out the singing of German troops in a memorable scene of resistance?

A) 'The Star-Spangled Banner'

B) 'Lili Marlene'

C) 'La Marseillaise'

D) 'Don't Let's Be Beastly to the Germans'

8. Conrad Veidt, who played the suavely menacing Major Strasser, was such a big star in his native Germany that he was on the same salary as Ingrid Bergman. He was best known back home for playing the villain of which film?

A) *Nosferatu*

B) *M*

C) *The Cabinet of Dr. Caligari*

D) *Metropolis*

9. Dooley Wilson, who played Sam the pianist, is famous for his rendition of 'As Time Goes By'. Which of the following songs did he NOT play in the film?

A) 'It Had to Be You'

B) 'Avalon'

C) 'Knock on Wood'

D) 'Take This Bottle'

10. Which item is symbolically binned by the French Captain Renault (Claude Rains) at the end of the film?

A) A beer stein

B) A bottle of Vichy water

C) A plate of bratwurst

D) A swastika-shaped birthday cake

11. What was the name of Herbert Ross's comic 1972 love letter to *Casablanca* that starred a Bogart-obsessed Woody Allen?

A) *Play It Again, Sam*

B) *A Kiss is Still a Kiss*

C) *The Fundamental Things Apply*

D) *The Same Old Story*

12. What gaffe is it hard to ignore when watching *Casablanca*?

A) Casablanca is actually in Mauritania, not Morocco

B) At one point Ingrid Bergman calls Rick 'Bogey'

C) The chessboard Rick is playing on has three kings on it

D) There were no German troops in Casablanca in 1941

13. Which Seventies TV star played Rick in the 1983 *Casablanca* TV series that was axed after three episodes?

A) Telly 'Kojak' Savalas

B) William 'T.J. Hooker' Shatner

C) Alan 'M*A*S*H' Alda

D) David 'Starsky & Hutch' Soul

14. What was the title of the lavish 1990 Sydney Pollack flop – starring Robert Redford and Lena Olin – that was a remake of Casablanca in all but name?

A) *Lisboa*

B) *Brasilia*

C) *Havana*

D) *Manila*

15. In 2008 Madonna was reportedly considering a *Casablanca* remake set in war-torn Iraq. La Ciccone would play Ilsa, naturally. But who did she have lined up to play Rick?

A) Robert Downey Jr.

B) Ryan Reynolds

C) Jason Statham

D) Ashton Kutcher

TEENAGE DREAM

Clueless

1. Which European designer was responsible for the yellow plaid outfit Cher (Alicia Silverstone) wears in the opening scenes of Amy Heckerling's 1995 teenpic?

2. Early on, we learn that Cher's mom died while undergoing a surgical procedure. Which one?

3. What's the significance of the name Bronson Alcott to the film's main characters?

4. For which member of the *Beverly Hills* 90210 cast is the 'hymenally challenged' Cher purportedly saving herself?

5. Complete the summation of Cher's big speech on American history: 'It does not say __________ on the Statue of Liberty.'

6. To which decade can the columns in Cher's 'classic' Beverly Hills home be dated?

7. The girls' slang term for a male hottie derives from which acting dynasty?

8. And what's the girls' painterly term for someone who looks good from a distance, but a mess close-up?

9. Which prominent Nineties actor completes Cher's plan for a perfect night out – 'go to the mall, have a calorie-fest, and see the new ______________'?

10. Cher's step-brother Josh (Paul Rudd) shares his full name with a prominent screen actor. Which Josh?

11. During their night in together, Cher and would-be squeeze Christian (Justin Walker) settle down to watch a tellingly queer double bill. Which two post-war studio classics does this double bill consist of?

12. Which none-more-Nineties band can be seen playing at the film's big party scene?

13. At what event can director Amy Heckerling be seen making an aggressive cameo?

14. The film entered the pop-cultural bloodstream very quickly. Which popular US sitcom's stars played Cher and co. in a tribute/spoof at the 1996 MTV Movie Awards?

15. It stuck around, too. Which singer's 2014 promo 'Fancy' paid homage to the film?

DOWN IN THE VALLEY

Magnolia

1. Upon being approached by P.T. Anderson to play the role of Earl Partridge, Hollywood veteran George C. Scott reportedly threw the script across the room, bellowing 'This is the worst fucking thing I've ever read. The _________ is terrible.' What?

A) Paper quality
B) Moral outlook
C) Soundtrack
D) Language

2. Croupier and weekend scuba diver Delmer Darion (Patton Oswalt) comes to an unusual end in the film's prologue. How does he meet his maker?

A) Swallowed by a crocodile
B) Brained by a bullfrog
C) Scooped from a lake and dropped on a forest fire
D) Decapitated by a shonky roulette wheel

3. What time does *What Do Kids Know?*, the quiz show hosted by Jimmy Gator (Philip Baker Hall), go out?

A) 12:30 PST
B) 3:30 PST
C) 5:30 EST
D) Midnight PST

4. What symbol appears on the set immediately behind Stanley (Jeremy Blackman), the show's most vulnerable contestant?

A) A Turkish sword
B) An open book
C) An angel's wings
D) A frog in a tutu

5. Complete the name of the program Tom Cruise's uber-alpha Frank T.J. Mackey runs for undersexed males – *Seduce &* _________?

A) *Conquer*
B) *Prosper*
C) *Cuddle*
D) *Destroy*

6. And what number would you need to call to pick up this program's brochure?

A) 1-877-TAME-HER
B) 1-877- GRAB-HER
C) 1-877-STALK-HER
D) 0898 50 50 50

7. There is a recurring reference displayed throughout the film – seen on a billboard, a sign in the quiz show's audience, and elsewhere. What does it say?

A) Clapton Is God
B) Exodus 8:2
C) Get Your Hair Cut
D) Boogie Nights

8. Which Nineties banger can be heard blasting from Quiz Kid Donnie Smith (William H. Macy)'s car as he ploughs into a convenience store window?

A) Des'ree's 'Life'

B) The Spin Doctors' 'Two Princes'

C) Strike's 'U Sure Do'

D) Gabrielle's 'Dreams'

9. Which singer – once romantically linked to Paul Thomas Anderson – created artwork seen on the walls of Claudia (Melora Walters)'s bedroom?

A) Aimee Mann

B) Edith Piaf

C) Fiona Apple

D) Dolly Parton

10. And which four-word phrase is revealed in the corner of one of these paintings as the frogs begin to fall from the sky?

A) But it did happen.

B) Satan Lives Inside Us.

C) And the Lord said.

D) Magnolia Makes No Sense.

11. Which member of the film's ensemble told PTA they'd once experienced a storm in Italy when rain, snow and – yes – frogs did indeed cascade down from the heavens?

A) Tom Cruise

B) Philip Baker Hall

C) John C. Reilly

D) Julianne Moore

12. The song 'One', as performed by Aimee Mann, plays over the film's opening credits. But who originally wrote the track?

A) Bill Clinton

B) Chris de Burgh

C) Harry Belafonte

D) Harry Nilsson

13. To whom did Cruise lose out in the Best Supporting Actor category at the 2000 Oscars?

A) Haley Joel Osment for *The Sixth Sense*

B) Michael Caine for *The Cider House Rules*

C) Jude Law for *The Talented Mr. Ripley*

D) Michael Clarke Duncan for *The Green Mile*

14. A major international director singled the film out for praise as 'proof of the strength of American cinema'. Which one?

A) Jean-Luc Godard

B) Mike Leigh

C) Ingmar Bergman

D) Georges Méliès

15. American filmmaker Kevin Smith was less positive about *Magnolia*, describing the experience of watching it as being like ...?

A) Break dancing on thumb tacks

B) A naked donkey ride to hell

C) Eating sand

D) Cinematic root canal

CHANGING FRAMES

A movie spot-the-difference

Can you find ten differences in these images from 1946's enduring heartwarmer *It's a Wonderful Life*?

LOST IN SPACE

2001: A Space Odyssey

1. What's the title of the Arthur C. Clarke short story that Stanley Kubrick's 1968 opus *2001: A Space Odyssey* is based on?

A) 'Encounter at Farpoint'

B) 'The Sentinel'

C) 'Galactic North'

D) 'Use of Weapons'

2. What was the last film Kubrick directed prior to 2001?

A) *Barry Lyndon*

B) *Spartacus*

C) *Dr. Strangelove*

D) *Lolita*

3. Perhaps the most famous of 2001's musical cues is 'Also Sprach Zarathustra'. Who composed the piece?

A) Richard Strauss

B) Wolfgang Amadeus Mozart

C) Pyotr Tchaikovsky

D) Richard Wagner

4. Gary Lockwood, who played jettisoned astronaut Frank Poole, can claim what other connection to the stars?

A) He was an unused standby astronaut on NASA's Mercury 7 program

B) He was a crew member on the *Star Trek* pilot

C) His father's sporting goods firm supplied the golf equipment that NASA used on the moon

D) His son David G. Lockwood was the first astronomer to discover a planet orbiting another sun

5. What's the *Shining*-related title of the 2012 documentary that explored – among many other curious theories – the possibility that Kubrick helped fake the 1969 moon landings?

A) *The Overlook*

B) *The Maze*

C) *Words of Wisdom*

D) *Room 237*

6. What do the initials of the *Discovery One* spaceship's all-controlling HAL 9000 onboard computer stand for?

A) Hargrave-Andrew Crystal Control Logic

B) Heuristically Programmed Algorithmic Computer

C) High-Order Machine-Assembly Language

D) Hypertext Aided Interfacial Learning Circuit

7. *2001* did not fare well with all critics of the day. Which of the following responses did the film NOT elicit upon release?

A) 'A monumentally unimaginative movie.'

B) 'Morally pretentious, intellectually obscure and inordinately long.'

C) 'What is this bullshit?'

D) 'If I wanted to be bored for hours with empty rhetoric about man's place in the universe, I'd go to church.'

8. Which song does HAL break into as astronaut Dave Bowman (Keir Dullea) attempts to shut him down?

A) 'Raindrops Keep Falling on My Head'

B) 'Puff, The Magic Dragon'

C) 'If I Had a Hammer'

D) 'Daisy Bell'

9. *2001*'s world premiere was held at the Uptown Theater in Washington, D.C. on 2 April 1968. What alteration did Kubrick make to the film before it was released eight days later.

A) He excised the role of Sergeant Fisher, played by Larry Hagman

B) He removed the jazz-theremin freak-out track that played over the 'Star Gate' sequence

C) He added *A Space Odyssey* to the title

D) He cut out 19 minutes of footage

10. A version of the monolith from *2001* features on the cover of the 1971 LP *Who's Next* by rambunctious rock royalty The Who. What disrespect is being heaped upon it?

A) The four of them appear to have just urinated on it

B) It is being used as the stumps in a game of freeform cricket

C) Drummer Keith Moon is defacing it with the words 'Zeppelin Suck'

D) They are throwing eggs at it

11. And what is 'Primate Homer's' reaction to the monolith in a 'Dawn of Man' daydream in *The Simpsons* episode 'Lisa's Pony'?

A) He takes a bite out of it

B) He takes it back to his cave and turns it into a pool table

C) He leans against it and takes a nap

D) He uses it as a surfboard

12. Launched in 2001 – and planned to remain in operation until 2025 – what is the name of the NASA mission that was dedicated to author Arthur C. Clarke?

A) *2001 Mars Odyssey*

B) *Mars Sentinel Orbiter*

C) *Clarke Discovery One*

D) *HAL 9000 Orbital Probe*

13. *2001*'s special effects supervisor Douglas Trumbull went on to direct which seminal Seventies sci-fi?

A) *Zardoz*

B) *Dark Star*

C) *Star Trek: The Motion Picture*

D) *Silent Running*

14. What's the name of 2001's long-awaited sequel, released in 1984?

A) *2002: The Year After*

B) *2010: The Year We Make Contact*

C) *2012: The Mayan Prophecy*

D) *2046: The Undiscovered Country*

15. Who pipped Kubrick to the 1969 Best Director Oscar?

A) Carol Reed for *Oliver!*

B) Franco Zeffirelli for *Romeo and Juliet*

C) Anthony Harvey for *The Lion in Winter*

D) Gillo Pontecorvo for *The Battle of Algiers*

WHO YA GONNA CALL?

Ghostbusters

1. Fraudulent sleazeball Peter Venkman would become Bill Murray's signature role, but who was his *Ghostbusters* character originally written for?

A) Richard Dreyfuss

B) Eddie Murphy

C) John Belushi

D) Billy Crystal

2. Sigourney Weaver's Dana Barrett is possessed by Zuul, the Gatekeeper. Rick Moranis's Louis Tully is possessed by Vinz Clortho, the Keymaster. Together they summon the shape-shifting God of Destruction known as ...?

A) Gozer the Gozerian

B) Locutus

C) Ivo Shandor

D) Furlo Roth

3. Which famous conductor and composer provided the film's score?

A) Andre Previn

B) Nelson Riddle

C) John Williams

D) Elmer Bernstein

4. *Ghostbusters* director Ivan Reitman had previously worked with Bill Murray and Harold Ramis in 1981 on which institutional comedy?

A) *Disorderlies*

B) *Police Academy*

C) *Stripes*

D) *Animal House*

5. Where do the Ghostbusters find their first ghost?

A) Trump Tower

B) The New York Public Library

C) The Chrysler Building

D) The American Museum of Natural History

6. Which of the following is an actual cartoon series that was produced in the wake of *Ghostbusters'* success?

A) *Turbo Ghostbusters*

B) *Ghostbusters Academy*

C) *Your Friendly Neighborhood Ghostbusters*

D) *The Real Ghostbusters*

7. What was the name of the villain of *Ghostbusters II*?

A) Morgo the Ligurian

B) Vigo the Carpathian

C) Drogo the Hessian

D) Sligo the Caledonian

8. What song soundtracks the Statue of Liberty's stroll through Manhattan in the *Ghostbusters II* finale?

A) 'She's a Lady' by Tom Jones

B) 'Good Golly, Miss Molly' by Little Richard

C) 'Walk Like an Egyptian' by the Bangles

D) '(Your Love Keeps Lifting Me) Higher and Higher' by Jackie Wilson

9. Who sued Ray Parker Jr for plagiarism over the film's number 1 hit song?

A) Huey Lewis

B) Thomas Dolby

C) Elton John

D) Gloria Estefan

10. Beaten only by the Taj Mahal and the *Millennium Falcon,* which famous Ghostbusters icon is – at 4,634 pieces – the third-largest Lego set commercially available?

A) The Stay Puft Marshmallow Man

B) The firehouse HQ

C) The rooftop battle set

D) The Ecto-1

11. Whenever the Ghostbusters encounter some new paranormal or supernatural phenomenon, what go-to encyclopedia do they consult?

A) *Theakston's Old Peculier*

B) *The Horrificata Illuminata*

C) *Byron's Ghost Atlas*

D) *Tobin's Spirit Guide*

12. What was the title of the 2008 Michel Gondry comedy in which Jack Black and Mos Def make – among other films – their own homemade version of *Ghostbusters*?

A) *Do Not Adjust Your Set*

B) *Be Kind Rewind*

C) *The Magnetic Theatre*

D) *Blockbusters*

13. Paul Feig's 2016 *Ghostbusters: Answer the Call* reboot was reportedly denied a release in which country, as it contravened rules that prohibit films that 'promote cults or superstition'?

A) China

B) Uganda

C) Saudi Arabia

D) Brazil

14. In what is – sadly – one of the better jokes in the 2016 film, what does Chris Hemsworth's Kevin reveal that his dog is called?

A) Fluffernutter

B) Canine O'Brien

C) Bark Wahlberg

D) Mike Hat

15. Paul Feig directed Ghostbusters Kristen Wiig and Melissa McCarthy to far greater success in which 2011 comedy?

A) *Bridesmaids*

B) *27 Dresses*

C) *The Heat*

D) *Trainwreck*

LA SHAKEDOWN

Short Cuts

1. From which writer's work were most of the strands of Robert Altman's 1993 tapestry drawn? Hint: he won a Pulitzer Prize for his 1983 volume of shorts, *Cathedral*.

2. Robert Altman cast Julianne Moore after seeing her in a stage version of which Chekhov classic?

3. In which comically inclined branch of the performing arts does Anne Archer's Claire Kane make her living?

4. Which actor plays unsmiling traffic cop Gene Shepard? Hint: he was also the star of Altman's 1992 Hollywood satire *The Player.*

5. Robert Downey Jr's Bill can be seen wearing a baseball cap emblazoned with the simple yet striking logo of another early Nineties movie by director Spike Lee that touched upon social division in LA (and elsewhere). Which one?

6. Young Casey (Zane Cassidy) is knocked down and hospitalized just hours before a birthday. Which birthday?

7. In a scene that takes place in a hospital, Casey's grandfather Paul (Jack Lemmon) performs a neat trick involving two shot glasses and which comestible?

8. Much of the jazz-oriented soundtrack is care of the Low Note Quintet. Which hellraising, oft-topless rock singer provides vocals for the track 'Evil California'?

9. Jennifer Jason Leigh prepared for her role as phone sex operator Lois by meeting real-life chatline employees. How many film directors did she apparently overhear while listening in to the women's work?

10. Which of the following cast members does not flash their naughtiest bit over the film's three-hour runtime – Julianne Moore, Frances McDormand, Madeleine Stowe or Huey Lewis?

11. The film's production designer was one Stephen Altman. What relation is he to director Robert?

12. Complete the name of the making-of documentary, showing Altman working closely with his ensemble, that received a theatrical and VHS release after the film became an arthouse talking point: *Luck, Trust & _________*? (Hint: think condiments.)

13. With which European film – the first part of a trilogy – did *Short Cuts* share the Venice Golden Lion in 1993?

14. One of the short stories adapted by Altman, 'So Much Water So Close to Home', received even fuller treatment in a 2006 Australian film called *Jindabyne*. Which Irish leading man played the starring role?

15. Altman confessed he'd accumulated another two films' worth of material in making *Short Cuts*. What was the title of the planned sequel, abandoned due to funding issues?

HOBBITS AND MORE

The Lord of the Rings movies

1. Ian McKellen ultimately made for the perfect Gandalf, but who was director Peter Jackson's first choice for the role?

A) Kelsey Grammer

B) Liam Neeson

C) Sean Connery

D) Pierce Brosnan

2. What role does Samwise Gamgee perform for Frodo Baggins before they are caught up in the quest to destroy the Ring of Power?

A) Live-in chum

B) Gardener

C) Gallerist

D) Cook

3. 'It is a strange fate that we should suffer so much fear and doubt over so small a thing ... such a little thing ...' Which character muses over the power of the Ring in one of the trilogy's most memorable lines?

A) Galadriel

B) Théoden

C) Arwen

D) Boromir

4. What's the name of the inn where the Hobbits first encounter Strider/Aragorn?

A) The Prancing Pony

B) The Good Mixer

C) The Green Dragon

D) The Lamb and Flag

5. What was the name of Aragorn's forebear who cut the One Ring from Sauron's hand in the epic prologue of *The Fellowship of the Ring*?

A) Berwhale

B) Isildur

C) Gil-galad

D) Titus Andromedon

6. Which big-time Tolkien fan expressed an interest in playing the part of Boromir that eventually went to Sean Bean?

A) John Travolta

B) Ben Affleck

C) Bruce Willis

D) Hugh Jackman

7. Dominic Monaghan, who played the Hobbit Meriadoc Brandybuck, went on to land a plum role in which hit TV show?

A) *Lost*

B) *Dexter*

C) *Heroes*

D) *Sons of Anarchy*

8. What is Shelob?

A) A spider

B) A sword

C) A drink

D) A language

9. What was notable about the casting of John Rhys-Davies as the dwarf Gimli?

A) His parents were both little people

B) He and Peter Jackson had come to blows on the set of 1996's *The Frighteners*

C) As a staunch Welsh nationalist, he speaks only rudimentary English

D) At 6 foot 1 inch, he was the tallest member of the Fellowship

10. By which name was Gollum known before the Ring ensnared him?

A) Precious

B) Dougal

C) Smeagol

D) Deagol

11. Who kills the fearsome Witch King – the leader of the Black Riders – at the Battle of Pelennor Fields in *The Return of The King*?

A) Faramir

B) Éowyn

C) Pippin

D) Legolas

12. Karl Urban, who played hunky helmed horsemaster Éomer, would go on to fill the helmet of which comic-book character?

A) Judge Dredd

B) Thanos

C) Magneto

D) G.I. Joe

13. What is the name of the Shire lass who Sam marries and sprogs out a couple of mini-Hobbits within one of *The Return of the King*'s many, many codas?

A) Lobelia

B) Rosie

C) Pam

D) Mary

14. What was director Peter Jackson's next film after the *Lord of the Rings* trilogy?

A) *The Lovely Bones*

B) *King Kong*

C) *Pacific Rim*

D) *The Hobbit: An Unexpected Journey*

15. Other than his magisterial performance as the wizard Saruman, what is Christopher Lee's claim to *Lord of the Rings*?

A) He once met author J.R.R. Tolkien

B) As an ordained minister, he presided over the marriage of Peter Jackson and *LotR* co-writer/producer Fran Walsh

C) His son Aldous wrote the classic 1980s home-computer text-adventure game The Hobbit

D) His single 'Middle-Earth Blues' topped the UK charts in 1967

BEAT THE DEVIL

Rockers' Revenge: *Bula Quo!*

1. On which Pacific island does this amiably duff 2013 vehicle for double-denimed rockers Status Quo take place?

2. What was the cheery name of the career-spanning, two-and-a-half-hour Quo doc that beat *Bula Quo!* into cinemas by six months?

3. Which US comedian was drafted in to narrate the opening newsreel, and thereafter play the nefarious mastermind of the island's deadly organ trafficking operation?

4. What is (somewhat inevitably) the first Quo song heard on the soundtrack?

5. Which Quo man is reported dead after being pushed off a waterfall in the film's opening minutes – frontman #1 Rick Parfitt, frontman #2 Francis Rossi, bassist John 'Rhino' Edwards, or keyboardist Andy Bown?

6. Original Quo bassist Alan Lancaster, who reunited with the band for their subsequent tour, cameos as which essential member of a hotel's staff?

7. At one point, the group's onscreen manager Simon (Craig Fairbrass) is seen battering a ne'er-do-well into submission with an item of footwear. Which?

8. The film's title song, 'Bula Bula Quo (Kua Ni Leqa)', represented a specific milestone for the band. What was it?

9. What does that subtitle translate into English as?

10. And at what number did the song eventually chart in the UK?

Road to Morocco: ***Casablanca***

1. c, 2. b, 3. a, 4. c, 5. d, 6. b, 7. c, 8. c, 9. d, 10. b, 11. a, 12. d (or at any other time during the Second World War), 13. d, 14. c, 15. d

Teenage Dream: ***Clueless***

1. Jean-Paul Gaultier, 2. Liposuction, 3. It's the name of the school they attend, 4. Luke Perry, 5. 'RSVP', 6. The 1970s (1972, to be precise), 7. Baldwin, 8. A Monet, 9. Christian Slater, 10. Josh Lucas, 11. *Some Like It Hot* and *Spartacus*, 12. The Mighty Mighty Bosstones, 13. A wedding, 14. *The Golden Girls*, 15. Iggy Azalea

Down in the Valley: ***Magnolia***

1. d, 2. c, 3. b, 4. c, 5. d, 6. a, 7. b, 8. d, 9. c, 10. a, 11. b, 12. d, 13. b, 14. c, 15. d

Lost in Space: ***2001: A Space Odyssey***

1. b, 2. c (in 1964), 3. a, 4. b, 5. d, 6. b, 7. d (critic Pauline Kael, celebrity intellectual Arthur Schlesinger Jr and Rock Hudson – upon walking out halfway through the film's premiere – respectively), 8. d (aka 'Bicycle Built for Two'), 9. d, 10. a, 11. c, 12. a, 13. d, 14. b, 15. a

Who Ya Gonna Call?: ***Ghostbusters***

1. c, 2. a, 3. d, 4. c, 5. b, 6. d, 7. b, 8. d, 9. a (for the song 'I Want a New Drug'), 10. b, 11. d, 12. b, 13. a (a failed attempt to find a loophole saw the film renamed *Super Power Dare Die Team*), 14. d, 15. a

LA Shakedown: ***Short Cuts***

1. Raymond Carver, 2. *Uncle Vanya*, 3. She's a clown, 4. Tim Robbins, 5. *Malcolm X*, 6. Eighth, 7. An egg, 8. Iggy Pop, 9. Two, 10. Madeleine Stowe (Stowe swapped roles with Moore at an early stage, so merely appeared topless), 11. Son, 12. Ketchup, 13. *Three Colours: Blue*, 14. Gabriel Byrne, 15. *More Short Cuts*

Hobbits and More: ***The Lord of the Rings*** **movies**

1. c, 2. b, 3. d, 4. a, 5. b, 6. c, 7. a, 8. a, 9. d, 10. c, 11. b, 12. a, 13. b, 14. b, 15. a

Rockers' Revenge: ***Bula Quo!***

1. Fiji, 2. Hello Quo!, 3. Jon Lovitz, 4. 'Rockin' All Over the World', 5. Rick Parfitt, 6. A porter, 7. A flip-flop, 8. It was their 100th single release, 9. 'No worries', 10. It didn't

---

Changing Frames

ANSWERS

13

Mad, bad and dangerous to KNOW

Cinematic curveballs and catastrophes

GOING FOR BROKE

The movies' most notorious flops

1. Michael Cimino's grand 1980 Western folly *Heaven's Gate* remains best known as the film that brought studio United Artists crashing down. But what, in the film, is Heaven's Gate?

A) A saloon
B) A ranch
C) A roller rink
D) A railway line

2. What was the title of Francis Ford Coppola's doomed 1982 bid to revive the movie musical?

A) *Fool for Love*
B) *Tender Mercies*
C) *One from the Heart*
D) *The Heart of Saturday Night*

3. Howard the Duck was quietly mothballed after the spectacular failure of his disastrous 1986 big-screen debut – but he made an ominous reappearance at the end of which recent blockbuster?

A) *Guardians of the Galaxy*
B) *The Lego Movie*
C) *Suicide Squad*
D) *Solo*

4. Who was hot-glued into a blond choirboy wig, handed a toga and told to look windswept and interesting in the title role of Oliver Stone's 2004 Macedonian misfire *Alexander*?

A) Ewan McGregor
B) Colin Farrell
C) Cillian Murphy
D) Tom Hardy

5. What was the full title of Andrew Dominik's flawed 2007 Jesse James retelling, which starred Brad Pitt, Sam Shepard and Casey Affleck?

A) *Have a Good Funeral My Friend … Jesse James Will Pay*
B) *Jesse James, Cole Younger and the Great Northfield, Minnesota Raid*
C) *The Assassination of Jesse James by the Coward Robert Ford*
D) *Jesse James Will Have His Just Revenge on the Culpepper Cattle Co.*

6. Director Paul Verhoeven's notorious NC-17-rated 1995 bomb *Showgirls* was, in part, intended to make a star of actress Elizabeth Berkley. From which squeaky-clean teen sitcom had she been plucked?

A) *Saved by the Bell*
B) *Hangin' with Mr. Cooper*
C) *Degrassi High*
D) *Salute Your Shorts*

7. 2000's *Battlefield Earth* was adapted from a book by which prominent 20th-century figure?

A) Leonard Nimoy
B) L. Ron Hubbard
C) Pelé
D) Buzz Aldrin

8. What distinction does *Life is Beautiful* Oscar winner Roberto Benigni's *Pinocchio* adaptation share with Adam Sandler's *The Ridiculous 6, Police Academy 4: Citizens on Patrol* and *Jaws 4: The Revenge*?

A) They are the only films to have swept the board at the Golden Raspberry Awards, winning twelve 'Razzies' apiece
B) They are the only four films in which Michael Caine's brother Rampton has acted
C) They are among the select few films to have a 0% rating on Rotten Tomatoes
D) They are all on Vladimir Putin's top ten US movies list, as stated on the Kremlin's website

9. Which wrong-headed effort sees Justin Timberlake miming along to the Killers' 'All These Things That I've Done' while drunkenly roaming through an amusement arcade?

A) *My Son, My Son, What Have Ye Done?*
B) *Darth Vader's Psychic Hotline*
C) *Southland Tales*
D) *Death Proof*

10. Who directed Robin Williams and Shelley Duvall in bizarro 1980 musical *Popeye*?

A) Dennis Hopper
B) François Truffaut
C) Robert Altman
D) Alan Parker

11. What role does Hugh Jackman NOT take on in Darren Aronofsky's triple-stranded 2006 tree-of-life curio *The Fountain*?

A) A First World War ambulance driver
B) A space traveller
C) A modern-day neuroscientist
D) A conquistador

12. After fifty years of trying, Disney finally manhandled John Carter (formerly *John Carter of Mars*, formerly *A Princess of Mars*) on to the screen in 2012. Who wrote the series of novels on which it was based?

A) William S. Burroughs
B) Edgar Rice Burroughs
C) Philip K. Dick
D) Arthur Conan Doyle

13. 2015's *Bombay Velvet*, Bollywood's biggest flop of recent years, was originally intended as the first film in a trilogy that would see directorial duties split between Anurag Kashyap and ...?

A) Sam Mendes
B) Danny Boyle
C) Ang Lee
D) Baz Luhrmann

14. The end credits of *The Postman*, Kevin Costner's 1997 love letter to himself, feature Kev and Amy Grant duetting on which song?

A) 'You're One in a Million'
B) 'A Post Officer and a Gentleman'
C) 'A Kindness that Can Never Be Repaid'
D) 'You Didn't Have to Be So Nice'

15. Who did the producers of 1999 Will Smith/Kevin Kline comedy Western *Wild Wild West* cast as the villain – a bewhiskered ex-Confederate mad scientist in a steam-powered wheelchair?

A) Steve Buscemi
B) Werner Herzog
C) Kenneth Branagh
D) John Waters

TALL TALES

Outlandish premises

1. Among other high/lowlights, John Waters' 1970 film *Multiple Maniacs* sees Divine being sexually assaulted by a grossly outsized item of sea life. Which creature?

2. In 1975's blaxploitation jawdropper *Soul Vengeance*, aka *Welcome Home Brother Charles*, Marlo Monte plays an avenging ex-con who slays his targets with a genetically modified body part. Which part?

3. What unlikely, generally chilly location gets converted into an impromptu brothel in 1982's jolly Ron Howard romp *Night Shift*?

4. Which Eighties horror introduced retching audiences to a sexual practice known as 'shunting'?

5. What was unusual about the cast of *Meet the Feebles*, Peter Jackson's X-rated pre-Tolkien provocation of 1989?

6. 2002's *Bubba Ho-Tep* saw Bruce Campbell's Elvis sprung from a Texan nursing home to see off a marauding mummy with a very much unassassinated JFK. Beyond his renewed existential status, what's atypical about this JFK?

7. A 2005 psychothriller took its title from a rodent whose chief narrative function was to block Charlotte Gainsbourg's kitchen sink. Which rodent?

8. The shut-in siblings of 2009's Greek headscratcher *Dogtooth* are instructed that the word 'telephone' refers to table salt and that the c-word means 'large lamp'. According to their dissembling parents, which crooner is their grandfather?

9. Which British comedian played the journalist investigating the making of a murky poverty-row offering (complete with Danny Dyer, Craig Fairbrass and Frank Harper cameos) in 2010's murkily meta poverty-row offering *Just for the Record*?

10. The same year's *Rubber*, an oddity about a runaway tyre that goes on a head-bursting killing spree, was directed by Quentin Dupieux, one of the very few French directors to have had a #1 hit in the UK pop charts. Under what alias?

11. Which glamorous American leading lady does Denis Lavant's Monsieur Merde kidnap and drag off to a dingy cave in 2012's one-of-a-kind imagining *Holy Motors*?

12. In 2014's *The Voices*, factory worker Ryan Reynolds is urged to kill by which of his pets?

13. How many prisoners does deranged warden Bill Boss (Dieter Laser) stitch together, anus-to-mouth, in 2015's inevitably grisly *The Human Centipede (Final Sequence)* – 100, 300, 500 or 1,000?

14. *Aaaaaaaah!*, the actor Steve Oram's directorial debut of 2015, imagines a world where humans live in the manner of which creature?

15. Michael St. Michaels, the magnificently named performer who made an impact as the oleaginous, willy-waggling psychopath of 2016's *The Greasy Strangler*, had previously made a living in which beauty specialty?

OPPOSITES ATTRACT

Unlikely screen pairings

1. Which Hollywood funnyman stars alongside John Wayne in the 1949 western *The Fighting Kentuckian*?

A) Buster Keaton

B) Jerry Lewis

C) Bob Hope

D) Oliver Hardy

2. In which film would you bump into both William Shatner and Judy Garland?

A) *The Haunting of Hill House*

B) *Le Mans*

C) *Judgment at Nuremberg*

D) *The Blackboard Jungle*

3. Marilyn Monroe was the showgirl in 1957's romance *The Prince and the Showgirl*. Which Knight of the Realm played the prince?

A) Sir Laurence Olivier

B) Sir Noël Coward

C) Sir Sidney Poitier

D) Sir Nigel Playfair

4. In which Tim Burton film would you find both Tom Jones and Natalie Portman?

A) *Sweeney Todd: The Demon Barber of Fleet Street*

B) *Mars Attacks!*

C) *Big Fish*

D) *Planet of the Apes*

5. Which film features the disparate talents of Joseph Gordon-Levitt, Cuba Gooding Jr, Helen Mirren and Mo'Nique?

A) *The Paperboy*

B) *Shadowboxer*

C) *The Salton Sea*

D) *Lucky Number Slevin*

6. Who was Prince's love interest in 1986's *Under the Cherry Moon*?

A) Ellen DeGeneres

B) Kate Winslet

C) Julianne Moore

D) Kristin Scott Thomas

7. What 1992 comedy tried to convince us that Dolly Parton and James Woods would make a sweet couple?

A) *Another Day in Paradise*

B) *Best Seller*

C) *Rhinestone*

D) *Straight Talk*

8. What 1990 comedy starred Marlon Brando, Matthew Broderick and a Komodo dragon?

A) *Men of Respect*

B) *The Island of Dr. Moreau*

C) *The Freshman*

D) *Night of the Iguana*

9. Dennis Rodman, Mickey Rourke, Jean-Claude Van Damme and Belloq from *Raiders of the Lost Ark* ... Which film?

A) *F.T.W.*

B) *Double Team*

C) *Monaco Forever*

D) *B*A*P*S*

10. In which film does Samuel L. Jackson's Gang Member No. 2 rub shoulders with James Cagney's Commissioner Rhinelander Waldo?

A) *Ragtime*

B) *Nashville*

C) *Serpico*

D) *New York, New York*

11. Which unlikely candidate is pitching woo to Jennifer Lopez in 2002's *Maid in Manhattan*?

A) Gary Sinise

B) Philip Seymour Hoffman

C) Gary Oldman

D) Ralph Fiennes

12. According to her autobiography, what was Dame Judi Dench's experience of 2004 Vin Diesel sci-fi actioner *The Chronicles of Riddick*?

A) 'Worst. Catering. Ever.'

B) 'I didn't really understand what was going on.'

C) 'I thought it was all a complete load of hogwash.'

D) 'For the entirety of the shoot Vin seemed to be of the mistaken belief that my name was Jodie.'

13. In which film would you find Clint Eastwood, Jim Carrey and Slash from Guns N' Roses?

A) *Pink Cadillac*

B) *Casper*

C) *The Dead Pool*

D) *In the Line of Fire*

14. Which of the following has NOT starred opposite Steven Seagal at one time or another?

A) Billy Bob Thornton

B) John C. Reilly

C) Michael Caine

D) Kurt Russell

15. John Cleese, Arnold Schwarzenegger, Steve Coogan, Macy Gray, Owen Wilson, Kathy Bates and Jackie Chan all star in ...?

A) *Around the World in 80 Days*

B) *Rat Race*

C) *EuroTrip*

D) *Muppets From Space*

TABLOID FODDER

Scandals and outrages

1. Which of the following is the evocative name attached to the blue movie Joan Crawford allegedly made before becoming a major Hollywood star – *Night Manoeuvres, Confessions of a Seductress, Velvet Lips or A Sailor's Return*?

2. Up-and-coming starlet Peg Entwistle earned the posthumous sobriquet the Hollywood Sign Girl after throwing herself to her death from the LA landmark. From which of the sign's letters did she take her fatal plunge?

3. How many cigarettes was Judy Garland smoking per day at the height of MGM's attempts to make her lose weight? (Hint: it falls between one and one hundred.)

4. Which Golden Age star's daughter knifed her mother's abusive mobster boyfriend in 1958 in what the coroner ruled as a justifiable homicide?

5. Womanizers John Huston and Errol Flynn came to blows over which *Gone with the Wind* actress?

6. Which gossipy 1959 tome, edited by avant-garde filmmaker Kenneth Anger, was described by the *New York Times* as 'a book without one single redeeming merit'?

7. Sly Stallone had Richard Gere fired from the set of 1974's *The Lords of Flatbush* for dripping a condiment on his trousers. Which one?

8. Rob Lowe's once-infamous sex tape of 1988 was recorded in a hotel room during which political event?

9. Robert Blake, found liable for the wrongful death of second wife Bonnie Lee Bakley in 2005, has a now doubly unnerving cameo in which David Lynch movie?

10. Which Angel wound up punching Bill Murray on the set of 2000's *Charlie's Angels* after the actor reportedly made a disparaging remark about her talents?

11. In 2004, a leaked video showed a furious David O. Russell going toe to toe with which incandescent performer on the set of that year's *I Heart Huckabees*?

12. Which offhand term did Mel Gibson use to address a female police officer after he was arrested for driving under the influence in July 2006?

13. Leaked audio from the set of 2009's *Terminator: Salvation* revealed Christian Bale quite spectacularly losing his rag with a crew member who'd broken his concentration. What kind of crew member?

14. Anthony Rapp, who prompted Kevin Spacey to issue his October 2017 apology after he accused the actor of inappropriate sexual behaviour at a party several decades before, starred in which movie musical adaptation of 2005?

15. Complete the name of the online tool, launched in 2017, which allows concerned viewers to check whether a film features any actors accused of sexual impropriety: Rotten _________?

FASCIST GROOVE THANG

Screen Nazis

1. Which high-ranking German general did director Erich von Stroheim embody in Billy Wilder's 1943 *Five Graves to Cairo*?

2. In the same year's animated short *The Commando*, a popular cartoon character gives Hitler what for with a mallet. Which character?

3. Another exiled director-turned-actor, Otto Preminger, promised he would give Wilder a special present if ever he messed up his lines while playing the prison-camp commandant in 1953's *Stalag 17*. Wilder ended up receiving jar upon jar of which delicacy?

4. What's the medical specialism of Laurence Olivier's fugitive Nazi Dr Christian Szell in 1976's *Marathon Man*?

5. Which generally upstanding leading man turned up as no-good Josef Mengele in 1978's *The Boys from Brazil*?

6. Christoph Waltz, who won an Oscar for Best Supporting Actor for his role as SS-Standartenführer Hans Landa in *Inglourious Basterds*, is pictured on a postage stamp issued by which country?

7. Which of the following actors has not yet portrayed Hitler on screen – Anthony Hopkins, Jürgen Prochnow, Armin Mueller-Stahl or Robert Carlyle?

8. Which early Noughties comedy takes an unexpected diversion through the Klaus Barbie Museum, a turn that results in Jon Lovitz taking the wheel of Hitler's staff car?

9. The 2002 documentary *Blind Spot* comprised of an extended interview with erstwhile Hitler employee Traudl Junge. Which role did Junge fill within the Hitler household?

10. Bruno Ganz, the much-memed Hitler of 2004's *Downfall*, isn't in fact German. What nationality is he?

11. Which Nazi-bashing studio blockbuster of 2004 made the claim Hitler lived on until 1958?

12. Which 1981 blockbuster features a sadistic and scarred Gestapo agent, played by Ronald Lacey, whose face is memorably melted off his skull in the film's climactic scene?

13. 2008's *Valkyrie* saw which action man heading up a plot to kill Hitler?

14. 2016's Berlin Olympics drama *Race* featured in passing an unusually saucy Leni Riefenstahl, played by which *Game of Thrones* performer?

15. Which of the following is not a dramatization of the attempted assassination of Reinhard Heydrich – *Hangmen Also Die!*, *Where Eagles Dare*, *Operation Daybreak* or *The Man with the Iron Heart*?

HEAVEN AND HELL

Memorable screen divinities – and devils

1. Morgan Freeman played Himself in the 2003 Jim Carrey comedy *Bruce Almighty* and its Carrey-free 2007 sequel *Evan Almighty*. Who played Evan?

A) Ben Stiller

B) Will Ferrell

C) Paul Rudd

D) Steve Carell

2. Always read the small print! Who played an especially pernickety Devil in *Bedazzled*, Harold Ramis's comic 2000 update of the Faust legend?

A) Uma Thurman

B) Demi Moore

C) Cameron Diaz

D) Elizabeth Hurley

3. Based on real events, the 2016 comedy *Army of One* sees the Almighty visit Nic Cage's unemployed Colorado handyman and send him on a lone mission to capture Osama bin Laden. Who plays God? (Note: this is a real film that actually exists.)

A) Ice-T

B) Hulk Hogan

C) Russell Brand

D) Kim Kardashian

4. Arnold Schwarzenegger attempts to stop the satanic Gabriel Byrne from siring the Antichrist in 1999 shocker *End of Days*. What subtly religious name does Arnie's character labour under?

A) Armageddon T. Zebedee

B) Jacob Methuselah

C) Jericho Cane

D) Saul Lazarus

5. 'What does God need with a starship?' Veteran character actor George Murdock played a God who is stranded on a distant planet in which sci-fi film?

A) *Event Horizon*

B) *Star Trek V: The Final Frontier*

C) *Saturn 3*

D) *Flight of the Navigator*

6. Which rock god played Old Nick opposite Jack Black and Kyle Glass in the 2006 comedy-musical *Tenacious D in The Pick of Destiny*?

A) Bono

B) Dave Grohl

C) Jack White

D) Axl Rose

7. Which singer played a mute, genderless God in Kevin Smith's 1999 comedy *Dogma*?

A) Billy Corgan

B) Tori Amos

C) David Bowie

D) Alanis Morissette

8. It had to happen eventually. Al Pacino finally chewed up the scenery as the Prince of Darkness in 1997 legal thriller *The Devil's Advocate*. Who plays said advocate?

A) Keanu Reeves

B) Charlize Theron

C) John Cusack

D) Edward Norton

9. The Lord (voiced by Graham Chapman) sends the Knights of the Round Table off on their quest in 1975's *Monty Python and the Holy Grail* only after rebuking King Arthur (also Graham Chapman) for what?

A) Smelling of elderberries

B) Not having brought him a gift

C) Grovelling

D) His haircut

10. Robert De Niro makes for a mighty frightening Mephistopheles in Alan Parker's 1987 chiller *Angel Heart*. What is his character's earthly pseudonym?

A) John Milton

B) Louis Cyphre

C) Daryl van Horne

D) Leland Gaunt

11. Who provides the voice of God for DreamWorks' 1998 animated film *Prince of Egypt*?

A) Glenn Close

B) Crispin Glover

C) Val Kilmer

D) Harrison Ford

12. Dustin Hoffman's insidious Devil torments Milla Jovovich's dreams in Luc Besson's 1999 film *The Messenger*. Who is the film's subject?

A) Elizabeth I

B) Eva Braun

C) Cleopatra

D) Joan of Arc

13. The voice of God inspires Rainn Wilson to become disastrously underpowered superhero the Crimson Bolt in 2010's blackest comedy, *Super*. Who voices this particularly reckless deity?

A) Nick Cave

B) Rob Zombie

C) Tom Waits

D) Marilyn Manson

14. In which film does Harvey Keitel play the Infernal One?

A) *Holy Smoke!*

B) *From Dusk till Dawn*

C) *Little Nicky*

D) *The Last Temptation of Christ*

15. How is God depicted in Cecil B. DeMille's 1956 epic *The Ten Commandments*?

A) As a lamb

B) As a shaft of sunlight

C) As a burning bush

D) As a dove

NO MARKS

The IMDb's lowest-rated films

1. Who has the distinction of having starred in two of the Internet Movie Database's ten worst-rated films of all time?

A) 50 Cent
B) Paris Hilton
C) Nicolas Cage
D) Jennifer Lopez

2. Tommy Wiseau's 2003 howler *The Room* – often referred to as the worst film ever made – is halfway down the bottom 100. Which star plays Tommy in *The Disaster Artist*, an adaptation of a book that charts the film's making?

A) Shia LaBeouf
B) Jared Leto
C) James Franco
D) Sean Penn

3. Who plays struggling comedian Schecky Moskowitz in 1989 cruise-ship comedy *Going Overboard*?

A) Adam Sandler
B) Chris Rock
C) Dave Chappelle
D) Rob Schneider

4. Which of these respected thespians does NOT have a film in the bottom 100?

A) Richard Burton
B) Jeremy Irons
C) Benedict Cumberbatch
D) Halle Berry

5. Which TV sitcom luminary starred opposite a baseball-playing chimp in 1996's *Ed*?

A) Julia Louis-Dreyfus
B) Ted Danson
C) Matt LeBlanc
D) Ray Romano

6. Which of the following well-regarded films does NOT have a sequel nestling in the bottom 100?

A) *Caddyshack*
B) *Donnie Darko*
C) *RoboCop*
D) *The Usual Suspects*

7. What did Michael Caine, star of 1987's *Jaws: The Revenge*, say about the film years later?

A) 'When my kids get out of line, they're sent to their rooms and forced to watch it. I've never had too much trouble out of them.'
B) 'I've never seen it, but by all accounts it's terrible. However, I have seen the house that it built, and it's terrific!'

C) 'When the worst job you've ever had involves sitting on a boat off the coast of Antigua drinking pina coladas all day, you have to just grin and bear it.'

D) 'I'd give it all back – the knighthood, the Oscars – to get that one chalked off.'

8. What was the name of the 2009 documentary that caught up with the cast and crew of 1990's *Troll 2*?

A) *The Butcher's Bill*

B) *Burden of Dreams*

C) *Best Worst Movie*

D) *Back to the Bridge*

9. What was the name of the Man of Steel's nemesis in *Superman IV: The Quest for Peace*?

A) Negatron

B) Doctor Chaos

C) The Atomic Skull

D) Nuclear Man

10. Guy Ritchie directed his then-wife Madonna in which 2002 flop?

A) *The Next Best Thing*

B) *Body of Evidence*

C) *Swept Away*

D) *Filth and Wisdom*

11. Which of the following is NOT one of the Friedberg/Seltzer movie spoofs that fill out the lower reaches of the IMDb?

A) *Epic Movie*

B) *Date Movie*

C) *Gangster Movie*

D) *Disaster Movie*

12. What 1993 video-game adaptation stars Bob Hoskins, Dennis Hopper and Lance Henriksen?

A) *Sonic the Hedgehog*

B) *Super Mario Bros.*

C) *Wing Commander*

D) *Doom*

13. What bottom 100 film begins with the weighty lines 'Greetings my friend. We are all interested in the future, for that is where you and I are going to spend the rest of our lives'?

A) *Battlefield Earth*

B) *Rollerball (2002)*

C) *Barb Wire*

D) *Plan 9 from Outer Space*

14. Which of these musicians' vanity projects does NOT crud up the bottom 100?

A) *Crossroads* starring Britney Spears

B) *Glitter* starring Mariah Carey

C) *Who's Your Caddy?* starring Big Boi from OutKast

D) *Hip-Hop o'Clock* starring Flavor Flav from Public Enemy

15. First it was a bus, then it was a boat. What's the title of the 1997 *Speed* sequel that starred Sandra Bullock and Jason Patric?

A) *Speed 2: Neptune's Candy*

B) *Speed 2: Cruise Control*

C) *Speed 2: Reverse Engines*

D) *Speed 2: Silent Running*

BEAT THE DEVIL

Avant-Gardians: Experimental film

1. The rebellious schoolboys of Jean Vigo's dreamy 1933 short *Zéro de Conduite* were a major inspiration on which late Sixties British film?

2. Which writer-director of 1943's enduringly spooky *Meshes of the Afternoon* gave her name to a prize awarded by the American Film Institute for excellence in experimental cinema?

3. *Scorpio Rising*, Kenneth Anger's homoerotic biker reverie of 1963, would inspire (among many other things) an identically titled Adam Ant track of 1985. With which two words does that track rhyme the phrase 'leather jackets'?

4. Which leading US film critic can briefly be glimpsed amid the semi-obscured action of Michael Snow's 1967 structuralist landmark *Wavelength*?

5. Which experimental filmmaker's work includes 1967's *Bottoms*, 1969's *Rape* and 1971's not-what-you-think *Erection*?

6. Jonas Mekas' autobiographical 1969 work *Diaries, Notes and Sketches* goes by an alternative title in some contexts. What is it?

7. What happens to the photographs Hollis Frampton puts before the camera in 1971's *(nostalgia)*?

8. Which Belgian coastal town, revisited in the 2016 doc *Exprmntl*, became known as the Cannes of the avant-garde thanks to its experimental film festival?

9. One of the more memorable scenes from Jørgen Leth's 1982 film *66 Scenes from America* was an extended take showing Andy Warhol eating an item of fast food. What was it?

10. Patrick Keiller's 1994 essay *London* and its two sequels follow the perambulations of an unseen character, known by which common surname?

Going for Broke: The movies' most notorious flops
1. c, 2. c, 3. a, 4. b, 5. c, 6. a, 7. b, 8. c, 9. c, 10. c, 11. a, 12. b, 13. b, 14. d, 15. c

Tall Tales: Outlandish premises
1. A lobster, 2. Penis, 3. A morgue, 4. *Society*, 5. They were puppets, 6. He's black (and played by the great Ossie Davis), 7. Lemming, 8. Frank Sinatra, 9. Rik Mayall, 10. Mr Oizo (of 'Flat Beat' notoriety), 11. Eva Mendes, 12. His cat, 13. 500, 14. Apes, 15. Hairdressing

Opposites Attract: Unlikely screen pairings
1. d, 2. c, 3. a, 4. b, 5. b, 6. d, 7. d, 8. c, 9. b, 10. a, 11. d, 12. b, 13. c (Carrey also pops up in the role of 'Lounge Entertainer' in *Pink Cadillac*. Slash, however, sat that one out), 14. b, 15. a

Tabloid Fodder: Scandals and outrages
1. *Velvet Lips*, 2. H, 3. Eighty, 4. Lana Turner, 5. Olivia de Havilland, 6. *Hollywood Babylon*, 7. Mustard, 8. The Democratic National Convention, 9. *Lost Highway* (1997), 10. Lucy Liu, 11. Lily Tomlin, 12. 'Sugartits', 13. A lighting technician, 14. *Rent*, 15. Apples

Fascist Groove Thang: Screen Nazis
1. Rommel, 2. Daffy Duck, 3. Caviar, 4. Dentistry, 5. Gregory Peck, 6. Austria 7. Jürgen Prochnow, 8. *Rat Race* (2001), 9. His secretary, 10. Swiss, 11. *Hellboy*, 12. *Raiders of the Lost Ark*, 13. Tom Cruise, 14. Carice van Houten, 15. *Where Eagles Dare*

Heaven and Hell: Memorable screen divinities – and devils
1. d, 2. d, 3. c, 4. c, 5. b, 6. b, 7. d, 8. a, 9. c, 10. c, 10. b, 11. c, 12. d, 13. b, 14. c, 15. c

No Marks: The IMDb's lowest-rated films
1. b (*The Hottie & the Nottie* and *Pledge This!*), 2. c, 3. a, 4. c (*Exorcist II: The Heretic*, *Dungeons & Dragons* and *Catwoman* respectively), 5. c, 6. d, 7. b, 8. c, 9. d, 10. c, 11. c, 12. b, 13. d, 14. d, 15. b

Avant-Gardians: Experimental film
1. 1968's *If ...*, 2. Maya Deren, 3. 'Big packets', 4. Amy Taubin, 5. Yoko Ono, 6. *Walden*, 7. They burn up on a hot plate, 8. Knokke-le-Zoute, 9. A Burger King Whopper, 10. Robinson

ANSWERS

14

Franchise

FRENZY

A series of questions about series

GALAXY QUEST

On the *Star Wars* franchise

1. George Lucas was so certain 1977's *A New Hope* was going to be a flop that he skipped the film's premiere to go on holiday to Maui. With which fellow director did he pack his bags and abscond?

2. Which actor provides the voice of the murderous Darth Vader, played in Episodes IV through VI by Dave Prowse – the Bristol-born bodybuilder?

3. How much taller is actor Peter Mayhew (Chewbacca) than Kenny Baker (R2D2) – 2ft, 3ft, 4ft or 5ft?

4. John Williams's son Joseph was drafted in to write lyrics for the Ewoks' songs in 1983's *Return of the Jedi*. For which chart-topping band is Joseph the vocalist? (Hint: think Judy Garland.)

5. From which household item, most often found in bathrooms, was Qui-Gon Jinn (Liam Neeson)'s communicator in 1999's *The Phantom Menace* constructed?

6. Which A-lister-to-be played Queen Amidala (Natalie Portman)'s decoy in that same episode?

7. Complete the foulmouthed phrase Samuel L. Jackson had inscribed on Mace Windu's lightsaber: 'Bad __________'. What?

8. What vocal tic connects Ewan McGregor in *The Phantom Menace* with Laura Dern in 2017's *The Last Jedi*?

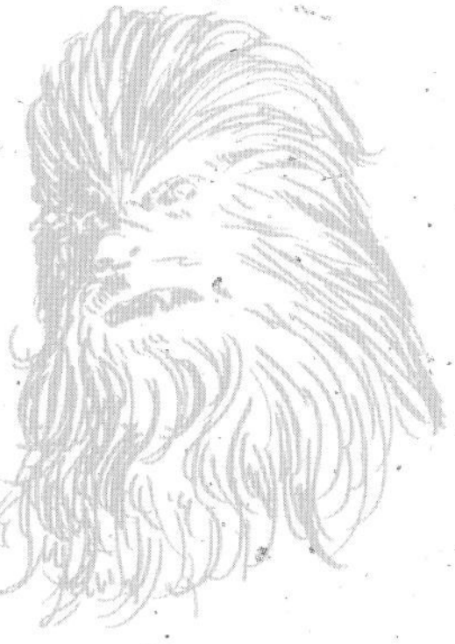

9. Which acclaimed playwright was brought in to polish the script for 2005's *Revenge of the Sith*?

10. And what was the generally unloved Jar Jar Binks' sole, apologetic line in that film?

11. Which specific limb did Harrison Ford break during filming for 2015's *The Force Awakens*?

12. In an age of online piracy, security has become a top Lucas film priority. Which recent *Star Wars* movie was shipped into cinemas under the title *Los Alamos*?

13. The Porgs in 2017's *The Last Jedi* were creations of necessity, the result of digital effects artists painting over creatures that kept finding their way into shot on the Skellig Island locations. Which creatures?

14. Which instalment's opening credit scroll begins with a single word – 'War!'

15. Which film did Lucas originally declare to be the weakest in the series, before walking his opinion back?

MARVELLOUS

Stan Lee's cameos

1. Stan Lee's first live-action Marvel cameo was as the jury foreman in 1989's *The Trial of the Incredible Hulk*. What was the green Goliath on trial for?

A) Tax evasion

B) Roughing up some well-connected hoodlums

C) Hospitalizing the Mayor of New York during a St Patrick's Day Parade freak-out

D) Flattening a tollbooth while being chased by a bee

2. Lee plays himself – as the head of Marvel Comics – in the deranged 1990 Eric Roberts vehicle *The Ambulance*. In which comic book adaptation would Roberts appear years later?

A) *The Death of Stalin*

B) *The Dark Knight*

C) *Ghost in the Shell*

D) *Blue Is the Warmest Colour*

3. What does Brodie (Jason Lee), the comic book-obsessed hero of director Kevin Smith's 1995's *Mallrats*, ask Lee?

A) If Tony Stark has a toilet built into his Iron Man suit

B) If superheroes go to 'normal heaven'

C) If The Thing's ... *thing* is also made of rock

D) If he can try on Lee's glasses

4. What do we find Lee doing during his cameo in 2000's *X-Men*?

A) Selling hot dogs

B) Shoplifting

C) Auditioning for the Blue Man Group

D) Busking

5. In 2003's *Daredevil*, our blind superhero (Ben Affleck) saves Lee after he steps into traffic while engrossed in which periodical?

A) *Unscientific American*

B) *Mustache Weekly*

C) *Braille World*

D) The *New York Post*

6. In the same year's *Hulk* (the Eric Bana one), Lee plays a security guard who is partnered up with ...?

A) Al Pacino

B) George Romero

C) Lou Ferrigno

D) Quentin Tarantino

7. 2007's *Spider-Man 3* saw Peter Parker (Tobey Maguire) bumping into Lee in which famous New York location?

A) Crazy Louie's European Art Kino on 42nd Street

B) Times Square

C) The crown of the Statue of Liberty

D) Sesame Street

8. For whom is Lee mistaken when walking the red carpet in 2008's *Iron Man*?

A) Dick Cheney

B) A vagrant

C) Ang Lee

D) Hugh Hefner

9. He also pops up in 2010's *Iron Man 2* (in which he is mistaken for Larry King). Which actors play the villains of that film?

A) Martin Freeman and Alan Alda

B) Sam Rockwell and Mickey Rourke

C) Jack Black and Sharon Stone

D) Brie Larson and James Woods

10. In 2011's *Captain America: The First Avenger*, Lee can be heard making a saucy remark about Captain America at a presentation ceremony. What is it?

A) 'You just gotta love eugenics ...'

B) 'What a beefcake!'

C) 'I thought he would be taller.'

D) 'Call me when he starts shaving.'

11. *The First Avenger* was the first Captain America film that Lee appeared in, but it wasn't the first that Marvel had produced. Which famous person's son starred in the less-than-super 1990 version?

A) Tina Turner

B) Colonel Sanders

C) J.D. Salinger

D) Grace Kelly

12. What is Lee seen reading on a bus amid the metaphysical trippiness of 2016's *Doctor Strange*? (Verdict: 'That is hilarious!')

A) Aldous Huxley's *The Doors of Perception*

B) Robert M. Pirsig's *Zen and the Art of Motorcycle Maintenance*

C) The Koran

D) Stephen Hawking's *A Brief History of Time*

13. In the same year's *Captain America: Civil War*, Lee plays a FedEx employee with a package to deliver to Tony Stark. How does he misread the esteemed recipient's name?

A) Toby Stork

B) Tony Stank

C) Teddy Shrek

D) Tory Spank

14. What does Lee deprive Chris Hemsworth's hulking Asgardian of in 2017's *Thor*: *Ragnarok*?

A) His wallet

B) His hammer

C) His interdimensional travel privileges

D) His hair

15. A member of which profession has Lee NOT played during the course of his cameo career?

A) A mailman

B) A librarian

C) A jockey

D) A disc-jockey

MORE MORE MORE

Unlikely sequels and spin-offs

1. Shortly before starring opposite Al Pacino in *Scarface*, which soon-to-be-A-lister followed in Olivia Newton-John's footsteps as the star of 1982's *Grease 2*?

2. Staying with music, which New York tough-guy wrote and directed 1983's *Staying Alive,* the belated sequel to *Saturday Night Fever*?

3. Who slips on the shades and (slightly larger) suit to play Dan Aykroyd's new partner in *Blues Brothers 2000*?

4. What was the title of the second entry in *The Fast and the Furious* franchise?

5. Steven Seagal vehicle *Under Siege* – arguably his one decent starring role – was basically *Die Hard* on an aircraft carrier. Its 1995 sequel *Under Siege 2: Dark Territory was Die Hard* on a ...?

6. Mila Kunis starred in the sequel to which 2000 film specializing in 'murders and acquisitions'?

7. In what year was 2017's *Blade Runner* sequel set? (It was in the title of the film, so you've got no excuse!)

8. What was the title of the 1990 sequel to *Chinatown*?

9. She won an Oscar for a different form of fighting, but before that she played *The Next Karate Kid* in the 1994 reboot/spin-off of the hit Eighties series. Who?

10. What was the subtitle to 1991's *The Naked Gun 2½*?

11. Who took over the role of Bruce Wayne's childhood friend/ladylove Rachel Dawes from Katie Holmes in 2008's *The Dark Knight*?

12. Hal Hartley's 1997 indie hit *Henry Fool* was a bittersweet character study. Its 2006 sequel *Fay Grim* was an international spy caper. Who starred in both as Fay?

13. Which French chart toppers provided the killer soundtrack to 2010's *Tron: Legacy*?

14. 2005's *Son of the Mask* was not the only film to top-line the offspring of one of Jim Carrey's movie characters. Which of his other famous roles spawned a son-centric spin-off?

15. In *The Godfather Part II* it is revealed that Corleone was the surname given to the young Vito when he arrived in America. It was originally Andolini. Who or what is 'Corleone'?

BACKSEAT DRIVERS

Supporting and guest stars in *The Fast & the Furious* franchise

Below you'll find fifteen facts alongside fifteen folks in the *F&F* family. Can you put a name to each one?

1. Danced in the promo for Janet Jackson's 1990 hit *Love Will Never Do (Without You)*
2. Won an Independent Spirit Award for playing a teen boxer in 2000's *Girlfight*
3. Made the US Olympic trials for taekwondo in 2000
4. Had a long-running beef with 50 Cent
5. Is the mother to two daughters, Esmeralda and Amada Lee
6. Is CEO of Disturbing Tha Peace Records
7. Is the son of a semi-legendary straight-to-video action star named Wings
8. Went on to star in the 2006 videogame adaptation *DOA: Dead or Alive*
9. Is scared of owls
10. Played one of Tim Allen's sons on sitcom *Home Improvement*
11. Married a Marvel hero in 2010
12. Counted the Atomic Legdrop among his signature moves
13. Took home a bronze medal for women's judo at the 2008 Beijing Olympics
14. Released the single 'Groundbreaking' in 2017
15. Ranked #12 in the world for platform diving in 1992

Zachery Ty Bryan
Dwayne 'The Rock' Johnson
Tony Jaa
Cole Hauser
Rick Yune
Devon Aoki
Ja Rule
Djimon Hounsou
Jason Statham
Elsa Pataky
Ludacris
Michelle Rodriguez
Eva Mendes
Tyrese Gibson
Ronda Rousey

DOUBLE-O HEAVEN

Arcane Bond facts

1. What links James Bond with Adolf Hitler?

A) They were both born in the Austrian spa town of Bad Homburg

B) Their choice of sidearm – the Walther PPK

C) Their shoes are/were made by the same Tuscan cobbler

D) Both remain on the official list of the Enemies of the Russian People

2. What was notable about the credit sequence for 1965's *Thunderball*?

A) Sean Connery's name was misspelled as 'Connerry'

B) It was the first in which Monty Norman's guitar-led 'James Bond Theme' is heard

C) It was the first to feature the gun-barrel sequence

D) It featured a female nipple – a first for a British film

3. Bond's grumpy gadget ace is known chiefly as Q. What does it stand for?

A) Quimbly

B) Quartermaster

C) Quality and Reliability Engineer

D) Queen's Armourer

4. What was the name of Bond author Ian Fleming's Jamaican estate?

A) Goldeneye

B) Blofeld

C) Skyfall

D) Pussy Galore

5. How might Roger Moore's admitted hoplophobia have hindered someone in Bond's line of work?

A) It's an allergy to alcohol

B) It's a fear of kissing

C) It's the chronic inability to keep a secret

D) It's a fear of firearms

6. What is the only Bond song to have made it to the top of the US charts?

A) 'Nobody Does it Better' by Carly Simon

B) 'Skyfall' by Adele

C) 'A View to a Kill' by Duran Duran

D) 'Live and Let Die' by Paul McCartney and Wings

7. Which of these screen tough guys has NOT appeared in a Bond movie?

A) Benicio del Toro

B) Michael Madsen

C) Ray Winstone

D) Charles Dance

8. And which of the following actors was NOT strongly considered for the role of James Bond at one point or another?

A) James Mason

B) Dominic West

C) Rob Lowe

D) Burt Reynolds

9. After being runner-up to Timothy Dalton for the role of Bond, who at least got a (temporary) licence to kill as rogue agent 006 in 1995's *GoldenEye*?

A) Clive Owen

B) Sam Neill

C) Liam Neeson

D) Sean Bean

10. As what does Madonna make a cameo in 2002's *Die Another Day*?

A) A nightclub singer

B) A fencing instructor

C) A librarian

D) A polo player

11. To what did Daniel Craig agree to waive his rights when signing the contract to become 007?

A) Skiing, parachuting, motorcycling and all other such Bondian activities

B) Using social media

C) Advertising products that do not appear in Bond films

D) Wearing a tuxedo in other films

12. On the plus side, which of the following perks did Craig secure?

A) He has been granted a diplomatic passport by the British government

B) An endless supply of Smirnoff vodka

C) The use of any Aston Martin car at any time – for life

D) His own four-storey penthouse in a skyscraper named after him in Abu Dhabi

13. Of what manly pre-Bond distinction can Sean Connery NOT boast?

A) He served in the Royal Navy

B) He placed third in the 1953 Mr Universe competition

C) He was a caber-tossing champion at the 1958 Highland Games

D) He was offered a contract to play for English football giants Manchester United

14. Sean Connery retired from the Bond franchise in 1971, but would make a lucrative return to the role in 1983 for an independently produced film that exists outside of the official 007 canon. What was it called?

A) *Twice Upon a Time*

B) *Against All Odds*

C) *Never Say Never Again*

D) *My Word is My Bond*

15. Finally, which 007 once said 'Bond is a brute! I've already put him behind me. Peace – that's the message now.'

A) Daniel Craig

B) Roger Moore

C) Sean Connery

D) George Lazenby

THE DOUBLE

Films that became TV series – and vice versa

1. Ed Harris plays the antagonist of TV's *Westworld*, but who played the implacable gun-slinging baddie in the 1973 film?

A) William Shatner
B) Yul Brynner
C) Charles Bronson
D) Lee Van Cleef

2. What show spawned the very first TV-to-feature-film adaptation?

A) *Dragnet*
B) *Captain Video and His Video Rangers*
C) *The Flintstones*
D) *The Honeymooners*

3. Netflix series *She's Gotta Have It* is based on which director's debut film?

A) Ava DuVernay
B) Spike Lee
C) Antoine Fuqua
D) Lee Daniels

4. TV to film to TV. Jonathan Harris played the cowardly Dr Smith in the TV show and Gary Oldman gave us a far darker take in the 1998 film. But who plays the character in the 2018 Netflix version of *Lost in Space*?

A) Jim Parsons
B) Parker Posey
C) Elizabeth Banks
D) Sebastian Stan

5. A record 105 million American viewers tuned in to see the very last episode of TV's *M*A*S*H* when it aired in 1980. Which of the following is the only broadcast to have attracted more viewers?

A) The Royal Marriage of Charles and Diana (1981)
B) The *Friends* finale (2004)
C) The moon landing (1969)
D) Super Bowl 50 (2016)

6. Tim Burton adapted which cobwebbed Sixties TV show into a 2012 film that starred Johnny Depp as a lovelorn vampire who escapes from the grave in order to save his distant family's fish canning business?

A) *13 Demon Street*
B) *Dark Shadows*
C) *Carnival of Souls*
D) *Sleepy Hollow*

7. Which of the following films did NOT get its own animated TV spin-off?

A) *Jurassic Park*
B) *Spaceballs*
C) *Rambo: First Blood Part II*
D) *Napoleon Dynamite*

8. And which of the following is NOT the title of a SpongeBob SquarePants spin-off movie?

A) *Atlantis SquarePantis*

B) *Truth or Square*

C) *SquidBob TentaclePants*

D) *Sponge Out of Water*

9. What's the name of the summer camp, introduced in 2001's *Wet Hot American Summer*, to which writer-director David Wain has returned for two Netflix series?

A) Lake Clambake

B) Especially for Youth

C) Camp Firewood

D) Beaver Falls

10. What was the title of Beavis and Butt-Head's 1996 big screen adventure?

A) *Beavis and Butt-Head Meet God*

B) *Beavis and Butt-Head Go to the Movies*

C) *Beavis and Butt-Head Do America*

D) *Beavis and Butt-Head: Foreign Exchange*

11. What's the nickname of the college football team in both the movie and TV adaptations of Buzz Bissinger's non-fiction bestseller *Friday Night Lights*?

A) Ridgemont Wolves

B) Permian Panthers

C) Langley Falls Bazooka Sharks

D) McKinley Titans

12. The TV show *Entourage* – which spawned a dire big-screen coda in 2015 – was loosely based around the Hollywood experience of which actor?

A) Mark Wahlberg

B) Andy Samberg

C) Seth Rogen

D) Seth Green

13. It's the title of the classic 1996 Coen brothers movie and the equally celebrated TV show it inspired, but in which US state would you find the city of Fargo?

A) Alaska

B) Minnesota

C) North Dakota

D) Nevada

14. The TV spin-off of Alan Parker's 1980 movie musical *Fame* was heavily sponsored, leading to which product being featured none-too-subtly throughout the series?

A) Nike sportswear

B) Yamaha keyboards

C) Kellogg's Pop-Tarts

D) Rubik's Cubes

15. Which late Nineties teen movie yielded a TV series – *Manchester Prep* – that was never aired, but instead re-edited to form the basis of a direct-to-DVD sequel to the movie?

A) *Clueless*

B) *10 Things I Hate About You*

C) *Cruel Intentions*

D) *Never Been Kissed*

BEAT THE DEVIL

Subtitled Series: Foreign-language franchises

1. Which high-minded director was responsible for *Les Bronzés*, a lowish-brow trilogy of holiday-camp comedies sometimes translated as *French Fried Vacation*?

2. 1993's *Les Visiteurs* spawned both a sequel and a US remake in 2001's *Just Visiting*. In which city did the time-travelling knights played by Jean Reno and Christian Clavier rematerialize in the latter?

3. 1998's *Taxi* – first cab off the rank in the five-film French franchise that beat *The Fast and the Furious* to the movie starting line – featured which international star-to-be as its love interest?

4. Sanjay Dutt's hulking Mumbai mobster Munna Bhai – focal point of two excellent Bollywood comedies – was pestered towards virtue by the ghost of a historical figure in 2006's *Lage Raho Munna Bhai*. Who?

5. The Amitabh Bachchan-starring *Sarkar* series – initiated in 2005, with sequels in 2008 and 2017 – was inspired by which US trilogy?

6. The *Doraemon* franchise, bigger than either *Pokémon* or *Digimon* on home turf in Asia yet comparatively under-exported, centres on a robotic variant of which animal?

7. What kind of monsters were the heroes of 2007's wobblycam horror *[REC]* – film zero of both a Spanish and US series – running in terror from?

8. Ip Man, the legendary martial artist lionized by Wong Kar-Wai in 2013's *The Grandmaster*, has been rather better served by a growing series of films (beginning with 2008's *Ip Man*) starring which ever-energetic action star?

9. Joel Kinnaman, square-jawed star of 2014's *RoboCop* remake, came to global prominence via a trilogy of Swedish films centred on a student involved in the drug trade. What was the trilogy called? (A bonus point for the original Swedish title.)

10. Hands across the ocean: 2017's *Wolf Warrior 2*, the actioner that became the first Chinese film to crack the top 100 grossing movies of all time, featured an American actor – himself no stranger to franchises – in a supporting role. Who?

Galaxy Quest: On the *Star Wars* franchise
1. Steven Spielberg, 2. James Earl Jones, 3. 3ft (3ft 6in, to be precise), 4. Toto, 5. A women's razor, 6. Keira Knightley, 7. Motherfucker, 8. Both make childlike noises when using their weapons, 9. Tom Stoppard, 10. ''Scuse me', 11. Left leg, 12. *Rogue One*, 13. Puffins, 14. *Revenge of the Sith*, 15. *The Empire Strikes Back*

Marvellous: Stan Lee's cameos
1. b, 2. b, 3. c, 4. a, 5. d, 6. c, 7. b, 8. d, 9. b, 10. c, 11. c, 12. a, 13. b, 14. d (in a cameo as a barber), 15. c (he was a postman in 2005's *Fantastic Four,* a librarian in 2012's *The Amazing Spider-Man* and a DJ in 2016's *Deadpool*)

More More More: Unlikely sequels and spin-offs
1. Michelle Pfeiffer, 2. Sylvester Stallone, 3. John Goodman, 4. *2 Fast 2 Furious*, 5. Train, 6. *American Psycho*, 7. 2049, 8. *The Two Jakes*, 9. Hilary Swank, 10. *The Smell of Fear*, 11. Maggie Gyllenhaal, 12. Parker Posey, 13. Daft Punk, 14. *Ace Ventura* (Ace's son got his own movie, *Ace Ventura Jr.,* in 2009), 15. It was the town in Sicily where he was born

Backseat Drivers: Supporting and guest stars in *The Fast & the Furious* franchise
1. Djimon Hounsou, 2. Michelle Rodriguez, 3. Rick Yune, 4. Ja Rule, 5. Eva Mendes, 6. Ludacris, 7. Cole Hauser, 8. Devon Aoki, 9. Tyrese Gibson, 10. Zachery Ty Bryan, 11. Elsa Pataky, 12. Dwayne 'The Rock' Johnson, 13. Ronda Rousey, 14. Tony Jaa, 15. Jason Statham

Double-O Heaven: Arcane Bond facts
1. b, 2. c, 3. b, 4. a, 5. d, 6. c, 7. c, 8. c, 9. d, 10. b, 11. d, 12. c, 13. c, 14. c, 15. d

The Double: Films that became TV series – and vice versa
1. b, 2. a (in 1954. *Captain Video* made it to the big screen in 1951 but only in serial form), 3. b, 4. b, 5. d (with 111.9m viewers), 6. b, 7. a, 8. c (this was the racy title of a season 4 episode), 9. c, 10. c, 11. b, 12. a, 13. c, 14. b, 15. c

Subtitled Series: Foreign-language franchises
1. Patrice Leconte, 2. Chicago, 3. Marion Cotillard, 4. Mahatma Gandhi, 5. The *Godfather* films, 6. Cat, 7. Zombies, 8. Donnie Yen, 9. *Easy Money* (aka *Snabba Cash*), 10. Frank Grillo

ANSWERS

15

Practical
MAGIC

The nuts and bolts
of moviemaking

NOSE JOBS

Notable prosthetics work

1. John Hurt spent untold hours in the makeup chair to play the title character of David Lynch's 1980 film *The Elephant Man*. What was his character's name?

A) Oliver Stone

B) Jack Horner

C) John Merrick

D) James Bell

2. Ian Holm's Scientific Officer Ash is revealed to be an android after he is brutally decapitated (and later revived) by Sigourney Weaver in 1979's *Alien*. What colour is his 'blood'?

A) White

B) Blue

C) Green

D) Black

3. Gary Oldman is a chameleonic actor who often dissolves into a role. For which film did one of these disappearing acts did he win his one and only Oscar?

A) *Bram Stoker's Dracula*

B) *JFK*

C) *Darkest Hour*

D) *Immortal Beloved*

4. Rick Baker won the inaugural Best Makeup Oscar in 1981 for *An American Werewolf in London*, but perhaps remains best known for his work on which music video?

A) 'Donkey Rhubarb' by Aphex Twin

B) 'Hungry Like the Wolf' by Duran Duran

C) 'Sledgehammer' by Peter Gabriel

D) 'Thriller' by Michael Jackson

5. Which leading American actor hams it up to such a degree that they are still highly identifiable beneath all manner of facial furniture in the role of Alphonse 'Big Boy' Caprice in 1990's *Dick Tracy*?

A) Al Pacino

B) Dustin Hoffman

C) Meryl Streep

D) Robert De Niro

6. Which actor spent so much time under layers of prosthetics during the filming of hit 1985 weepie *Mask* that the security guards at the film's wrap party failed to recognize him?

A) Kiefer Sutherland

B) Emilio Estevez

C) Crispin Glover

D) Eric Stoltz

7. 'Finally, a man who can satisfy two women at once!' One of the many nasally based witticisms reeled off by generously schnozzed fire chief C.D. Bales (Steve Martin) in 1987's *Roxanne*. On which classic text is the film based?

A) *Ulysses*

B) *The Mahabharata*

C) *Love's Labour's Lost*

D) *Cyrano de Bergerac*

8. Emma Thompson went the warts-and-all route when transforming into Nanny McPhee for the 2005 children's fantasy of the same name. What was the name of its 2010 sequel?

A) *Nanny McPhee's Arctic Adventure*

B) *Nanny McPhee: International Woman of Mystery*

C) *Under the Sea with Nanny McPhee*

D) *Nanny McPhee and the Big Bang*

9. What is Mrs Doubtfire's first name?

A) Fanny

B) Euphegenia

C) Hortensia

D) Gertrude

10. The 2008 Brad Pitt/Cate Blanchett romantic fantasy *The Curious Case of Benjamin Button* was based on a 1922 short story by which esteemed American writer?

A) F. Scott Fitzgerald

B) Harper Lee

C) Flannery O'Connor

D) Edith Wharton

11. Who plays Edgar, the farmer who is killed and then used as a rapidly decomposing flesh puppet to disguise an invading alien bug monster in 1997's *Men in Black*?

A) Tony Shalhoub

B) John Turturro

C) Stephen Baldwin

D) Vincent D'Onofrio

12. Which blue-skinned, red-haired, yellow-eyed mutant does Jennifer Lawrence play in the *X-Men* films?

A) Psylocke

B) Domino

C) Mystique

D) Gambit

13. Steve Carell was virtually unrecognizable under mounds of makeup as 'wrestling enthusiast' John du Pont in which 2014 drama?

A) *Foxcatcher*

B) *Cockfighter*

C) *Greenberg*

D) *Demolition*

14. The same can be said of Tilda Swinton as the 84-year-old Madame D. in which comedy of the same year?

A) *Hail, Caesar!*

B) *The Best Exotic Marigold Hotel*

C) *Birdman*

D) *The Grand Budapest Hotel*

15. Which big-name British actor's nose, chin and ears were tweaked to make him look more like a young Patrick Stewart for 2002's *Star Trek: Nemesis*?

A) Henry Cavill

B) Jude Law

C) Tom Hardy

D) Christian Bale

SLOW CINEMA

Cinema's more extreme takes

1. What's unusual about the extended 'You Are the World to Me' sequence in Stanley Donen's 1951 musical *Royal Wedding*?

A) Fred Astaire dances on the ceiling

B) It was shot covertly on London streets

C) Astaire pauses for breath halfway through

D) Queen Elizabeth takes an unexpected twirl

2. Orson Welles's grim crime saga *Touch of Evil* starts with an unbroken opening tracking shot, but what specific item dictates the length of the shot?

A) An over-ripe orange

B) A ticking timebomb

C) A loaded six-shooter

D) A bottle of Tequila

3. Michael Snow's 1967 experiment *Wavelength* is comprised of an uncompromisingly slow, 45-minute zoom from one side of an apartment to the other. On what image does the camera eventually alight?

A) The director's own smiling face

B) A photograph of the sea

C) A poster of a shirtless David Cassidy

D) A Polaroid of the same room we've travelled through

4. Jean-Luc Godard's 1967 provocation *Weekend* features an eight-minute tracking shot along what?

A) A traffic jam

B) The queue for a funfair rollercoaster

C) The hind leg of a mongoose

D) The totality of space and time

5. What's the name of the nightclub through which Henry Hill (Ray Liotta) passes unhindered in a famous three-minute single take from 1990's *GoodFellas*?

A) The Boom Boom Room

B) Sid's

C) The Copacabana

D) Lassiter's

6. Three of the following projects can be heard being pitched during the eight-minute opening shot of 1992's Tinseltown satire *The Player*. Which is the odd pitch out?

A) *Ghost* meets *The Manchurian Candidate*

B) *The Graduate Part II*

C) *Out of Africa* meets *Pretty Woman*

D) *Mutiny on the Bounty* with cows

7. The serpentine opening of 1998's *Snake Eyes* sees director Brian De Palma staging a typically grandiose, thirteen-minute introductory recce of the venue for which event?

A) A goat autopsy

B) A prize fight

C) A Presidential manicure

D) The Superbowl

8. 2002's *Russian Ark* was Alexander Sokurov's grand, single-take tour of which iconic institution?

A) The Russian Museum

B) The National Portrait Gallery

C) The Hermitage

D) Keswick Pencil Museum

9. With the aid of computer trickery, David Fincher established the vulnerability of Jodie Foster's home in 2002's *Panic Room* by setting his camera to snake through a bannister, a serving hatch, and – in one especially show-offy manoeuvre – what?

A) A keyhole

B) The crevice of a cello

C) A coffee pot handle

D) The eye of a needle

10. What is the ever-handy Tony Jaa attempting to retrieve in the spectacular four-minute multi-storey action scene in the middle of 2005's *The Warrior King* (aka *The Protector* in the US)?

A) The arc of the covenant

B) A cheque for $5,000

C) A copy of Shonen Knife's 1992 album *Let's Knife*

D) An elephant

11. These things are hard work: how long did the five-minute single-take attack on the car carrying Clive Owen, Pam Ferris and expectant mother Kee (Clare-Hope Ashitey) in 2006's *Children of Men* take to film?

A) Five minutes

B) One day

C) Twelve days

D) Fourteen weeks

12. The three-minute closing shot of Mike Leigh's 2008 film *Happy-Go-Lucky* leaves heroine Poppy (Sally Hawkins), the Pollyanna of Primrose Hill, where exactly?

A) On a boating lake

B) At a driving test centre

C) At the gates of hell

D) Paraguay

13. How many attempts did it require for director Sebastian Schipper to get 2015's one-take, two-hour-plus thriller *Victoria* in the can?

A) One

B) Two

C) Three

D) 57

14. Which of the following was shot in one uninterrupted take, as opposed to being merely edited to look that way?

A) Alfred Hichcock's *Rope*

B) Gaspar Noé's *Irreversible*

C) Alejandro González Iñárritu's *Birdman*

D) Mike Figgis's *Timecode*

15. Finally, which of the following motion pictures has the shortest average shot length?

A) *Speed*

B) *Run Lola Run*

C) *Fast & Furious 6*

D) *Crank*

RED OR DEAD

Cinema's favourite colour

1. Maggie Cheung sparked renewed interest in the traditional Chinese cheongsam dress after modelling several examples – particularly a startling little red number – in which 2000 crossover hit?

A) *Infernal Affairs*
B) *Chungking Express*
C) *In the Mood for Love*
D) *Raise the Red Lantern*

2. What is everyone looking for in 1990's *The Hunt for Red October*?

A) A computer chip
B) A diamond
C) A submarine
D) A painting

3. Anthony Hopkins reprised his role as Hannibal Lecter for Brett Ratner's 2002 adaptation of Thomas Harris's novel *Red Dragon*. But the book had already been filmed by Michael Mann in 1986, with Brian Cox as the Doc. What was Mann's version called?

A) *Manhunter*
B) *Jagged Edge*
C) *Black Moon Rising*
D) *Tightrope*

4. What red item of clothing is central to the plot of Nicolas Roeg's chilling 1973 puzzler *Don't Look Now*?

A) A hat
B) A dress
C) A child's anorak
D) A pair of shoes

5. Where is Gene Hackman's paranoid PI Harry Caul disturbed and horrified to see blood suddenly emerge from in 1974's *The Conversation*?

A) Between the floorboards of his apartment
B) A sandwich
C) A fountain
D) A toilet

6. What was the make and model of the impossibly sleek blood-red car that filled the title role of John Carpenter's 1983 Stephen King adaptation *Christine*?

A) A 1957 Plymouth Fury
B) A 1966 Cadillac DeVille
C) A 1974 Chrysler Hunter
D) A 1982 Dodge Charger

7. Around which area of the Overlook Hotel, the setting of Stanley Kubrick's 1980 chiller *The Shining*, should guests be on the alert for sudden tidal waves of blood?

A) The squash court
B) The Gold Rush Lounge
C) The main staircase
D) The elevators

8. Character actor J.T. Walsh – described by *Playboy* magazine as 'everybody's favourite scumbag', and co-star of *A Few Good Men*, *The Grifters* and *Good Morning, Vietnam* – is perhaps best known for playing the villainous Red Barr in which Kurt Russell vehicle?

A) *U Turn*

B) *Used Cars*

C) *Running on Empty*

D) *Breakdown*

9. Bruce Willis, Helen Mirren and John Malkovich all star in superior 2010 action comedy *RED* and its inferior 2013 sequel. What does the acronym RED stand for in their world?

A) Rusty but Exceptional Dinosaurs

B) Regulation Elderly Downgrade

C) Retired, Extremely Dangerous

D) Recalled: Error Detected

10. A perfectly respectable Rhode Island housewife starts rubbing her crotch, talking dirty and projectile-vomiting cherries before her husband beats her to death with a poker ... Which charming Eighties comedy?

A) *The Man With Two Brains*

B) *Throw Momma from the Train*

C) *The Witches of Eastwick*

D) *Gremlins*

11. What is Robert De Niro's vocation in the 2012 film *Red Lights*?

A) A news cameraman

B) A celebrity psychic

C) An air traffic controller

D) A clown

12. You awake in an opulent bed. You feel something sticky under the sheets. It's blood – blood from a severed horse's head! You're in *The Godfather*! What is your occupation?

A) Mafia boss

B) Nightclub owner

C) Movie producer

D) Police Commissioner

13. Who won the 1982 Best Director Oscar for *Reds*, the star-studded epic in which an American journalist charts the beginnings of the 1917 Russian Revolution?

A) Oliver Stone

B) Robert Redford

C) Warren Beatty

D) Richard Attenborough

14. What is Morgan Freeman's mind-your-business reply to Tim Robbins when asked why he's called 'Red' in *The Shawshank Redemption*?

A) 'Come by my cell tonight and I'll show you.'

B) 'Maybe it's because I'm Irish.'

C) 'Well, I have this rash ...'

D) 'I'm a communist. But keep it to yourself.'

15. Clint Eastwood literally – literally! – paints the town red in which film?

A) *Pink Cadillac*

B) *Blood Work*

C) *High Plains Drifter*

D) *Paint Your Wagon*

IMAGE FINDERS

The great cinematographers

1. Orson Welles claimed 'Everything I know about the art of photography I learnt from a great cameraman in half an hour.' Who was this expert teacher?

A) James Wong Howe

B) Robert Surtees

C) Gregg Toland

D) Harold Rosson

2. Mid-century shotmaker Robert Burks was most closely associated with which major director?

A) John Ford

B) Alfred Hitchcock

C) Howard Hawks

D) Anthony Mann

3. France's Henri Alekan had an extraordinarily wide-ranging, fifty-year career. On which of the following was he not the cinematographer?

A) *La Belle et la Bête*

B) *Roman Holiday*

C) *Jules et Jim*

D) *Wings of Desire*

4. Freddie Francis revealed in his memoir *The Straight Story* that the candles he deployed as cinematographer on 1961's horror classic *The Innocents* were specially formulated to burn bright enough to light any scene. How so?

A) They were made from gelignite

B) They had multiple wicks

C) They contained LED bulbs

D) They were wired up to the mains

5. Gordon Willis's work with simultaneously forbidding and seductive, low-lit interiors in the three *Godfather* films earned him a nickname within the industry. What was it?

A) The Godfather of Gloom

B) The Mafiosi of Murk

C) Gordy the Squint

D) The Prince of Darkness

6. The great Italian cinematographer Vittorio Storaro won the Oscar three out of the four times he was nominated. For which of his nominated films did he miss out?

A) *Apocalypse Now*

B) *Reds*

C) *The Last Emperor*

D) *Dick Tracy*

7. Michael Chapman, Scorsese's director of photography on *Taxi Driver* and *Raging Bull*, made his directorial debut with which early Eighties Tom Cruise starrer?

A) *Taps*

B) *Endless Love*

C) *All the Right Moves*

D) *Risky Business*

8. Christopher Doyle – a key figure in Wong Kar-Wai's early, neon-lit visions, and in recent Asian cinema in general – also goes under the Chinese name Du Ke Feng. How does that phrase translate?

A) Dances with Spotlights

B) Eye on the Prize

C) The Visualizer

D) Like the Wind

9. Harris Savides defined the look of key films by Gus Van Sant, David Fincher and Sofia Coppola before his tragically early death in 2012. Yet he earned his first cinematography credit shooting which bestselling fitness video?

A) *Jane Fonda's AM/PM Yoga*

B) *Cindy Crawford: The Next Challenge Workout*

C) *Elle Macpherson: The Body Workout*

D) *Shape Up with Mad Lizzie*

10. What's the title of the essential 1992 doc that did so much to promote cinematography as an art?

A) *Visions of Light*

B) *Masters of Light*

C) *Light in the Dark*

D) *Strike a Light*

11. In the 2010 doc *Cameraman*, Jack Cardiff suggests of one painter that his use of light might have made him 'the greatest cameraman that ever lived'. Which one?

A) Van Gogh

B) Rembrandt

C) Turner

D) Caravaggio

12. What unconventional item did star British cinematographer Robbie Ryan wear on the Moors while filming Andrea Arnold's bold 2011 take on *Wuthering Heights*?

A) A stab-proof vest

B) Snowshoes

C) A hazmat suit

D) Football boots

13. Emmanuel Lubezki, the extraordinary Mexican shotmaker who became the first cinematographer to win three successive Oscars in 2015, is known on set as 'Chivo'. How does this translate?

A) Little Master

B) The Boss

C) Happy

D) The Goat

14. Bradford Young is one of this field's most versatile and accomplished new talents. For which film did he earn the first ever Oscar nomination for a black cinematographer?

A) 2013's *Ain't Them Bodies Saints*

B) 2014's *A Most Violent Year*

C) 2014's *Selma*

D) 2016's *Arrival*

15. Roger Deakins broke an awards-night curse in 2018 when he won the Oscar for his work on *Blade Runner 2049*. How many nominations – from 1994's *The Shawshank Redemption* to 2015's *Sicario* – had he previously racked up without winning?

A) Seven

B) Eight

C) Twelve

D) Fifteen

CARTOON NETWORK

Spotlight on animators and animation

1. Why does Christopher Lloyd's Judge Doom want to tear down Toontown in 1988's *Who Framed Roger Rabbit*?

A) Spite

B) To build a freeway

C) To drill for oil

D) To build the world's first adult-oriented theme park

2. What kind of animal was Fritz, the unrelentingly horny hipster hero of Ralph Bakshi's X-rated 1972 hit?

A) A cat

B) A crow

C) A fox

D) A bear

3. Why was Hayao Miyazaki not in attendance when his 2001 film *Spirited Away* won the Oscar for Best Animated Feature?

A) He boycotted the show in protest against the Iraq War

B) Sunday night is family night in the Miyazaki household – no exceptions

C) He had slipped and broken his leg hours before the show

D) He has never accepted an award for any of his films

4. 'When you're drawn, in a way it says more about how children are going to see you than anything else, and I so care about that.' Which actor's reason for turning down the role of Shrek?

A) Hugh Grant

B) Sean Connery

C) Dan Aykroyd

D) Nicolas Cage

5. Who were the baddies of the lysergic 1968 Beatles animation *Yellow Submarine*?

A) The Orange Nasties

B) The Fiendish Four

C) The Awful Nigels

D) The Blue Meanies

6. Which actor provides the voice for Rocky Rhodes, the laid-back rooster hero of Aardman Animations' 2000 smash hit *Chicken Run*?

A) Mel Gibson

B) Brad Pitt

C) Tommy Lee Jones

D) Jeff Bridges

7. Anime .... Impenetrable to those who don't get it, glorious to those who do. Which of these is NOT an actual anime?

A) *Project A-ko 2: Plot of the Daitokuji Financial Group*

B) *Creamy Mami, the Magic Angel: Forever Once More*

C) *Violence Jack: Harem Bomber*

D) *Lucifer and the Biscuit Hammer*

8. Against what backdrop is 2003's *Belleville Rendez-Vous* (aka *The Triplets of Belleville*) set?

A) The construction of the Eiffel Tower

B) Nazi-occupied Paris

C) The Tour de France

D) The opening night of the Moulin Rouge

9. The short *Destino*, also released in 2003, went into production 58 years earlier as a collaboration between Walt Disney and which other artist?

A) Pablo Picasso

B) Frida Kahlo

C) Salvador Dalí

D) Jackson Pollock

10. Who is the effeminate, clothes-obsessed Ken to Jodi Benson's Barbie in 2010's *Toy Story 3*?

A) Ray Liotta

B) Robin Williams

C) Matthew McConaughey

D) Michael Keaton

11. Who bodyswaps with his own animated creation in Henry Selick's 2001 flopperoo *Monkeybone*?

A) Brendan Fraser

B) Jim Carrey

C) Mike Myers

D) Steve Martin

12. 2007's *Persepolis* described a young girl's coming of age in which country?

A) Afghanistan

B) Northern Ireland

C) Iran

D) Venezuela

13. 2009 stop-motion charmer *Coraline* was adapted from a book by which author?

A) Roald Dahl

B) Neil Gaiman

C) Philip Pullman

D) Philip K. Dick

14. Which of the following animated films has NOT raked in more than $1 billion at the box office?

A) *Frozen*

B) *The Lion King*

C) *Minions*

D) *Finding Dory*

15. He was directed by Gore Verbinski and voiced by Johnny Depp, but what kind of creature was the star of 2011's *Rango*?

A) A gibbon

B) A chameleon

C) A ferret

D) A buzzard

FANTASTIC BEASTS

Animal wrangling

1. Which of the following is NOT the title of a Lassie movie – *Lassie Come Home*, *The Return of Lassie*, *Son of Lassie* or *The Magic of Lassie*?

2. Which pest ran wild in both 1971's *Willard* and a 2003 remake?

3. Prolific pooch Benji gained a celebrity voice in 1980's *Oh! Heavenly Dog*. Which *Saturday Night Live* graduate found himself spirited into the lovable mixed-breed scamp?

4. What was the title of the notorious 1981 production in which practically every member of cast and crew, from leading lady Tippi Hedren to cinematographer Jan de Bont, was mauled at some point by the leonine performers?

5. Hambone, the canine hero of 1983's *Hambone and Hillie*, made a cross-country journey to be reunited with his owner. But which screen legend occupied the role of Hillie?

6. Everybody knows that Hooch was Tom Hanks's dog in 1989's *Turner & Hooch*. But what was the rockin' good name of Jim Belushi's dog in the same year's *K-9* (and sequels)?

7. For which animal is Jim Carrey's eagle-eyed Ace Ventura on the lookout in 1994's *Ace Ventura: Pet Detective*?

8. Which animal takes centre stage in 1994's *Andre*?

9. Bonzo from 1951's *Bedtime for Bonzo* and Dunston of 1996's *Dunston Checks In* are prominent movie examples of what?

10. What were Michael Douglas and Val Kilmer hunting in 1996's *The Ghost and the Darkness*?

11. What's the real name of the bear who, in a career longer than that of some performers, broke through with the title role in 1988's *The Bear* before going growl-to-growl with Anthony Hopkins in 1997's *The Edge*?

12. Big question: why were there snakes on the plane in 2006's *Snakes on a Plane*?

13. Which Hollywood A-lister provided the voice of thoughtful spider Charlotte in the 2006 version of *Charlotte's Web*?

14. What's the name of the dragon in the *How to Train Your Dragon* franchise?

15. Finally, which is the odd dog out, and why – Beethoven, from *Beethoven*; Hachi, from *Hachi: A Dog's Tale*; Marley, from *Marley & Me*; Skip, from *My Dog Skip*?

CREDIT WHERE CREDIT'S DUE

Stellar production companies

More movie stars than ever have their own production company to help develop material for themselves and others. Below, you'll find fifteen of today's most prominent production outfits – can you match them to the performers listed?

Amen Ra Films
Appian Way Productions
Flower Films
Gary Sanchez Productions
Green Door Pictures
Hello Sunshine
Irish DreamTime
JuVee Productions
Malpaso Productions
Plan B Entertainment
Playtone
Point Grey Pictures
Purple Pebble Pictures
Rabbit Bandini Productions
Red Chillies Entertainment

Pierce Brosnan
James Franco
Brad Pitt
Leonardo DiCaprio
Idris Elba
Shah Rukh Khan
Reese Witherspoon
Clint Eastwood
Viola Davis
Drew Barrymore
Tom Hanks
Will Ferrell
Priyanka Chopra
Wesley Snipes
Seth Rogen

BEAT THE DEVIL

Call Me By My Name: Cinema's oddest closing credits

1. In a further example of Beatle wackiness, 1965's *Help!* is dedicated to Elias Howe, real-life inventor of what household device in 1846?

2. Which late Seventies Burt Reynolds vehicle originated the now common practice of rounding a middling-to-fair night's entertainment up with a blooper reel?

3. Which 20th-century dictator earned the credit 'Worst Boy' (it's just below Best Boy) on 1980's *Airplane!*

4. 1985's *Sesame Street Presents ... Follow That Bird* ends with the Count totting up the total number of credits. How many credits does the Count count (to the nearest ten)?

5. James Dearden earned an unusual screenplay credit on 1987's *Fatal Attraction* 'for the screenplay based on __________'. What?

6. Why can't Michael Moore's 1989 documentary *Roger & Me* be shown on its home turf of Flint, Michigan, according to a final disclaimer?

7. Which writer-director once gave closing credit thanks to 'Mum and Dad, for having sex all those years ago'?

8. Which 2004 release featured credits for such characters as Shelf-Humping Sex Addict, Croquet Mallet Whacker, Tire Lick Boy, and Fat Fuck Frank?

9. Which Coen brothers venture reassured us with a closing disclaimer that 'no Jews were harmed in the making of this motion picture'?

10. In end credit terms, which film is the odd one out, and why – *Seven*, *Memento*, *Run Lola Run* or *Irreversible*?

Nose Jobs: Notable prosthetics work

1. c, 2. a, 3. c, 4. d, 5. a, 6. d, 7. d, 8. d, 9. b, 10. a, 11. d, 12. c, 13. a, 14. d, 15. c

Slow Cinema: Cinema's more extreme takes

1. a, 2. b, 3. b (Wave-length. Geddit?), 4. a, 5. c, 6. d (which was the original pitch for 1948's *Red River*), 7. b, 8. c, 9. c (the shot does enter a keyhole, but is repelled by the burglars' arrival), 10. d, 11. c, 12. a, 13. c, 14. d, 15. c (at 1.5 seconds; by contrast, *Run Lola Run* plods along at 4.9 secs, *Speed* holds steady with 3.5 secs, and *Crank* flies by at 2.7 secs)

Red or Dead: Cinema's favourite colour

1. c, 2. c, 3. a, 4. c, 5. d, 6. a, 7. d, 8. d, 9. c, 10. c, 11. b, 12. c, 13. c, 14. b, 15. c

Image Finders: The great cinematographers

1. c, 2. b, 3. c, 4. b, 5. d, 6. d, 7. c, 8. d, 9. d, 10. a, 11. c, 12. d (for grip), 13. d, 14. d, 15. c

Cartoon Network: Spotlight on animators and animation

1. b, 2. a, 3. a, 4. d, 5. d, 6. a, 7. d (this popular manga has, at time of writing, not yet been adapted into an anime), 8. c, 9. c, 10. d, 11. a, 12. c, 13. b, 14. b, 15. b

Fantastic Beasts: Animal wrangling

1. *The Return of Lassie*, 2. Rat, 3. Chevy Chase, 4. *Roar*, 5. Lillian Gish, 6. Jerry Lee, 7. A dolphin, 8. A seal, 9. Apes, 10. Lions, 11. Bart, 12. It was a plot to kill off a gangland witness, 13. Julia Roberts, 14. Toothless, 15. Beethoven, from *Beethoven*, as he's the only canine who survives to the end credits

Credit Where Credit's Due: Stellar production companies

Amen Ra Films: Wesley Snipes; Appian Way Productions: Leonardo DiCaprio; Flower Films: Drew Barrymore; Gary Sanchez Productions: Will Ferrell; Green Door Pictures: Idris Elba; Hello Sunshine: Reese Witherspoon; Irish DreamTime: Pierce Brosnan; JuVee Productions: Viola Davis; Malpaso Productions: Clint Eastwood; Plan B Entertainment: Brad Pitt; Playtone: Tom Hanks; Point Grey Pictures: Seth Rogen; Purple Pebble Pictures: Priyanka Chopra; Rabbit Bandini Productions: James Franco; Red Chillies Entertainment: Shah Rukh Khan

Call Me By My Name: Cinema's oddest closing credits

1. The sewing machine, 2. 1978's *Hooper*, 3. Adolf Hitler, 4. 278 (so anywhere between 270 and 280 gets you the point), 5. 'His earlier screenplay', 6. Because the city's only cinema closed down, 7. Kevin Smith (at the end of 1995's *Mallrats*), 8. John Waters' *A Dirty Shame*, 9. 2009's *A Serious Man,* 10. *Memento* – it's the only one whose credits roll from the bottom of the screen to the top, as per convention

ANSWERS

GUIDE TO THE ILLUSTRATIONS

Happy Feet
66. Mickey Rooney
67. Gene Kelly

Attack
68. Der Führer

Trading Post
70. John Wayne

The Women
73. Lauren Bacall

The Big Man
74. Orson Welles

Make 'Em Laugh
76. Harold Lloyd
77. (top) Henry Fonda
77. (bottom) John L. Sullivan

First Contact
82. Jennifer Aniston

Self-Portraits
84. John Malkovich

Get Carter
86. Helena Bonham Carter
87. Tim Burton

Brief Encounter
88. Robert De Niro

Uncaged
90. Nic Cage

Backup
94. Allison Janney

Crossing Over II
96. Mia Farrow
97. Quentin Tarantino

Role Play
102. Peter Cook
103. (top) Charlize Theron
103. (bottom) Leonardo diCaprio

The Incredibles
104. (top) Randall (voiced by Steve Buscemi)
104. (middle) Dory (voiced by Ellen DeGeneres)

Method Mayhem
108. Jared Leto

Neat Eats
110. Gene Wilder

New Rules
112. Thomas Vinterberg

Hack Attack
114. John Turturro

The Two Bergmans
124. Ingmar Bergman
125. Ingrid Bergman

Thunder Down Under
126. Nicole Kidman
127. Mel Gibson

Bollywood and Beyond
128. Deepika Padukone

South of the Border
130. Jennifer Lopez
131. Sofia Vergara, Dolores del Río

The Oscar Oddities
138. Liza Minnelli

Riviera Days
140. Terry Jones
141. Cher

Thanksgiving
142. J.K. Simmons
143. Chris Rock, Sean Penn

MTV Movie Awards
144. Jon Heder

Breakouts
146. Whoopi Goldberg

On the QT
152. Quentin Tarantino
152. (bottom) Randy Crawford
153. (top) Nancy Sinatra
153. (bottom) Jack and Meg White (The White Stripes)

Movies Take the Mic
154. Russell Crowe

Key Themes
156. Pharrell Williams
157. Public Enemy

Roll Over Beethoven
158. (top) John Lennon
158. (middle) Tupac
159. (top) Beyoncé
159. (bottom) Cate Blanchett

Vérité Virtuosos
160. Bob Dylan

Multiple Threads
162. Gwen Stefani
163. (top) Bruce Springsteen
163. (bottom) Victoria Beckham

Videotheque
164. Kate Bush

What's My Line
170. Rachel McAdams
171. (top) Jake Gyllenhaal
171. (bottom) Dolly Parton

Entrances and Exits
172. Ray Liotta

PR Exercise
174. Paris Hilton

Bard Influence
176. The Bard of Avon (aka William Shakespeare)

King's Game
180. Stephen King

Burn Hollywood Burn
182. Charlie Sheen
171. (top) Harrison Ford
171. (bottom) Nick Nolte, Julia Roberts

Search Party
189. Macaulay Culkin

Festive Fun
190. Will Ferrell
191. (bottom) Colin Farrell

Our Kansas
194. Judy Garland

Money Spinners
196. Leonardo da Vinci

Monster Mash
198. Jeff Goldblum

Rittertainment
200. John Ritter

Road to Morocco
208. Humphrey Bogart

Teenage Dream
210. Alicia Silverstone
211. Paul Rudd

Lost in Space
216. Stanley Kubrick

LA Shakedown
220. Robert Altman
221. Julianne Moore

Hobbits and More
222. Ian McKellen

Going for Broke
228. Howard the Duck (voiced by Chip Zien)

Tall Tales
230. Ryan Reynolds
231. Bruce Campbell

Opposites Attract
232. Natalie Portman
233. Tom Jones

Tabloid Fodder
234. Kevin Spacey
235. Mel Gibson, Robert Blake

Fascist Groove Thang
236. Cristoph Waltz
237. (top) Gregory Peck
237. (bottom) Bruno Ganz

Heaven and Hell
238. Morgan Freeman

No Marks
240. Tommy Wiseau

Galaxy Quest
246. George Lucas

Marvellous
248. Stan Lee

More More More
250. Al Pacino
251. (top) Jim Carrey
251. (bottom) Mila Kunis

Backseat Drivers
252. Dwayne 'The Rock' Johnson
253. Ludacris

Double-O Heaven
254. Daniel Craig

The Double
256. Ed Harris

Nose Jobs
262. Tilda Swinton

Slow Cinema
264. Sally Hawkins

Red or Dead
266. Clint Eastwood

Image Finders
268. Roger Deakins

Credit Where Credit's Due
274. James Franco
275. Viola Davis, Brad Pitt

ACKNOWLEDGEMENTS

Mike McCahill would like to thank all at Team TCO/LWL, but especially to David Jenkins, the best kind of editor (and source of many of this book's better ideas), and to Clive Wilson, an expert pointman who kept everything on track through this book's many incarnations.

A special shoutout to those friends, colleagues and family members who suggested ideas for topics or individual questions while preventing me from banging my head against brick walls; and eternal gratitude to Shanika Morris for her love, support and (in particular) her patience, which proves as much a virtue during the compilation of quizbooks as it is in any other field.

ACKNOWLEDGEMENTS

Adam Lee Davies would like to thank Paul Auster, the Estate of Rodney Dangerfield, whoever left that cassette tape of rocking klezmer music at his house and the staff and regulars of the Neon Teepee, Berlin – 'Liquor in Front, Poker in Rear!' – for their help in writing this book.

Little White Lies would like to thank Mike and Adam for their mad trivia skills, the maestro Sophie Mo for amazing illos and layouts, the wizard Clive Wilson, Laurène Boglio for initial design work, the LK cru Andrew Roff and John Parton, plus the team LWLies: Adam Woodward and Hannah Woodhead (wordsearch maven).

THE

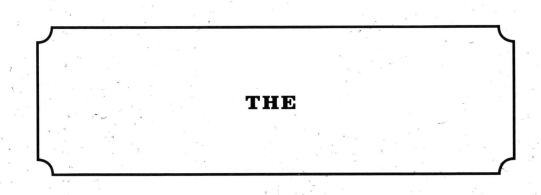

END

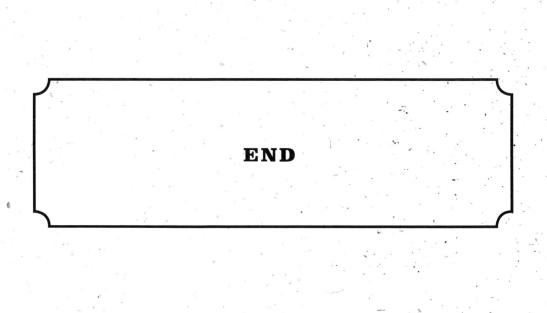

Published in 2019 by
Laurence King Publishing Ltd
361–373 City Road
London EC1V 1LR
enquiries@laurenceking.com
www.laurenceking.com

A catalogue record for this book is available
from the British Library

ISBN: 978-1-78627-519-6

Design and illustrations by Sophie Mo

Printed in China

Laurence King Publishing is committed to ethical and sustainable
production. We are proud participants in The Book Chain Project®
bookchainproject.com

BOOK
CHAIN
PROJECT